The English
prison officer
since 1850

International Library of Social Policy

General Editor   Kathleen Jones
Professor of Social Administration
University of York

Arbor Scientiæ
Arbor Vitæ

A catalogue of the books available in the **International Library of Social Policy** and other series of Social Science books published by Routledge will be found at the end of this volume.

The English prison officer since 1850

A study in conflict

J E Thomas

Department of
Adult Education (Sociology)
University of Hull

Routledge & Kegan Paul
London and Boston

First published 1972
by Routledge & Kegan Paul Ltd,
Broadway House, 68–74 Carter Lane,
London EC4V 5EL and
9 Park Street, Boston, Mass. 02108, U.S.A.
Printed in Great Britain by
Western Printing Services Ltd, Bristol
© J. E. Thomas 1972

ISBN 0 7100 7280 5

For Olwen

gwar uetwl ueith
gorne gwawr vore ar uor diffeith

Contents

Figure

Tables

Acknowledgments

This book is the outcome of research I carried out for a doctorate at the University of York. I must first express my gratitude for the help and direction I received from my supervisor, Professor Kathleen Jones, who gave a good deal of priority to my work, applying herself rigorously to its development. I am also much indebted to Professor Norman A. Jepson and Peter L. Nokes, both of the Department of Adult Education and Extra Mural Studies of the University of Leeds, for much help in the difficult initial stages.

Without the indirect help of one person, I could never have carried out this research. This is Nicholas J. Tyndall, once a governor in the prison service, now Chief Officer, National Marriage Guidance Council. He initiated, and built up, the library at the Staff College of the prison service at Wakefield. He consolidated a piece of very hard work by negotiating with the Home Office to deposit a large number of Reports, some of which are rare, some of which, as far as I can discover, cannot be found elsewhere. My debt to him, to David Hewlings and R. S. Llewelyn, college principals who allowed me to use the library after I left the service, and to the Librarian, Mrs P. Johnson, will quickly become apparent. Like so many other pockets of excellence in the prison service, this fine specialist library deserves to be more widely known.

I would like to thank Mrs B. Young of the Staff College for typing the first draft of the early chapters of the thesis. I owe an especial debt to Miss Susan Cornall of the Department of Adult Education, University of Hull, for working so hard in typing the final manuscript.

Introduction

'There should be no conflict in an ideal prison system between security and rehabilitation.' This was the opening sentence of a leading article in *The Times* on 27 November 1969. It is a frequently expressed view. The theme of this account is that there is such a conflict, that it is generic in prison systems and that it can be demonstrated through examination of the English prison system, which has tried to carry out both tasks. My analysis of this conflict is centred round the role of the basic grade uniformed officer. Variously called 'dubsman', 'turnkey', 'warder' and 'officer', his grade is always in the majority on any prison staff. The problem of coping with conflicting tasks is his.

A role cannot exist in a vacuum; to exist it has to be relative and derivative. It cannot be separated either from the social structure which forms its environment, or from other key roles from which it derives. If, therefore, the role of the modern prison officer is to be comprehensible, it must be analysed within the context of the development of the prison service, and in relation to other staff roles, especially those of the governor and the borstal housemaster. But neither the prison system, nor these key roles, have been described in terms which can provide a structure for an examination of the officer's role. It will be necessary therefore to describe both the evolution of the prison system and, where appropriate, the roles of other staff, notably the two already mentioned. Hence the basic structure, the backbone of this analysis, is the chronological development of the prison system.

Because writers have found the prisoner more interesting, very little has been written about the uniformed prison officer. His role is the product of a complex historical process, which has its roots in the Victorian prison system. Since the persisting features of the officer's role were established during that period, the first chapters are substantially descriptive of the life and work of the officers at that time. Details are included which may appear minor, and incidental, to the central themes of the analysis. This is deliberate. I hope to convey something of the officer's world, a world which has remained remarkably intact over the last hundred years. Each of three important documents will be examined in some detail, two of which have never been mentioned in prison literature before. These are the Rosebery Report and the De Ramsey Report. The third is the Gladstone Report. The three provide a valuable source of information about the nature and problems of the officer's work.

After this essentially descriptive introduction, designed to lay a foundation of understanding of the background and traditions of the prison officer's job, I shall go on to discuss the confusion over organisational goals which has dogged the prison service in the twentieth century, and the response of the officer to it. It will become apparent that the crises leading to the Mountbatten Inquiry had their source in the recommendations of the Gladstone Committee, seventy years before.

It will also become clear that as the prison system has declared increasingly reformative goals, the prison officer has been excluded from their implementation. In spite of assertions that the officer has been, and is associated with, these goals, it will be shown that his role has always been to control, and that his success or failure as an officer is measured against his ability to do that. In fact, his opportunities to take on work which is not solely custodial, have been *narrowed* in the past ninety years.

The hypotheses which I develop, and the conclusions I draw from the evidence, are novel, and may appear unduly pessimistic and perhaps unacceptable. Because they are novel, I have tried to support statements with substantial, in some ways excessive, amounts of evidence. I have done so because the novelty of my hypotheses needs this. Without such evidence, which I have tried to show is overwhelming, this analysis joins the tradition of unsupported assertion which is general in literature on prisons. I do not believe that my conclusions are pessimistic. They are realistic. It is quite impossible to introduce reformative measures into prisons, or indeed change into any organisation, unless the constraints are examined objectively and taken into account. If these constraints are acknowledged, then real change is at least possible. If they are not, a reformative prison system will exist only in official literature.

Although this account is about the English system, it is substantially relevant to prison systems of all advanced societies. England, Scotland, and Northern Ireland have separate prison systems. Their structures are different and they are almost entirely independent of each other. I shall discuss the English system, which includes three institutions in Wales.

The women's prisons in England deserve separate study. Although much of what I will discuss applies to them, they are, and always have been, very different. Except therefore where I specifically mention them, they are usually excluded.

1   The organisation and the task

The theoretical problem

There is a good deal of literature on prisons, the bulk of which seeks only to describe. Apart from this descriptive category, which includes official publications and reminiscences, there are some historical accounts, and a very few sociological investigations. Almost all the literature is confined to two themes—prisoners and penal reform.

In the historical accounts, with the singular exception of R. B. Pugh, *Imprisonment in Medieval England*, the classical debate about reformation and deterrence is usually central. Typically, historical literature describes a pattern of 'progress' from the capricious cruelty of the eighteenth century, through the cold barbarity of the nineteenth, to the enlightened policies of the twentieth. On the one side are the villains led by Du Cane, and on the other are the heroes, Howard, Elizabeth Fry, Paterson. The history of the English prison system thus appears as a battle between those who wished for reform, and those who opposed it. Accounts are reminiscent of the Marxist dialectic when, as in L. W. Fox, *The English Prison and Borstal Systems*, the present system is seen as a kind of synthesis of the struggles which inexorably brought the prison system to the Criminal Justice Act of 1948.

This exclusive interest in penal reform has led to two major deficiencies in historical writing. There is no account of the evolution of the English prison staff structure, and no account of the development of the prison service as an administrative or organisational entity, except in the barest outline.

Such sociological writing as there is on prisons has inherited these classical interests in prisoners and reform. The main contribution of the sociologists has been in describing the inmate community, exploring such topics as leadership, communication, and adjustment to imprisonment. This is a valuable contribution. But almost all sociological literature has three shortcomings.

First, most sociologists who have written on prison have been American, and their research has very limited relevance to the

English system, which is centralised, staffed by civil servants (not by political appointees) and is set in a vastly different social context. Next, there is not nearly enough stress on the relationship between the prison system and society. This relationship is crucial and dynamic, and must be taken into account if a prison system is to be understood. Most sociological work presents prison as an isolated phenomenon.

Above all, the generic weakness of most sociological writing on prisons is the heavy commitment to reform. This commitment leads to a discussion of the wrong issues. Since there is an underlying assumption that the prison organisation ought to be reformative in task, reasons have to be sought as to why it is not. It is assumed that there must be blockages in the achievement of this task. If reformation is not being carried out, what is it that the prison is doing? It is being punitive. Thus, like the historian, the sociologist assumes that the primary conflict in prison is between reformation and deterrence. A notable exception is Gresham Sykes's, *The Society of Captives*.

Galting sums up the theme of most sociological literature as follows:[1]

> Probably the most frequently contemplated topics in the entire field of penological theory is the functional incompatibility of such ends as, for example, retribution and therapy.

It is easy to see how this definition tends to distort the function of the staff structure, and the roles of staff members. Generally the staff are seen as agents of punishment, and are categorised as impediments to reformation. Cressey expresses a representative American view:[2]

> The institutional program ideally becomes one in which non-professional employees, who remain as custodians or foremen, assist the professional staff in this rehabilitative work.

Cressey makes clear his view of the work content of the staff in the traditional structure. Apparently he considers that they have no professional expertise, and he contrasts them with the professionals, to whom they are 'ideally' to be subordinated. Cressey goes on to suggest that:

> Guards who are punitive or repressive must be considered unable to exhibit affective neutrality in relation to inmates because of some personality characteristic. The usual diagnoses

are 'rigid', 'punitive', 'sadistic', 'maladjusted' and 'neurotic'—
terms that are used somewhat opprobriously. But such
difficulties call for education and therapy, not punishment.

This view of staff has, as its source, values about treatment which
Cressey brings to the sociological investigation of the prison. Cressey
uses highly pejorative words—'punitive', 'repressive' and so on—
without either defining them, or asking if they are appropriate attitudes for the achievement of the prison task. He suggests in his last
sentence, that guards may be ignorant or sick. The whole of Cressey's
argument rests on the belief that 'therapy' is the desirable institutional goal:

> Third, supervisors, guards, and foremen are not trained for
> social work or psychiatric practice, nor are they prepared to
> receive a professional education even if there were time to
> provide it.

Sociologists tend to bring to their investigation a commitment to
reform which results in a judgment of the *actual* role of staff against
an *ideal* situation. They are mainly concerned with the relationship of
the custodial staff structure to therapeutic policies. While this is a
question which is of importance both theoretically and practically, its
dominance tends to bar the way to understanding the role of staff. It
also accounts for the animosity shown towards staff in varying
degrees. For instance, it explains the distaste expressed by many
people for the 'para-military' structure, and the recruitment of ex-
servicemen, which is a feature of most prison systems. This militarism
is regarded as irreconcilable with the needs of a reformative regime.

These criticisms arise because the structure is examined in a
vacuum. No attempt is made to examine the reason for this structure.
The relationship between staff and prisoner might be better understood (though not necessarily approved), if the role of staff in relation
to organisational tasks were assessed. And so more fundamental
questions have to be asked, untrammelled by interest in the prisoner,
or commitment to reform. Why does the staff structure take the form
it does? Why does it persist? Above all to understand the prison
system as an *organisation*[3] and the role of the staff in it, it is necessary
to ask first why it exists at all.

This interest in the prisoner community, and concern with penal
reform, have been so dominant as to have an inhibiting effect on the

development of historical analysis, or sociological theorising about prisons. As a result, much writing about the English prison system is repetitive. What is needed is a conceptual framework which will enable the circle to be broken. There are three theoretical concepts, drawn from the sociological theory of organisations, which together provide such a framework.

The first is the concept of the primary task. This term is suggested by A. K. Rice, and is defined by him as: 'The task which it [the organisation] is created to perform.'[4] Clearly the attempt to define the primary task is an essential preliminary to any investigation of organisational structures.

The second is the conceptual framework described by Wilfred Brown which is useful for close examination and clarification of some subtle, persistent, contradictions in organisations. He enumerates four aspects of organisations:[5]

Manifest—the situation as formally described and displayed.
Assumed—the situation as it is assumed to be by the individual concerned. There may, or may not be consistency between the 'assumed' and the 'manifest' situation.
Extant—the situation as revealed by systematic exploration and analysis. (It can never be completely known.)
Requisite—the situation as it would have to be to accord with the real properties of the field in which it exists.

But one is left with the problem of how to decide what is the primary task. In some organisations there may be more than one goal, there may be conflict about priorities in the allocation of resources, but there can only be one primary task. Which is it? The definition of the primary task becomes easier when the question is asked as to what constitutes failure. How is it recognised that the organisation is unsuccessful?

The test is to try to define the 'manifest disaster criterion'. Peter Nokes defined this concept in his exploration of the meaning of professionalism.[6] While Nokes uses it mainly in respect of the performance of the individual, this valuable concept can usefully be extended to the performance of organisations. When, for example, is disaster manifest in the industrial situation? When a firm is bankrupt, since in the industrial situation the primary task is to make profits—that is, to ensure 'the long-term financial stability of an enterprise'.[7] When the firm ceases to do this, its failure is clear to everyone. The situation in respect of non-profit-making organisations is more complex. Does the English prison system have a manifest disaster criterion, definition of which could lead to a definition of a primary task? The prison system is usually described as an organisation which has conflicting goals. If, however, the principle of demonstrable failure is applied to the examination of the goals, then the primary nature of one goal becomes evident.

For several hundred years English society has agreed that people who reject certain social values must be removed from that society. Outlawry in the middle ages, transportation from the seventeenth century, and imprisonment from the nineteenth are all expressions of that agreement. Imprisonment, other than as a preliminary to transportation or death, is a relatively new method of dealing with offenders. Society has defined the need for removal of the criminal, and the prison system, as an organisation, has come into being to achieve this task. The court warrants instruct the prison authorities to hold the prisoner. These documents say nothing about treatment.

If society has called the prison system into being to ensure removal of recalcitrant members of society, the question arises as to how success or failure is measured. The manifest disaster criterion must be failure at successful containment and control of prisoners. However, because the prison system is a public service, expressions of concern about lack of control result in correctives being applied before the stage of complete organisational disaster is reached. In the English system, the escape of George Blake and Frank Mitchell in 1966 drew the attention of society to the manifest failure of the organisation to carry out its primary task. Because of the public outcry, Lord Mountbatten carried out an inquiry, and resources were mobilised to prevent further failure. Allocation of resources is also an indication of the priority of an organisational task, and this allocation of resources is an important clue to the understanding of the prison organisation.

The hypothesis that the prison system has control as its primary organisational task, does not mean that discussion about the treatment of prisoners is not necessary or appropriate. Restatement of the primary task, on the contrary, can be a helpful preliminary to such discussion, since aspirations can be realistically defined, through full account being taken of the constraints on a treatment programme. In fact society appears to agree on a *secondary* task for the prison system. It is that the prisoner, having undergone the experience of imprisonment, should not return to prison. And it is at this point that there is sharp disagreement, and it is here that most of the literature about prison begins. The debate about the treatment of prisoners is a debate about the means of achieving a *secondary* goal. The place which this debate has occupied in the forefront of writing about prisons has limited understanding of the dynamics of prison.

The prison officer—task and structure

The prison officer in the English prison system stands at the centre of the debates about prison policy. As the various attempts to implement the means of secondary task achievement have been made, the role of the officer has had to be discussed, however briefly. Since rehabilitation was defined as a means in the Gladstone Report, it has been declared that he has a vital contribution to make, and that he should be involved in the training of prisoners. This has been the view of several interested parties including the Howard League,[8] and the body which represents the officers, the Prison Officers' Association. The latter has set out its formulation of a new role in its memorandum entitled 'The Role of the Modern Prison Officer'. The ACTO report, *The Organisation of After Care* also emphasises the need for the prison officer's involvement in preparation for release. A detailed account of these developments in the role of the officer will be the subject of this study. For the purpose of this introduction it is necessary only to outline these pressures, because in spite of them, the officers remain, for the most part, 'mere fetchers and carriers of men for the people who come inside from the various bodies which interest themselves in prison work'.[9]

The para-military structure remains intact, and has recently been reinforced by the introduction of another grade, as was recommended in the Mountbatten Report. Except in borstals and junior detention centres, officers wear uniform; all are subject to a discipline code, and can be dealt with by senior staff for offences against discipline. They generally parade for duty, and salute senior staff (although the quality of the salute varies considerably).

The question with which this analysis is concerned is why the structure, and organisational culture, of the prison staff remains essentially the same as it was in 1877. This question can only be answered by examination of the primary task, which I have suggested is *control*. The stability of the staff structure is an indication of the persisting priority of this task, in spite of all pressures to change it. The prisoner population, for the most part, does not wish to be locked up. Therefore, in the total prison community, which includes the staff, there is not likely to be a universal consensus of agreement about behaviour which might result in an acceptance of the desirability of 'good order'. In a community which at times might see no virtue in 'good order', it is necessary to use coercion. Because of these differing attitudes to 'good order', and because of the existence of a coercive atmosphere, staff and inmates are in a relationship of hostility, potential, or actual. The degree and expression of this hostility will clearly vary from prison to prison, and from time to time. As a generalisation it may be said that the staff can never expect maximum co-operation from the inmates in the achievement of the institutional task. Martin describes something approaching a state of war in the American prison: 'They [the guards] are surrounded by depravity, brutality and cunning . . . he is never more than a few feet from dangerous men who hate him.'[10]

In this setting, therefore, loss of control must be avoided. The signs of this loss of control are escape or riot, both of which are easily visible to society. They are the manifest disaster criteria which demonstrate task failure. In England the criterion has generally been escape. In America, because of tighter perimeter security, the riot has been the visible sign of crisis. Faced with evidence of task failure, society is likely to respond in two ways. First, it will observe that the organisation is not achieving its task, and second, it will deplore the use of severity to regain control. If a crisis does erupt, therefore, socially acceptable, physical means of subduing it are limited. In the English system firearms have not been used since 1954, although they were employed before that date. Bodily restraints such as canvas jackets are used, but these cannot be used for control of the 'community', and anyway their use is restricted. Nor can the prison resort to the large-scale use of drugs as can the mental hospital, since prisoners are not 'sick' as are psychiatric patients. The mental hospital has been able to change its entire system of control of patients with the introduction of drug therapy. The locked ward is now a relative rarity. The mental hospital is able to argue, however, that the drug is primarily a means of treatment. This is acceptable with respect to the psychotic or neurotic patient, but is not tenable as an argument for administering drugs to apparently normal prisoners. The prison officer has only his 'stick', a short baton which is similar to a police truncheon. Physical aids to control have, until very recently, been confined to this weapon, a larger 'riot stick' and the architecture of the prison. As a result of the Blake escape, since 1966 several prisons have closed-circuit television and dog patrols.

Some means of control must therefore be built into the staff structure itself to deal with crisis or incipient crisis. Crisis is a hazard of many organisations. Mooney and Reiley describe the 'critical character' of the military situation and the necessity that all plans and their execution should be rushed in consequence.[11] They go on to point out parallel situations in the industrial firm. The mental hospital too has a structure which is able to cope with the crisis situation:[12]

> The hospital was organised so as always to be ready for an emergency, and at times of crisis both patients and staff relied on this formal organisation of power.

Just how quickly a crisis can arise in prison may be illustrated from this account of the riot in Jackson Prison, Michigan in 1952:[13]

> One quiet Sunday evening in the spring of 1952 Harold W. Tucker, the captain in charge of guards on the 2-to-10 shift at the state prison at Jackson, Michigan, answered the telephone at the Main Hall office in the rotunda just inside the prison gates and heard a man say, 'This is Ward talking in 15-block'. Tucker knew Earl Ward and he knew Earl Ward shouldn't be talking on the telephone; he should be locked in his cell, the cell that he never left except once a week to take a bath. Ward was a homicidal psychopath, considered one of the most dangerous convicts in the institution.

The crisis in this case has erupted. In prison the threat of crisis is always real, and the state of war analogy is accurate. Since the armed services have been manifestly evolved to deal with critical situations, it is no accident that the military structure has been adapted for use in other organisations, such as prisons, which have a controlling task. The para-military staff structure of the prison system is a means not of repressive punishment (although this may be an incidental effect), but of control. In prison services the para-military structure is above all a *crisis-controlling structure*, which can be quickly mobilised to deal with threats to that control. It is therefore inaccurate to explain away the para-military structure as an example of 'structural inertia'.[14] Nor is it designed primarily to satisfy the errant emotional needs of the people in it:[15]

> Further, in institutions the immature and unstable are to be found in positions of control and the result is that they mask their insecurity and insufficiency with rigid rules and authoritative discipline.

The structure exists to achieve a primary task of containment and control, and as long as the prison task is so defined by society, this structure is likely to persist. The analysis which follows, of the history of the English prison system, and evolution of the officer's role, will produce evidence which will support these several hypotheses.

Notes

1 In Cressey (ed.), *The Prison: Studies in Institutional Organisation and Change*, p. 122.
2 In Johnston *et al.* (eds), *The Sociology of Punishment and Correction*, p. 181.
3 'Organisations are social units (or human groupings) deliberately constructed and reconstructed to seek specific goals' (Etzioni, *Modern Organizations*, p. 3).
4 Rice, *Productivity and Social Organization*, p. 32.
5 W. Brown, *Exploration in Management*, p. 24.
6 See Nokes, *The Professional Task in Welfare Practice*, especially pp. 7, 19–22, 112–14.
7 Rice, op. cit., p. 32. See also Etzioni, op. cit., p. 78: 'The organisational goal of private business is to make profits.'
8 See Rose, *The Struggle for Penal Reform*, ch. 8.
9 Prison Officers' Association, 'The Role of the Modern Prison Officer', p. 1.
10 Martin, *Break Down the Walls*, p. 162.
11 Mooney and Reiley, *Onward Industry!*, p. 355. These writers discuss at length the organisational links between government, church, army and industry.
12 Stanton and Schwarz, *The Mental Hospital*, p. 248.
13 Martin, op. cit., p. 11.
14 'A built-in tendency for structures appropriate to an irrelevant organisational strategy to persist.' T. Lupton, *Journal of Management Studies*, vol. 2, p. 221.
15 Vaizey, *Scenes from Institutional Life*, p. 109.

2 The background to the centralisation of the prison system

The erosion of local power

The main contemporary source of information about the English prison system before 1800 is *The State of the Prisons* by John Howard.[1] This exposition of conditions in English and foreign prisons is well known, and has often been described. The end of the eighteenth century saw the beginning of serious debate about the prison system, and therefore forms a convenient starting point for this description of events leading to a centralised prison service.

When Howard wrote, neither the prisons nor the 'bridewells' were administered by the central government. They belonged to a mixture of authorities, predominantly the local justices. Bridewells, the first of which had been established in London between 1552 and 1557, differed from prisons because they were intended for the relief of destitution, not for punishment. A difference of some importance to the inmates was that in bridewells they were not entitled to food. By Elizabeth I's reign the common gaol prisoners had acquired a legal right to sustenance.[2] From about 1700 onwards their differences narrowed, and in most areas they became indistinguishable. Their formal differences were eliminated by the Prisons Act 1865.[3]

At the end of the eighteenth century there were three principal methods of punishment for serious offenders. They could be executed, they could be confined in the local prison or they could be transported. It was transportation and its problems which first involved the the central government directly in prison administration. When Howard was writing, transportation as a sentence was well established. The Webbs state that the earliest case of transportation occurred in 1619,[4] but Shaw records transportation to Virginia after its foundation in 1607.[5] Although in the beginning the numbers involved were small, it became an increasingly popular practice, happily providing para-slave labour for the American colonies. By the outbreak of the American War of Independence in 1776, about a thousand criminals a year were being transported.[6]

10

The war put a stop to this expedient, and the central government was therefore compelled to make alternative provision, since it was not likely that the inadequate resources of the local prisons could have coped with this new problem. The problem was solved by putting the transportees in 'hulks', old vessels converted for the purpose, and intended to be temporary. In 1776 the Hulks Act was passed which authorised their use for a period of two years. The first two were at Woolwich, but, echoing other 'temporary' expedients in the penal system of this country, the hulks proved to be more permanent than had originally been envisaged.

There are many contradictions and errors in the various accounts of the ending of the hulk system. The Webbs, for example, state that the last hulk was closed in 1858,[7] and Fox writes that 'the last hulk in this country was destroyed in 1857'.[8] The Gladstone Report states that: 'the very last hulk in fact to be closed was the *Stirling Castle* at Portsmouth in 1860, which was used for invalids. A new invalid prison was opened in Woking in that year.'[9] All of these are wrong. The hulks had always been extremely unsatisfactory places and the Convict Directors, as well as the staff in them, frequently expressed concern. Their end was expedited when the *Defence* at Woolwich was burned out and had to be scuttled on 14 July 1857.[10] On 1 September, the old county prison at Lewes, which had been bought by the government, was lent by the Admiralty to be an invalid convict prison. The convicts from the *Defence*, who had been temporarily housed at Millbank Prison, and those from the hulk *Unité*, were transferred to Lewes. There remained one hulk, the *Stirling Castle*, which was closed in 1859. This hulk was used incidentally for prisoners sent home from Bermuda and Gibraltar for discharge, not for invalids as the Gladstone Report stated.[11] The very last hulk to be administered by the English government was at Gibraltar, and it was closed in 1875.[12]

Until 1850 when the convict prisons and the hulks were centralised, and put under the Directors of Convict Prisons, the hulks were administered by a variety of authorities:[13]

The hulks were at first placed under the Local Justices; the overseer was appointed by them, and the other officers by the overseer; the maintenance of the establishment was committed to a contractor. . . . An inspector of the hulks was provided for in the Act but was not appointed until 1802.

This inspector had to report to the Court of King's Bench. In 1815 the Inspector was succeeded by a Superintendent of the hulks, a clerk in the Secretary of State's office, and a very powerful figure. The first was a man called Capper. The post of Superintendent was abolished in 1847, and until 1850 the duty of management was performed by 'a person' with an un-named office.

The hulks were not, however, the only solution to problems consequent upon the cessation of transportation. There was discussion about proposals to build a national penitentiary, and this discussion led to the Penitentiary Act of 1779. This Act proposed the building of penitentiaries and the establishment of a regime which was to include labour of the hardest and most servile kind, and compulsory attendance at religious services.[14] The Act authorised the appointment of three people to select a site for the penitentiary. The three men who were chosen, Howard, Fothergill and Whatley, could not agree on a site, and this failure to agree was the first impediment in a complex of blockages, which was to include the abortive 'Panopticon' proposal of Jeremy Bentham.[15] Much of the impetus was lost when the decision was taken to transport convicts to newly discovered Australia. The first expedition was in 1787.[16]

In spite of the renewal of transportation, interest in the setting up of a penitentiary was maintained, as were efforts to raise standards in the local prisons. In 1784, and 1791, Prison Acts were passed which applied the principles of the proposed national penitentiaries to all prisons. But the local authorities could safely ignore these principles, since the central government had no sanctions with which to support either its mandatory or voluntary exhortations. As Wedderburn wrote in 1793: 'It is not so much from want of good laws, as from their inexecution, that the state of the prisons is so bad.'

This was to be the response of the local authorities, with very few exceptions, until total centralisation. The prison history of the period has, as its pivot, the rejection by the local authorities of bold principles of administrative reform. The beginning of the nineteenth century saw the emergence of a pattern of refusal to reassess priorities in the management of prisons which was to characterise the operation of the prisons by local government. It became increasingly evident as the central government developed its own network of convict establishments, that divided responsibility for prisons was unworkable.

Eventually, in 1816, the proposed penitentiary, Millbank, was started on the site of what is now the Tate Gallery. The Gladstone

Report is wrong when it states that Millbank was *opened* in 1816. It was completed in 1821,[17] but it was:[18]

> One of the most costly of all the buildings that the world had then seen since the pyramids of Egypt, the total expense from first to last amounting to not far short of three quarters of a million sterling.

Historically Millbank was of the greatest significance since it brought the central government into the mainstream of English prison administration. Although the government had undertaken the cost of maintaining prisoners in the hulks in 1779,[19] these were in spite of their apparent permanence, at least theoretically, temporary. Millbank demonstrated that the government was taking a manifestly permanent share in prison management. The new prison was the corner-stone of an organisational development which was to culminate in the establishment of the convict service, which, in turn, was to be the basis of a comprehensive national prison system. And so from 1821 there were two prison 'services' in England. The central service, which consisted of the hulks and Millbank, paid its staff and so broke with the tradition that they had to earn salaries by exploiting the prisoners. The hulks were administered by a Superintendent, and Millbank was managed by an eminent Committee, including the Speaker of the House of Commons. The local 'service', or more correctly 'services', were controlled by the justices. They continued to exercise restraint in reforming their prisons, since this meant added expenditure, and a resultant burden on the rates. The salaried gaoler was a rarity. In the early years of the nineteenth century there was little evidence that the local authorities would be likely to allocate more money to prisons as a result of any reassessment of the treatment of prisoners. In 1815 the Aldermen of the City of London declared that: 'their prisoners had all they ought to have, unless gentlemen thought they should be indulged with Turkey carpets'.[20]

During the period when Millbank was being built, organised and articulate pressure for prison reform was powerful. Especially noteworthy are the reports of James Neild, and Thomas Fowell Buxton, and the work of Elizabeth Fry. It is extremely difficult to know how much real difference the work of legendary figures like Mrs Fry made to the lives of prisoners. There is no assessment by the prisoners, and most accounts come from her, and sympathetic friends. Fox puts her, along with Florence Nightingale, 'among the greatest English-women'.[21] The Reverend Sydney Smith, a contemporary, was more restrained: 'Mrs Fry is an amiable and excellent woman . . . but hers are not the methods to stop crimes.'[22] Du Cane, characteristically, evaluated her impact on prisoners, after a scrutiny of the arithmetic of the situation:[23]

> It came to such a point that at the religious services held by the ladies there were twenty-three visitors, many of them gentlemen, to twenty-eight prisoners.

In the same passage Du Cane wrote of the 'difficulty' of the 'irregular authority' which had been given to the ladies since their efforts made 'a visit to the female department of Newgate one of the fashionable sensations of the day'.

In 1820 there was a Select Committee which strongly recommended action on prison reform. In 1822 Peel became Home Secretary, and in 1823 the Gaol Act was passed. This 'was the first measure of general prison reform to be framed and enacted on the responsibility of the national executive.'[24] The Act provided for quarterly reports by the justices to the Home Secretary, systematic inspection by the justices, payment of a salary to gaolers, abolition of private trading by gaolers, improved accommodation, supervision of females by females, and the keeping of work journals by the gaoler, the chaplain, and the surgeon, which were to be presented to the Quarter Sessions. There was also insistence upon productive labour, education, and religious observance.

Although the Act was a very impressive statement of progressive policy, it was only marginally successful. It had three major defects which militated against real success: there was no machinery for enforcement, there was no inspectorate to supervise or advise on implementation, and the measure applied only to a minority of prisons—those of the county justices, of the Cities of London and Westminster, and seventeen provincial towns. The London debtors' prison and 150 gaols in minor municipalities were excluded. The Webbs draw attention to the inexplicable fact that, for example, Bristol, Hull, Worcester and York were included, but Leeds, Dover, Oxford and Cambridge were excluded.[25] With such defects the Act was largely unsuccessful in its attempt to stabilise the erratic prison system. The whole problem seemed so insoluble that Peel wrote on 14 March 1826 to Sydney Smith: 'I despair of any remedy but that which I wish I could hope for—a great reduction in the amount of crime.'[26] In spite of the exceptional reformative work of isolated local authorities such as Gloucestershire, which had pioneered improvements under the leadership of Sir George Onesiphorus Paul[27] for thirty years, it became clear during the 1820s that the condition of the local prisons was not likely to improve without further direction from the central government.

In 1832 a Whig government came to power in a reformed Parliament:[28]

> In all its projects of reform, [it] was dominated by two leading assumptions—the value of uniformity of administration throughout the country and the impossibility of attaining this uniformity without a large increase in the activity of the central Government.

A House of Commons Committee in 1832 was followed by a House of Lords Committee in 1835, which was chaired by the Duke of Richmond. As well as producing substantial reports on the prisons, the investigation led to another very important Act in 1835. This Act was: 'for effecting greater uniformity of practice in the government of the several prisons in England and Wales, and for appointing inspectors of prisons in Great Britain'. Five inspectors were appointed, and this inspectorate was a further major step to centralisation. Although the central government could still not enforce the advice given to local authorities, the published reports of the inspectors performed a valuable function, by constantly exposing to public view defective administration when it occurred. Their first report on Newgate, for example, gives ample evidence that the prison was in a very unsatisfactory state. The Inspectors found prisoners with considerable authority over other prisoners, drunkenness, 'rioting, uproar, and fighting' and breach of the '2nd, 3rd and 6th and 7th Rules of the Gaol Act, which require that female prisoners shall be constantly attended by female officers'. There was 'utter absence of all employment for the prisoners'.[29] And in 1853 it was an Inspector, J. G. Perry, who uncovered the scandals which led to a Royal Commission being appointed to investigate the use of illegal punishments in Birmingham Prison.[30]

The Secretary of State extended his influence further by an Act of 1839 which gave him certain powers over the design of new prisons, or the renovation of existing ones. This new, and very important area of central influence was consolidated in 1844 by a further Act, which authorised the appointment of a Surveyor General of Prisons. All proposed building plans, and alterations to existing plans had to be referred to him. The government had increased its own resources by building Pentonville 'model' prison, which was opened in December 1842. There were now two convict prisons as well as the juvenile prison at Parkhurst. The work was carried out by 'Mr Crawford, Mr Whitworth Russell, the two first inspectors, both very prominent prison reformers, and Captain, afterwards Sir Joshua, Jebb, RE.'[31] Jebb was also to become first Surveyor General, and first Chairman of the Directors of Convict Prisons.

In the six years after the building of Pentonville, no fewer than 'fifty-four new prisons were built . . . affording 11,000 separate cells.'[32] The extent of this building makes the period one of the most remarkable in the history of the prison system:[33]

> One is lost, in these lean years, in admiration and envy of the formidable energy and resources which could thus produce great new prisons at the rate of one every year or so.

In 1850 the convict service was established. An Act gave the Secretary of State authority to appoint Directors of Convict Prisons, who were to take over the management of the hulks from the 'person' in charge, and of Millbank and Pentonville from the Committee and Commissioners. The first Chairman was Joshua Jebb. The institutions which the Directors had to manage, and which were to be the embryo of the later centralised service were, on 31 December 1850:[34]

> Prisons for separate confinement: Millbank and Pentonville.
> Cells for separate confinement rented in eight local prisons: Wakefield, Preston, Leeds, Leicester, Northampton, Bath, Reading and Bedford.
> Prisons for public works: Portland (opened 1849), Dartmoor (reopened 1850).
> Prisons for juveniles: Parkhurst.
> Hulks: Woolwich—*Warrior, Justitia*; Portsmouth—*York, Stirling Castle*.
> Invalid depots: Shorncliff Barracks and *Defence*.

The early years of the convict service will be discussed later.
A second major event in 1850 was a Select Committee on Prison

Discipline under Sir George Grey. This Committee was especially important because it examined the question of the relative merits of the 'silent' and 'separate' systems. There had been intense argument about these systems for thirty years. This discussion appears to be about 'reforming' criminals. I shall suggest later that in fact there were other more subtle and sophisticated issues in the discussion, and it is necessary therefore to describe what the 'systems' were. The silent system allowed 'association' for certain purposes, work for instance, but prisoners were forbidden to speak. The separate system kept prisoners in cellular isolation. They were not allowed to speak to each other, but they could talk to the governor and other officials who visited them in their cells. This rather limited concession distinguished the separate system from solitary confinement, where isolation was complete.[35] Although the opinions offered to the Committee reflected conflicting views about the systems, the Committee expressed itself in favour of separation, as indeed had previous influential groups:[36]

> The Inspectors' Third Report of 1838 was preceded by a hundred pages of introduction devoted to the defence of cellular isolation in which all the arguments in its favour are marshalled.

All kinds of reasons were given for preferring it to a silent system: for example that a silence rule, in association, is impossible to enforce without excessive punishment. In the Second Report of the Inspectors of Prisons on Coldbath Fields for 1836, it is pointed out that in the year there were 'no less than 5,138 punishments for talking and swearing'.[37]

While these debates about regimes were going on, there was increasing pressure on the convict prisons. Once again transportation was proving difficult. The concern in England about the justice and efficacy of transportation, was matched by an increasing reluctance on the part of Australia to take any more convicts. A Parliamentary Commission on Transportation, the Molesworth Committee, in 1837–8 condemned the practice and recommended detention in penitentiaries instead. In 1840, the government announced that no more convicts would be sent to New South Wales and the last ship arrived there on 18 November 1840.[38] In 1853 an Act was passed which allowed substitution of a sentence of penal servitude,[39] which could be served in England, for all crimes punishable by transportation for less than fourteen years. In 1852 transportation to Van Diemen's Land (now Tasmania) was stopped.[40] In that year 1,844 convicts were transported.[41] The crisis was slightly eased by the co-operation of South Australia, which agreed to continue taking convicts in 1850.[42] Less successful was a remarkable attempt to land 300 convicts on the Cape of Good Hope. This was 'resisted to the point of rebellion'.[43] In 1867 transportation to Western Australia ceased,[44] although ten years later, there were still 630 convicts there in various stages of imprisonment.[45] In 1850 Sir George Grey reported to Parliament that there was accommodation for only 12,900 convicts, 'while nearly 5,000 were sentenced to transportation every year'. For a number of reasons the situation did not become desperate[46] but it was clear that the convict service was going to have to develop resources to cope with all long-sentence prisoners in England.

During the years 1837–60, while methods of dealing with offenders were being adapted, the local prisons were still in a very unsatisfactory state. Grey's Select Committee of 1850 had stated that: 'Several prisons are still in a very unsatisfactory condition and proper punishment, separation or reformation in them is impossible.' The Royal Commission on Birmingham Prison has been mentioned, and there was another which investigated similar allegations at Leicester prison. Together they: 'Contributed not a little, though at an interval of a quarter of a century, to popular acquiescence in the measure of 1877.'[47] Fear of criminals who could no longer be transported, concern at the brutality and incompetence of many local prisons, and 'a sudden increase in the number of robberies with violence in the streets of London'[48] in the early 1860s, all contributed to the establishment of one of the most important prison committees of the century. This was the Select Committee of the House of Lords on Prison Discipline, 1863. The Committee which was chaired by Lord Carnarvon made recommendations which were to have drastic effects on English prisons. They rejected many of the principles which had been advocated by the Inspectors, 'especially Mr Perry'. It was Perry who had first reported the irregularities at Birmingham which led to the Royal Commission. Roberts, writing of the Victorian Inspectors, rather surprisingly describes Perry as 'one of the most indifferent'.[49] The tone of their views is summed up in the following statement (p. XIV of the Report):

They do not consider that the moral reformation of the offender holds the primary place in the prison system; that mere industrial employment without wages is a sufficient punishment for many crimes; that punishment in itself is morally prejudicial to the criminal and useless to society, or that it is desirable to abolish both the crank and treadwheel as soon as possible.

The 'terrible recommendations'[50] of the Report 'against which no protest was made'[51] were duly implemented. These have often been described.[52] For the purpose of examining the events leading to centralisation, the Report is important because it catalogued yet again the chronic deficiencies of the local administration—'unrestrained association', dormitories, questionable accounting systems and so on.[53] In 1865 a Prisons Act was passed which intruded even further into the administrative independence of the local authorities It 'constituted the turning point of English prison administration in the second half of the nineteenth century.'[54] The provisions of the Act were based on the recommendations of the 1863 Committee.[55] Two are of especial relevance to this account. The first is that the Act decreed a staff complement which had to include a gaoler, a chaplain, a surgeon and a matron for women (job specifications were set out in great detail in Schedule I) and forbade the employment of prisoners as staff. The second is that the grant from the central government to the local authority could be withdrawn if the latter failed to comply with the Act. The Secretary of State was also empowered to close an inadequate prison. But, as Du Cane points out,[56] this could not have been done unless another authority was willing to receive the 'redundant' prisoners. The government seems to have decided in the light of its experience with local authorities, that the only effective sanction would be withdrawal of finance. It was to be claimed in the debates about the Act of 1877 that the 1865 Act was not effective in bringing about the uniformity of management and treatment which seemed desirable. Nevertheless it marked clearly the end of an aspect of local autonomy which had been characterised primarily by a refusal to observe even the minimal conditions of care for prisoners which the government laid down. Nor was the central government going to let the matter rest.

The Prisons Act 1877—the end of local administration

This increasing influence of the central government in the administration of prisons, had its parallels in other developing social and welfare services. In fact, the prisons were a minor issue compared with more important controversies, such as the administration of the poor law, or education. Nevertheless the several Prison Acts, and the activities of the inspectors, all contributed to the increasing involvement of the central government in what had hitherto been local affairs.[57] After 1832 this involvement gained momentum quickly.

Centralisation was not the policy of any one party or group. Nor was the opposition to it, which was widespread, articulate, and often powerful, based upon any political ideology or philosophical dogma.[58] It was an issue which found supporters and detractors in groups which usually were homogeneous in their views. The Howard Association, for instance, in the discussion about the Act of 1877 was confused over the issue of centralising prisons.[59] In the absence of clear-cut party divisions based on firm political consensus there arose a mood of 'presumptuous empiricism'[60] with each reform between 1833 and 1854 being passed 'to meet an observed fact, not to accord with a principle'.[61] The political pragmatism which grew up may be illustrated by the fact that it was Disraeli and his party, with their long record of hostility to centralised administration,[62] who passed the most extreme centralising legislation of the century—the Prisons Act of 1877.

The Conservative government which was returned in 1874 was committed to a reduction in the rates.[63] The centralisation of the administration of prisons was one of the ways in which this could be achieved. Other possibilities, such as greater control over lunatics or the police, were not as suitable.[64] The Queen's Speech on 8 February 1876 contained an announcement that the prison system was due for further major administrative reorganisation: 'Your attention will be called also . . . to a measure for promoting economy and efficiency in the management of prisons and at the same time effecting a relief of local burthens.' On 1 June 1876, Assheton Cross, the Home Secretary, introduced a Prisons Bill for first reading.[65] It proposed the transfer of the management of the local prisons to the central government. Cross dealt with two issues—'the condition of our prisons' and 'the expense of their management'. These issues had been brought to his attention as an MP, and as a magistrate. Further, in 1874 concern about the prisons had been expressed, 'by a deputation which waited on me at the Home Office from the Social Science Association'. This deputation had pointed out that there was a great want of uniformity of discipline, a great want of efficiency, and a great amount of unnecessary expense, 'owing to the excessive number of our prisons'. Cross went on to describe the financial waste in the system. Forty-nine of the small prisons, for instance, had a daily average population from 49 to 2. Finally he outlined proposals for a Prison Commission.

This speech contained the two principal arguments in favour of centralisation. They were relief for the local rates, and achievement of a uniform system of discipline. Previous Prison Acts had not met with much opposition. The Act of 1835 received no attention from the press and little debate in Parliament.[66] How extensive was the opposition to this Bill? Rose states that 'it was obvious the Bill would go through without much difficulty'[67] and the Webbs consider that the Act encountered 'even less opposition than had been expected'.[68] There was, in fact, fierce opposition although it is difficult to gauge its extent or how representative it was. If it was lacking in quantity, it more than made up for it in quality.

In the main, the opposition mobilised arguments which had been made to resist government interference in factories, poor law, education and other services. The essence of these arguments was that the central government was incompetent, that costs would rise, that 'patronage' would increase, but above all that local government should be inviolate. The advice given to the editor of the *Spectator* of a hundred years before, was now offered to Cross. He was warned to:

> Take care how he meddled with the county squires for they
> were the ornament of the English nation—men of good heads
> and sound bodies.

One of the most vocal opponents of the Bill was John Rylands, Member for Burnley, and a member of the general committee of the Howard Association. His persistent opposition caused Cross to remark that in Rylands's speech could be found:

> A valuable index to the debates and anyone referring to [his
> speech] will find a summary of everything that can be said, or
> suggested, or imagined against the Bill.

The supporters of the Bill in general disagreed with the view that rule by the magistrates was 'local control'. It was pointed out that power would be taken from the magistrates, who were answerable to nobody, and given to the Home Secretary, directly responsible to Parliament. A more pedestrian note was introduced when it was suggested that the objections were in some way associated with the purveying of meat and stores for the prisons.

As well as these arguments for and against the Bill, which had been marshalled when other measures for government control had been proposed, there was some discussion about matters peculiar to prisons. During the committee stage of the Bill, a group of Irish Members played an active part in trying to ameliorate conditions in prison. Some of these had been in prison,[69] and so were able to speak with a rare authority on the subject. Led by Parnell, and supported by a small group of radicals, they were not very successful with their various suggestions, which ranged from abolishing flogging, to establishing a complaint book in which prisoners could write, and which the public could see. Parnell did manage to gain two concessions. People convicted of contempt of court were to be classified as first-class misdemeanants, which meant rather more congenial circumstances in prison, and tests of malingering could be made only by the authority of the justices. Finally, in the Act people convicted of sedition and seditious libel were classed as first-class misdemeanants. This extra category has all the hallmarks of pressure exerted by the Irish group. The impact of the Irish on the prison system was to be considerable during the next forty years. They were generally violent, unco-operative, and the subject of several investigations. Their contribution to the evolution of the English prison system may be as significant as their contribution to other facets of English life, and is worthy of special study.[70]

There were only two other components in the debates both of which were consonant with public interest at the time. The first was a brief suggestion that Communism was at work in the bill since: 'burdens would be taken off those who were of the poorer sort and put on the wealthy in the land'. The second was the view, expressed notably by G. H. Whalley, a noted anti-Catholic Member, that a Catholic conspiracy was at work, which, he suggested, was mainly inspired by anger that the local authorities had been slow to appoint Roman Catholic chaplains in the prisons.

There was some evidence in the debates of opposition from the local authorities, but again it is difficult to be certain how widespread this was. A petition from the Corporation of Nottingham was mentioned, and *The Times* (6 March 1877, p. 8) reported that, of the various municipalities and courts of Quarter Sessions, '10 were for, 13 were indifferent, and 2 were neutral'. Birmingham was declared to be unanimously against the Bill. During 1877 some local authorities continued to actively oppose the Bill. Oxford City Council affixed the City Seal to a petition to Parliament against the Bill, complaining that it was only a few years since they spent £3–4,000 on their gaol. At a meeting of the Association of Municipal Corporations at Westminster Palace Hotel, Mr Chamberlain moved a resolution that the objects of the Bill could have been achieved without interference with principles of local self-government, and that expenses to be met out of taxes as a result of the changes would be increased. The resolution was carried 'almost without opposition'.

The opposition was unsuccessful. After a brief debate in the House of Lords, the Bill received the Royal Assent on 12 July. The earlier prison legislation had been part of the 'imperfections, the confusions, and the weaknesses' of the earlier Victorian administrative state of the years 1833–54. The Prisons Act of 1877 like other legislation, such as the Education Act of 1870, the Mining Act of 1877, and the Factory Act of 1878, was an inevitable 'consolidating measure'.[71] Nevertheless in its transfer of power it went further than any other had ever done, or would ever do. *The Times*, which in principle consistently deplored centralisation, supported the Act in practice, as it did almost every other similar reform.[72] In approving its enactment on 12 September 1877 it pointed out that it had taken: 'all the vigour and energy of Mr Cross to get it through'.

The kernel of the Act was the transfer of every aspect of prison administration to the Secretary of State. He became responsible for all the prisons, their furniture and effects, the appointment of all the officers, and 'the control and safe custody of the prisoners'. To him went all the powers which had been held by the justices in respect of Acts, charters, and common law. A new body, the Prison Commission, was appointed to operate the new department. There was to be a maximum of five Commissioners, one of whom could be appointed chairman. To the Commission was delegated the organisation of the new prison service, and the detailed administration which had hitherto been carried out by the justices, In particular the Commissioners were to appoint 'subordinate officers' and had to make an annual report to the Home Secretary. This was to include details of manufacturing work carried on, and particulars of punishment which had been administered. The Inspectorate was to remain to assist, and its members were to be appointed by the Home Secretary.

The justices were not entirely excluded from the local prisons. Any justices who had jurisdiction in either the place where a prison was, or where an offence had been committed by a prisoner, could visit at any time, could inspect the prison, and could enter observations in the visitors' book. In addition there was to be a Visiting Committee of Justices, appointed by the Quarter Sessions or Magistrates' Benches. The duties prescribed for this Committee have remained substantially unchanged in the last ninety years. They were to visit regularly, listen to complaints—in private, if requested—report on abuses and so on. Ideally therefore they could act as a restraint on the excesses of the administration. A prisoner could complain to them, and since they were no longer in charge, they could afford to be impartial. In theory, prisoners were given extra protection because of the establishment of the Visiting Committee.

Apart from provision for prisoners convicted for sedition, seditious libel or contempt of court being classified as first-class misdemeanants, and for tests of malingering to be given only with the authority of the Visiting Committee or Prison Commissioner, there were not, in the Act, a lot of new rules and orders about the management of prisons. There were already plenty of those.[73] The importance of the establishment of a Commission was that now they could be enforced.

With this Act, about 800 years of local control over prisons was brought to a close. The English prisons had been insecure and squalid even by the standards of the age. The names of some— Newgate for instance—were bywords for corruption and misery for hundreds of years. Prison administration had not been one of the brightest episodes in the history of local government, and it was difficult to imagine how prisoners could fail to be better off under the central government.

Notes

1 The first edition was in 1778. There were several editions which varied in content. A short edited version was published by J. M. Dent & Sons in the Everyman's Library series in 1929. For an account of the man, see D. L. Howard, *John Howard—Penal Reformer*. Contemporary accounts of the system predating Howard's are in Pugh, *Imprisonment in Medieval England* and Clay, *The Prison Chaplain*, pp. 22–30.

2 Clay, op. cit., pp. 22–3.

3 S. and B. Webb, *English Prisons under Local Government*, ch. 1, gives

a detailed account of the development of both institutions, with a valuable list of sources about their operation.

4 Ibid., p. 44. In footnote 1 there is an extensive bibliography of the subject. See also Du Cane, *The Punishment and Prevention of Crime*, ch. 5.
5 Shaw, *Convicts and the Colonies*, p. 23. This book gives a very full account of transportation.
6 S. and B. Webb, op. cit., p. 44.
7 Ibid., p. 45.
8 Fox, *The English Prison and Borstal Systems*, p. 38.
9 Gladstone Report, p. 460. Woking, in fact, was opened on 28 April 1859—see Convict Report 1859, p. 298.
10 Convict Report 1857, p. 304 et seq.
11 Convict Report 1859, p. 148.
12 Du Cane, op. cit., p. 118.
13 Du Cane, op. cit., p. 122.
14 The Act is discussed in Fox, op. cit., p. 31; and the consequent legislation by S. and B. Webb, op. cit., ch. 4.
15 Details of the sequence of events are described by S. and B. Webb, op. cit., p. 46 et seq.
16 Shaw, op. cit., p. 51; S. and B. Webb, op. cit., p. 46.
17 Du Cane, op. cit., p. 125.
18 S. and B. Webb, op. cit., pp. 48–9. The precise figure in the Gladstone Report, p. 459, is £458,310. Du Cane (op. cit., p. 125) quotes an expenditure of £458,000.
19 Du Cane, op. cit., p. 184.
20 Clay, op. cit., p. 91 (quoted in Fox, op. cit., p. 27).
21 Fox, op. cit., p. 28.
22 Quoted by Shaw, op. cit., p. 135.
23 Du Cane, op. cit., p. 48.
24 S. and B. Webb, op. cit., p. 73.
25 Ibid., p. 73, n. 3.
26 Parker (ed.), *Sir Robert Peel*, vol. 1, p. 402.
27 For information about Sir George Onesiphorus Paul, see S. and B. Webb, op. cit.
28 S. and B. Webb, op. cit., p. 110.
29 Parliamentary Papers 1836, XXXV.
30 An outline is given in S. and B. Webb, op. cit., p. 170. For an account of the various government inspectorates, see Roberts, *Victorian Origins of the Welfare State*, especially ch. 6.
31 Du Cane, op. cit., p. 52.
32 Ibid., p. 56.
33 Fox, op. cit., p. 41.
34 *Report on the Discipline and Management of the Convict Prisons*, 1851.
35 For a full description of the two systems, see S. and B. Webb, op. cit., ch. 9; Fox, op. cit., pp. 32–9.
36 For a defence of the separate system, see Burt, *Results of the System of Separate Confinement as Administered at the Pentonville Prison*.

37 Parliamentary Papers 1837, XXXII.
38 Shaw, op. cit., p. 275.
39 For a description of penal servitude, see Du Cane, op. cit., ch. 6; S. and B. Webb, op. cit., ch. 10.
40 Shaw, op. cit., p. 275.
41 This is calculated from the reception and discharge figures given in the reports of individual establishments in the Convict Report for 1852.
42 Du Cane, op. cit., p. 147.
43 Ibid., p. 147. For an account of the incident, see Shaw, op. cit., p. 327.
44 Shaw, op. cit., p. 358.
45 Convict Report 1877, Western Australia, p. 586.
46 Shaw, op. cit., p. 348.
47 S. and B. Webb, op. cit., p. 170.
48 Ibid., p. 187.
49 Roberts, op. cit., p. 209.
50 S. and B. Webb, op. cit., p. 189.
51 Ibid., p. 188.
52 See S. and B. Webb, op. cit., ch. 11; Fox, op. cit., p. 46 and app. C (which gives extracts from the Report).
53 Report, p. XV.
54 S. and B. Webb, op. cit., p. 191.
55 Du Cane, op. cit., p. 58. The detailed provisions are discussed by S. and B. Webb, op. cit., pp. 188–92.
56 Du Cane, op. cit., p. 62.
57 Roberts, op. cit., p. 45.
58 Ibid., p. 101.
59 Rose, *The Struggle for Penal Reform*, pp. 39–41.
60 Roberts, op. cit., p. 96.
61 Ibid., p. 101.
62 Ibid., p. 96.
63 S. and B. Webb, op. cit., p. 198; Du Cane, op. cit., p. 66.
64 Rose, op. cit., p. 38.
65 The Bill is first reported in Hansard, vol. 229, col. 1536 et seq. There was not time to deal with it and it was reintroduced in February 1877 and is reported in Hansard, vol. 232, col. 133 et seq.
66 Roberts, op. cit., p. 45.
67 Rose, op. cit., p. 38.
68 S. and B. Webb, op. cit., p. 200, n. 1.
69 As had many of their countrymen. Proportionately, 'Ireland gives us above five times its proper number' of prisoners (Seventh Local Report, p. 10).
70 For the Irish contribution to the trade union movement, for example, see Jackson, *The Irish in Britain*, ch. 6.
71 Roberts, op. cit., p. 95.
72 Ibid., p. 100.
73 See, for example, Schedule I to the Act of 1865, which lays down very detailed rules.

3 Building the prison service

The new Prison Commission

On 17 July 1877, five days after the Act received the Royal Assent,[1] the three newly appointed Commissioners and their Chairman, Lieutenant-Colonel Edmund Frederick du Cane, met for the first time.[2] Du Cane was the obvious choice for the post. After a distinguished training at the Royal Military Academy at Woolwich, where he passed out at the head of his term, he was commissioned in the Royal Engineers. In 1851 he was employed in a very responsible position, alongside other Sappers, in the organisation of the Great Exhibition. When this was finished he was sent to Western Australia, and there supervised the building of extensive public works with convict labour until 1856. His exceptional skills as an engineer, and as a magistrate, resulted in a special report being made by the Governor.

When Du Cane returned to England in 1856 he was selected to take part in very important and highly skilled work on the fortification of dockyards and arsenals. Some of the biggest of these defence systems were constructed from his own designs, including those of Dover and Plymouth. His ability drew another special commendation, this time from the Committee which reported on the work.

In 1863 he was made a Director of convict prisons, mainly because of the extensive public works which were being built with convict labour. At the same time he was appointed Inspector of military prisons. In 1869 Captain du Cane was appointed Chairman of the Board of Directors of Convict Prisons, and quickly established an international reputation as an expert in penal administration. He continually drew the attention of the government to the unsatisfactory state of the local prisons, and in fact the Home Secretary's speech upon introducing the Prisons Bill in 1876, was virtually a reproduction of an address which had been given by Du Cane to the Social Science Congress at Brighton in 1875. On 6 August 1877 he was appointed a Knight Commander of the Bath. When he became Chairman of the Commissioners, he was forty-seven, and a Lieutenant-Colonel in his corps.[3]

The Royal Engineers established a considerable reputation as administrators and inspectors in the emerging Victorian government departments. The first three chairmen of the Board of Directors of Convict Prisons were all Sapper officers. The esteem in which they were held was summed up by Henry Labouchere at the Board of Trade, who said:[4]

> Whenever the government was in difficulty in finding an officer of high capacity for civil administration, the right man was sure to be obtained among the officers of the Royal Engineers.

Accounts of the English prison system express great distaste for Du Cane and his work. The most charitable remark to be found is that he was carrying out the wishes of Parliament.[5] He is usually regarded as the symbol of all that was harsh in the Victorian system. Actually he is the greatest figure in the history of the English prison system. His phenomenal capacity for hard work and attention to detail, his certainty of action when action was necessary, his many skills, and his scrupulous integrity made him a personification of all the Victorian virtues. He created the English prison service with all its strengths and weaknesses, and a proper evaluation of his achievements is long overdue. Du Cane's advent was not altogether devoid of advantages for prisoners. He increased the number of paid Catholic chaplains, and abolished flogging parades and shot drill. There were many other beneficial changes.[6]

The administrative task facing Du Cane and the Commissioners was formidable. As late as 1895 the enormity of the task excited wonder, even from an experienced administrator like Sir Godfrey Lushington, Permanent Under Secretary at the Home Office at the time of the Gladstone Committee Report:[7]

> The work of taking over nearly 120 prisons, all on a single day and consolidating them into about 60; organising the staff, every member of which had statutory rights reserved to him; re-arranging the buildings and establishing uniformity, has really been a work of prodigious magnitude, on which an immense amount of thought, contrivance, and skill has been expended.

The Gladstone Committee agreed, grudgingly perhaps, that: 'The long and able administration of Sir E. Du Cane has achieved a large measure of success.'[8]

The essential prerequisite for administrative success is a balance between authority and accountability. No administrator can be effective unless he has the executive power which springs from this balance. Much of the malaise which occurs in various grades of the prison service in the course of its history, can be traced to the lack of co-ordination of these two components of administration. Du Cane was fortunate. He had this executive power. He was accountable for what happened, as the events of 1895 were to show, but he was given corresponding authority to rationalise the system. The Commissioners were in a position to review the historical development of the prisons, to examine and clarify society's expectations of the system, and to act. Not only was the new Commission extremely powerful, it was administratively unique:[9]

> A great administrative service, extending through the whole country, which had been for centuries within the sphere of Local Government, was transferred en bloc to a department of the National Government. In no other branch of public administration has such a change been made in England.

Two reasons had been given as justification for this singular concentration of power—'economy' and 'uniformity'. It is necessary now to examine the relationship and relative importance of these, since they provided terms of reference for the new Commission.

'Economy and uniformity'

Du Cane constantly emphasises the priority of 'economy' as a mandate emanating from the Act, as did *The Times* in its final comment when it was operational.[10] In their early reports the Commissioners often point out how much money was being saved. In the debates, however, the financial advantages apparently became less important as the discussion developed. It was soon claimed that the saving would be slight; '$\frac{3}{4}d$ in the pound' became something of a term of abuse, and in any case *someone* would still have to pay for the prisons. Chamberlain was one of several who pointed out that 'the bribe would be a very small one',[11] to which Cross replied, incredibly, that 'he had never brought it forward as a measure especially intended to promote economy'.[12] The financial justification for the Bill became so unimportant during the third reading, that a Member commented that as, 'the discussion of the measures had gone on, less and less was said about economy in the transfer of the prisons to the government'.[13] The Webbs point out that the financial arguments, although they may have been 'the determining factor', were not really sound. They show that the much admired reduction in rates could have been achieved in other ways, such as 'an extension of the system of grants in aid'.[14] How important then was the question of finance?

In reality while the financial aspects of the administration of prisons loomed large in discussion and debate, 'economy' was not the central issue. There had been long-standing arguments about whether or not prisons ought to be profitable, but while the government felt that they should not, this issue did not justify centralisation. The change in the financing of the prison system was not an end in itself. It was a necessary prelude to the second aim—'uniformity'. Without centralised direction, 'uniformity' was not possible. And without uniformity, the real defect in the prison system could not be remedied. This defect was 'contamination'.

Reformers such as Howard and Fry, administrators such as Jebb and Du Cane, inspectors such as Perry, while they may have differed over some questions, were agreed that the universal, single, depressing feature of prison life, from which most other weaknesses sprung, was contamination. Everyone was worried because society took people, many of whom were criminally unsophisticated, and propelled them into a situation where they faced physical and moral danger. Society had called into being the prison community, but felt uneasy because society's agents, the prison staff, lost control of what was happening to people who had been put in a position of enforced dependency. On the hulks, for example, where association was inevitable, there was 'terrorism'.[15] Contamination was made possible by this 'association', especially where young and old, male and female were herded indiscriminately, and it followed that the reduction or elimination of social contact was necessary to eliminate contamination.

Two regimes, the 'silent' and the 'separate', had been developed to deal with the problem of contamination, and during the nineteenth century there was sharp disagreement about the merits and defects of each. But it became clear that, in association, silence rules are unenforceable. Not only do prisoners talk in spite of them, but they develop non-verbal means of communication, notably by tapping or knocking. The existence of such codes is mentioned occasionally. The Irish prisoners in Chatham in 1890 used a code to communicate with each other,[16] and a prisoner giving evidence to the Gladstone Committee observed that no matter how strict a silence rule was, 'it would be utterly impossible to keep prisoners from communicating in some way or other.'[17] And it is from the silent era that the most famous prison slang word comes—'snout' for tobacco: a request for this was communicated by touching the nose.

Physical association therefore resulted in communication, which in turn led to contamination. To reduce both to a minimum it was necessary to eliminate physical association; and it was this which the separate system was primarily intended to effect. But central control was necessary before it could be universally employed. Local authorities were laggardly in introducing it sometimes because they disapproved of it, sometimes because they were unwilling to spend money on the necessary rebuilding or alteration.

It is worth noting that the separate system, whatever its defects, *does* eliminate contamination. The bulk of commentators on the system view it with great distaste, seeing in it only a punitive function. To many it is the symbol and the essence of all that was deplorable about the Victorian prison. Association would appear to be intrinsically more desirable. Observers, generalising from their own feelings, often express the hope that association would civilise what is essentially an uncivilised experience—imprisonment. But whether or not separate confinement for most of the day, and all of the night, is more tedious and punitive than enforced association with unstable and aggressive companions, is at least debatable. It is possible that many prisoners would prefer even the excessive privacy of the separate system to the jungle of the open wing, ward or dormitory: 'There are a large number of prisoners who strongly dislike association in any shape or form whatever?—Yes, that is true.'[18] But, as is often the case with assumptions made about what is desirable for, or desired by, prisoners, there is very little evidence.

But the separate system, while it served to reduce society's concern about contamination, was of even greater significance to the staff, since the restriction of communication which prevented contamination, also prevented collaboration. If prisoners were kept apart physically, then the perennial threat of 'combination' would be kept at bay. So that although some officials were conscious of its possible adverse effects,[19] they: 'like it; it gives them very little trouble, so without pretending to understand its complicated effects, moral or mental, they almost all swear by it.'[20] The staff approved of separation because of this correlation between it and control: 'The mere fact of the isolation of the prisoner within four walls, by rendering contamination difficult, so far supersedes the necessity for supervision.'[21] The separate system thus prevented 'combination' by depriving it of its essential fuel, communication.

The system also inhibited the development of another danger which fosters a threat to control: an inmate sub-culture. If prisoners are allowed to associate, as well as 'contaminating' each other they develop a social system, which has as its central tenet, hostility to staff. This hostility, linked to the numerical advantage held by inmates, can easily disturb the control exercised by staff.

Most institutions have experience of an inmate culture although in some there are factors which hinder the development of a stable culture. In the mental hospital, for instance, the psychotic patient is unable to co-operate with his peers to achieve a common end, whilst the child in a residential home is too unsophisticated to do so. It is in the prison, above all, where the possibility of concerted action is greatest, and where the need to control the intra-group behaviour of the inmate community is greatest. Where the staff abrogate all control, other than at the security perimeter, a highly complex society develops, characterised by great brutality.

Because it prevented both collaboration, and the development of an inmate community, the physical separation of the prisoners was of great importance to the establishment of cohesion in the staff group. Because prisoners could no longer associate, there emerged, in each prison, a social system in which the staff group became an élite as described by Mosca:[22]

> —the dominion of an organised minority, obeying a single impulse, over the unorganised majority is inevitable. The power of any minority is irresistible as against each single individual in the majority, who stands alone before the totality of the organised minority. At the same time, the minority is organised for the very reason that it is a minority. A hundred men acting uniformly in concert, with a common understanding, will triumph over a thousand men who are not in accord and can therefore be dealt with one by one.

Mosca goes on to say that 'ruling minorities are usually so constituted that the individuals who make them up are distinguished from the mass of the governed by qualities that give them a certain material, intellectual, or even moral superiority.'

Two other factors contributed to this increasing 'dominion' by staff. The first was the perennial differences of all kinds between prisoners which militate against revolt, a factor which is commented upon in other prison situations:[23]

> The inmate population is shot through with a variety of ethnic and social cleavages which sharply reduce the possibility of continued mass action called for by an uprising.

The second factor was the introduction of the silence rule. Originally intended to induce 'that calm contemplation which brings repentance', silence became institutionalised as a device to effect control. The inmate community was thus unable to combine to disturb institutional equilibrium, while at the same time its social disorganisation contributed to staff cohesion.

The restriction of communication and consequent restriction of information put the prisoners at a great disadvantage. The contribution of this factor to the power of the staff as an élite has also been noted in other situations. In his examination of the function of communication McCleery remarks that:[24]

> The monopoly of information established the guards (some of whom had little natural advantage over inmates) as a relatively intellectual élite, and thus gave legitimacy to their authority.

The relationship between separation and control when stated, seems obvious. It needs stressing, because it is of the greatest significance to the understanding of the breakdown of the prison system in the mid-twentieth century. Separation stopped contamination, but it was a corner-stone of control. It put an end to situations like those described by the Carnarvon Committee:[25]

> In the event of a disturbance at night amongst the prisoners, the warder on duty would not be allowed to enter the room, for fear of an assault being made upon him.

This hypothesis about the place of separation in the task of control can be supported by an examination of an important difference between the local prisons and the convict prisons. In some of the latter the inmates worked outside the walls in quarries, dockyards and so on. In this situation there is a threat to control. So, in those prisons, the staff structure was different in one important respect from that of the local prisons, and convict prisons which did not carry out public works. In the public works prisons there was a body called the civil guard. Originally, in 1850, the guard consisted of regular soldiers, but in 1854, a guard of pensioners was substituted.[26] Because these were incompetent, the civil guard proper from 1857 consisted of younger men. The hierarchy of the guard varied from time to time but in 1857 at Dartmoor the force comprised a superintendent, two sergeants, and twenty-seven privates.[27] They carried guns, which they used, and, according to the evidence given to the Gladstone Committee, they stood some distance away from the outside working parties, and guarded the walls when prisoners were outside the cell blocks.[28] The reasons for these differences in the staff structures of the two kinds of prison, were lost sight of as the pressure for a more reformative regime gained strength. The starkly coercive function of the civil guard was incompatible with developing concepts of reformation of prisoners. In 1919 it was abolished. There is no discussion about the abolition in the annual report. It can only be deduced from a comparison of the estimates for 1891 and 1919. Its abolition is a particularly visible example of the organisational confusion in the prison service in the twentieth century. As prisoners were given more freedom, the need for effective perimeter security grew, not diminished. But oddly, the *raison d'être* of the guard was lost sight of, and abolition resulted in a weakening of security.

At first sight it seems odd that in the early days of a centralised service there was singularly little comment on the problem of 'security', or safe custody. Only very occasionally is the question even mentioned, as, for example, in the following statement by Charles Pearson, a well-known reformer:[29]

> I propose that he shall wear a coarse parti-coloured dress. I have no sympathy for the humanity that spares the nice feelings of a criminal by rejecting a prison dress; *it is necessary for security* [my italics].

The Commissioners did, of course, pay attention to security, but did not often discuss it: 'A general inquiry into the security of the prisons has led to the removal of many defects which carelessness and inexperience had allowed to grow up.'[30]

The reason for this dearth of comment about security is that its priority was taken for granted. Imprisonment meant the removal of the offender to a place of safe custody, until he could legally be released. No Victorian prison official would have made the slightest concession to a suggestion that security was not the primary task of the system. The prisons, copied from the 'model' prison at Penton-ville were very secure. The buildings, the staff structure, and the regime—based on the separate system—combined to ensure that the chances of successful escape or riot, were cut to a minimum. Inability to secure prisoners was to be a problem for a later age.

The principal staff problems inherited from the local services

Du Cane had to tackle three major problems in the formation of the new service. These were the chronic phenomenon of the prisoner who was given authority which properly belonged to staff, the regularising of appointments, and the setting up of a comprehensive and compre-hensible promotion structure.

By 1877 all staff were salaried. One of the reforms that Howard had advocated was that all staff ought to be paid by the authority responsible for the prison. This would end the situation where gaolers had to earn their incomes by exploiting prisoners. The methods of raising personal revenue had varied. They included 'farming out' prison labour to private contractors, making prisoners pay fees before release even if they had been acquitted in the courts, selling liquor to prisoners, and using the women's wards as brothels. Many of these practices were very old, and seem to have been per-missible as a method of augmenting meagre and uncertain stipends even in medieval times.[31] The Gaol Building Act of 1784 gave justices permission to pay salaries in lieu of profits from liquor sales. In the same year the justices of Wiltshire gave the gaoler of Fisherton Anger near Salisbury a salary, prohibited trafficking, stopped the sale of drink, and excluded all visitors.[32] In Gloucestershire, guided by Sir George Onesiphorus Paul, a local Act was passed in 1786 which included the abolition of fees, exactions, and perquisites, and instituted a salaried staff consisting of a governor, male and female warders, a surgeon and a chaplain.[33] This movement was given impetus in 1815 and 1816 by Acts which made all prison fees illegal, and made it an offence for an officer to exact a fee from any prisoners. The Act of 1823 included instructions to the justice to make gaolers into the salaried servants of the local authority. There was to be no private trading, no 'farming out', supervision of females by females, and the gaoler, chaplain and surgeon had to keep journals to be presented to the Quarter Sessions.

The increase in expenditure on staff was offset by the employment of prisoners as turnkeys, wardsmen, and monitors. This practice had been deplored by Sir William Blizard in 1785, but it persisted, and seems to have been acceptable to at least some of the reformers at the beginning of the nineteenth century. The Society for the Improvement of Prison Discipline and for the Reformation of Juvenile Offenders published an interesting document in 1820 entitled *Rules proposed for the Government of Gaols, Houses of Correction and Penitentiaries.* This document is probably the first to set out in some detail a job specification for each member of staff: keeper, chaplain, surgeon, taskmaster, matron, turnkeys and wardsmen. The wardsmen were to be prisoners, but their duties were limited to cleaning and similar tasks. They were to have no authority.

The Act of 1835 expressly forbade the employment of convicts as staff, and the excesses of the practice were reduced. In 1836, however, the new Inspectors reported that in Newgate allocation of prisoners to their wards was frequently carried out by 'the inner gateman of the second station', a convicted prisoner.[34] The extent of prisoner employment in some prisons may be judged from the fact that, as a result of the Act, the Middlesex magistrates had to recruit 'eighty-two new officers under the designation of sub-warders' to replace prisoner guards in the Coldbath Fields House of Correction.[35] Predictably, the various methods of avoiding a heavy wages bill continued in spite of criticism, and of legislation. The principal way was the prisoner/ officer, but there was another which is noteworthy because it was resurrected in 1967. This was the use of dogs. In Gloucestershire from 1810 to 1820 there were two dogs in the county prison.[36]

The 1865 Prison Act also contained sections which sought to professionalise prison staff. It laid down that each prison had to have a governor or gaoler, a doctor, and an Anglican chaplain, and every women's prison had to have a matron. It also specified that no prisoner should be employed in the discipline of the prison, or in the service of any officer, or in the service or instruction of any other prisoners. But prisoners continued to be employed as staff, mainly as clerks. This area was the last official stronghold of the prisoner/ officer. The new Commissioners eradicated the last traces of it. In the Fourth Report of the Commissioners for 1880–1, it is noted: 'the employment of prisoners as clerks has been put an end to.' At the same time the practice was finally stopped in the convict service. The Superintendent of Fremantle Prison in Western Australia reported in

1878 that 'the employment of prisoners as writers has, in accordance with instructions, entirely ceased'.

Although this powerful inmate influence was formally abolished, it is unlikely that the division between staff and inmates was complete, although the English prisoner probably wielded less power in the prison at this time than before or since. The evidence that inmates were given some power is slender, and the extent of the power is a matter for speculation. In the detailed description of the 'System of Progressive Stages' it is reported that: 'A prisoner in the fourth stage will—(a) Be eligible for employment of trust in the service of the prison.'[37] In his accounts of the system, Du Cane nowhere mentions this privilege, and consequently there is little detail available about its content.

The problem of the involvement of inmates in the authority structure of institutions is not confined to prisons, or to the nineteenth century. The pressure to give authority to inmates is considerable, and has four sources. The first is the pressure to save money. The next comes from inmates, since the kinds of jobs allocated are more convivial and pleasant than sewing mailbags, breaking stones, or working on the land. A modern source is the group in society who feel that it is therapeutic to involve inmates in the management of their environment; but perhaps the greatest and most effective pressure comes from staff. Institutions are often apparently understaffed, though this may be because of bad deployment. Since many staff jobs are routine and repetitive, inmates can do them perfectly adequately. Thus it is usual to find within institutional structures a hierarchy of prefects, Kapos, red bands, and leaders, in approved schools, concentration camps, prisons and borstals respectively, exercising authority, some of which is official, some of which is not. Other institutional experience indicates that, while the new Commissioners after 1878 were able to substantially reduce inmate authority, it is not likely that at the 'extant' level they eliminated it. It is highly likely that some prisoners would have been in a position to breach the caste division between staff and inmates. Nevertheless the abolition of the prisoner/clerk was of great significance, not only because it formally destroyed the last stronghold but because it led to the establishment of an administrative service in prisons, which has had far-reaching effects on the prison service, and on the role of the basic-grade officer. This development will be dealt with later.

The Commissioners had to be extremely wary in their approach to the other problems—appointments and promotions within the service. During the debates several Members had expressed concern about the 'patronage'[38] which would be wielded by the Home Secretary. It was pointed out that this patronage would consist of 149 appointments for gaolers, 132 for chaplains, 118 for surgeons and 111 for matrons; 510 in all. In addition there were nearly 2,000 subordinates whose appointment would rest with the Commissioners, and with 1,700 posts in convict prisons the Home Secretary would have patronage 'of upwards of 4,000 appointments'.[39] Rylands reported a friend's view of what was likely to happen. About 50 applications had been received for the post of Governor at Kirkdale prison, 'a very large number of which were made up of naval and military men'. The best qualified candidate was appointed but this friend had said:[40]

> Had the patronage been in the hand of the Government, each
> of these naval and military officers would have had some
> political influence, and it would have been 50 to 1 against the
> best man being appointed.

There was, however, abundant evidence that appointment methods under the local authorities were not quite as systematic and objective as Rylands, and others, claimed. The evidence of J. B. Manning, Governor of Pentonville, to the Gladstone Committee is worth quoting in full since it reflects the experience of others of the pre-1877 system:[41]

> I can tell you a tale of the old days when a particular prison
> governorship was considered the plum of the service and half a
> dozen Governors were selected after careful enquiry by the
> Visiting Justices, but when the matter came before Quarter
> Sessions a gentleman who had had nothing to do with the prison
> before whipped up the whole of the County Magistrates and they
> put the whole of the six Governors on one side and selected him
> as governor, the result of which was that the Committee resigned
> in a body. Take my own case. I was a Deputy Governor for
> five years and a candidate for the governorship of Chester
> Castle. I sent a circular round and I said I could not from my
> position canvass the magistrates for the appointment. An
> adjutant who was stationed at Chester Castle was also a
> candidate, and the whole of a bench of magistrates voted for

him because I had not canvassed them for their votes, although
I had sent a circular round. That was the old style of
appointment.

From the beginning, the Commissioners stressed that staff would
be selected on merit, and that political influence would no longer be
taken into account. There were parallel movements away from
political formation to civil service examinations in other sectors of
the public service.[42] Three weeks after the Act came into force Du
Cane issued a circular which had originally been directed to the
convict service. This made clear that promotions as well as appointments would not be influenced by political considerations:

> Whereas it has happened in several instances, that officers in the
> convict service have attempted to obtain their promotion by
> means of applications from private friends, and whereas such
> practices are injurious to the good order and discipline of the
> service, notice is hereby given, that all officers in the convict
> service must understand that their prospects of promotion must
> depend on the report which their supervisors may make as to
> their qualifications for, and as to their conduct in the perform-
> ance of their duties.
> Merit and not favour will thus be the ground of advancement,
> and any officer who may attempt to bring private interest to
> bear, for the purpose of influencing the directors to promote
> him, will be considered as having disqualified himself for the
> promotion which he may thus have sought to obtain.
> 10 September 1853   (signed) Palmerston

The new local prison service, since it was administered by the one
authority, would mean much more job mobility, and a more extensive career structure:[43]

> It has been before remarked that the larger field of promotion
> and selection which arises from all the prisons being under one
> authority, may be considered one of the most important results
> of the Prison Act of 1877, and certainly it is felt by officers to be
> one from which they may derive the greatest advantage.

This standardisation was not achieved without a colossal amount
of work, which called for a detailed grasp of very diverse situations,

shrewdness in coping with the inevitable resistance to drastic change, and great administrative skill. The problems may be illustrated by the complex of conditions of service which the Commissioners inherited. Not only did the actual rates of pay vary for comparable posts but the perquisites were extensive and, much to Du Cane's alarm, often unspecified:[44]

> Our enquiries showed that a considerable number of officers claimed as part of their emoluments the issue from the prison stores free of charge of certain articles for their private use, also the advantage of prison labour, either quite free or at a rate of remuneration very much below its true value as, for instance, where 4/- is charged for making up a suit of clothes. As regards the issue of stores such as coals, gas, brushes, soap etc., it was found on inquiry that in most cases there was no written authority from the various prison authorities for these issues, and in most cases also they were not recorded in the store books, where there were any.

Where there was written authority, the perquisites were often rather strange. At Coldbath Fields Prison in 1872 the warder/cooks were allowed two pints of porter daily.[45]

This very complicated pattern of rewards was standardised by the payment of cash for allowances of stores where it could be established that officers were 'fairly entitled to them'. Pay was standardised throughout the service[46] and allowances were precisely laid down. The Act specified that people who were discharged, or transferred to the new service, lost none of their rights:[47]

> We were required to keep in view that the Act secured to them the same terms and conditions of service as they would have enjoyed if the Act had not passed.

While the problems posed by these widely differing local variations were being tackled so that terms and conditions of service could be standardised, a staff structure was being set up which was, in all important respects, the same in every prison. It has come to be known as a para-military structure.

The para-military structure

The para-military staff structure had been the backbone of the convict service since its inception in 1850. With one major difference (there was no civil guard in the local service) it was adopted by the new local service in 1877, and it has persisted, substantially unchanged, for the last ninety years. It is found, in its essentials, in every prison service in the world.

The reason for the universality and the persistence of this form of staff organisation is that it is a 'crisis-controlling structure' (see pp. 8–9), and as such highly suitable for a prison system having control as its primary task. It is appropriate now to examine more closely the characteristics of the para-military structure. Like most organisational concepts, it is an 'ideal type' in the Weberian sense; it does not exist in a pure form. It is best regarded as a continuum, along which staff structures may be ranged according to the degree of approximation to the 'ideal'. Any staff structure can only be described empirically in terms of *tendencies*. It follows that the features of the para-military structure which will be described did not exist, devoid of any 'impurity', in 1877, any more than they would today.

There are two easily visible characteristics of the para-military structure. The first is that it is 'pyramidal', as may be illustrated from a description of the formal 'line' structure of the uniformed grades in the service of 1877, shown in Figure 1.

Figure 1   Structure of a prison staff in 1877

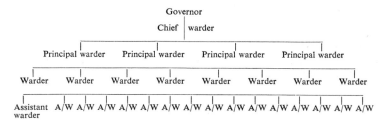

The second easily observable characteristic is that the staff wear uniforms, which serve a dual purpose. They serve to emphasise the uniformity of role of all the people wearing the same clothes, and emphasise the disparity of role of people wearing different clothes. Thus in a prison where high status is not readily conceded to a *personality*, especially by prisoners, the uniform is a valuable role sign, ascribing status, high in the case of staff, low in the case of prisoners, to people wearing it. The importance of uniform as a role sign can be seen in the advice traditionally given to the soldier reluctant to salute: 'You are not saluting the man, you are saluting the uniform.' In the prison service the most status accrues to staff who wear *no* uniform—the governors. In this case the *not* wearing of uniform serves as a role sign.

As staff are promoted, uniform, badges of rank, and in some situations weapons, are changed. In the British Army for many years the private soldier carried a rifle; the officer a revolver. The Victorian convict warder carried a bayonet, the principal warder a cutlass. Further, there is a complex pattern of saluting, and other courtesies, which varies according to a person's place in the hierarchy.

There are of course other characteristics of the structure which are not as obvious as these. The most noteworthy of these are: the presence of strong leadership; clarity of role; the nature of communications and the use of information; and a sense of group cohesion.

Prison work always provokes anxiety, and in 1877 this generic anxiety was added to by the confusion over the setting up of the service. There was therefore a need for strong leadership. At the head of the service Du Cane provided this; at the local level power was delegated to the governor and he was expected to exercise it.[48] As a result the staff were able to identify the person who exercised authority. In recent years the governor has still 'formally' had considerable power;[49] in reality he has not (see Chapter 10). The reducing power of the governor in this century has coincided with an increase in staff anxiety due to confusion of task. But in 1877 the head of the para-military structure was able to offer the positive leadership which is one of its most important features.

Clarity of task led to clarity of role. A work role has been defined by Banton as 'a set of norms and expectations applied to the incumbent of a particular position'.[50] It may be usefully divided into two parts; the 'prescribed' and the 'discretionary'. This framework was defined, and used, in accounts of organisation and management by Jacques and Brown.

The prescribed part of the work role consists of those duties which are routine and explicit. A prison officer's prescribed duties include, for example, locking and unlocking prisoners, and checking bars. He may also have to 'take applications'. When he carries out the latter task he merely passes on the application to a senior officer. If he were to decide on whether an extra letter was to be given, he would be performing the discretionary part of his role. The para-military structure limits the degree of discretion which is exercised. The core of a prison officer's job is composed of this prescribed component. In 1877 this was very much the case. Precision of job specification, which is associated with a heavily prescribed role, means that individuals in the same grade are interchangeable. An officer in a prison can work in any part of the prison, or in any other prison without a great deal of difficulty, after learning minor local idiosyncracies. So in the para-military structure: 'every sergeant must be able to do any sergeant's job'.[51] This restriction on the exercise of discretion is usually viewed as intrinsically undesirable. Banton has suggested that 'it is hard for individuals to identify with their jobs'.[52] But the appropriateness of freedom and discretion in an organisation must depend on the task. It is impossible to say whether 'discretion' in the abstract is desirable or not. In work situations a person can be as unhappy having freedom he does not want, as not having freedom he does want. This is especially true of prisons when, as in the English system in this century, an invitation is issued to use discretion and initiative, without reassessment of the effects on the total organisational configuration.

In the para-military structure there is a premium on downward communication. Orders are transmitted down the hierarchy, and staff are expected to obey. At its crudest this pattern of communication is summed up in the service adage 'you are not paid to think; you are paid to do as you're told'. It follows that there is little room for what is today called 'consultation'. Why is this so?

First, because of the 'critical situation'. In a crisis, or incipient crisis, there is little time for discussion. Decisions have to be made in the light of rapidly changing situations, and these have to be carried out swiftly.[53]

Second, such a pattern of communication can be acceptable in a structure where there is an acknowledged equation between experience and expertise. Time brings skill, given a modicum of sound judgment. As experience accumulates, so does ability to function effectively as a prison officer. There is no body of theory which can be mobilised to ensure that prisoners do not riot or escape, which is why training for prison officers, as for other occupations where the work is simple and repetitive, is often regarded as irrelevant. To reinforce the acceptability of this communications pattern to staff, experience and skill together bring promotion, so that the English prison staff structure consists today, as in 1877, of people arranged in bands of prestige, allocation to each being dependent, fundamentally, upon length of service.

As with communications, so with the possession of information. Orders flow down readily, information less readily. In a job of relatively little technical skill, and almost devoid of any theoretical base, one of the substitutes for a body of knowledge is the hoarding of information, often of a very simple kind. Generally, for example, junior prison staff have never been able to have unlimited access to Standing Orders (neither have the public). If they have a problem they have to ask a more senior member of the staff for the answer, which is often given unwillingly. Unwillingness to impart information is the most memorable feature of the reception given to newly joined staff. See for example Cronin's account of his early experience as an officer in *The Screw Turns*. On the other hand it goes almost without saying that junior staff who are given important information by inmates, have to transmit it upwards at once. There is no place in the para-military structure for the debates about confidentiality which beset the social work agency, or the conference of psychiatrists.

In the para-military structure, therefore, the communications system is appropriate to the task, and is accepted by the staff with as little grumbling as any other system, in most other organisations. Since there is little room for discussion, orders and instructions are clear and must be obeyed. Failure to obey them is attended with punishment. In 1877 prison officers were warned that: 'any instances of improper behaviour or ill-treatment of a prisoner' would be severely dealt with.[54] And the proliferation of orders constraining the behaviour of staff seem to have been respected, as can be evidenced from a variety of sources, especially, significantly, from prisoners' autobiographies: 'He insisted upon having the discipline of the prison carried out to the letter, but any abuse on the part of the warders was immediately checked and severely reprimanded.'[55] Officers could be subjected to a range of punishments ranging from dismissal to fining, all the punishments in fact which are usually found in the para-military organisation.

This supervision of *staff*, which is a feature of the para-military system, was most important. The tightening up of control over the prisoners through separation, made them especially vulnerable to staff misconduct. There is a built-in danger in a prison system, as there is in any organisation where authority wields almost un-challengeable power, that this power might be misused. Du Cane had thought about this, especially about the events leading up to the Royal Commission on Birmingham Prison. After drawing attention in *The Punishment and Prevention of Crime* to the weakness of a generalised, diffuse responsibility for supervision which was char-acteristic of the local justices' rule in prisons, a lack of clarity which was worsened by their lack of practical experience, he goes on:[56]

> Supervision so liable to be delusive in fact lends itself most
> easily to the establishment and cloaking of abuses, for it relieves
> those who are likely to commit them of responsibility, and even
> provides them with defence—the more effective in proportion as
> the supposed combined checking and managing power resides in
> persons who are powerful and important, and independent of
> any superior authority.

The new authority was vested in a body of full-time committed pro-fessionals, who would ensure that staff would obey orders which were *set down primarily to protect prisoners.*

There is plenty of evidence that the Directors and Commissioners checked this dangerous built-in tendency to excess by governors, in the same way as the latter checked their staffs. For instance, they watched the nature and scale of punishments very closely. As early as 1853, Convict Directors expressed concern over 'the number of prisoners punished with three days' dark cell and bread and water'. The 1853 Report goes on:

> the Directors thought the punishments out of proportion to
> the degree of the offence. They therefore intimated their opinion
> to that effect to the Governor, who at once acceded to their
> wishes, and diminished the severity of the punishments.

The new Commissioners were to be as direct in their instructions about punishment. Standing Order No. 94 of 7 January 1881 points out that 'discipline is not better maintained by resorting commonly to severe punishments' and officers should 'clearly and patiently explain the regulations or orders to which they are expected to conform' rather than too readily 'resort to the infliction of punish-ment'. The Order concludes: 'The Commissioners will look with satisfaction on any efforts the Governors may make to reduce the amount of prison punishments.'[57]

All of this aspect of the process of supervision is negative, in the sense that it consists merely of issuing orders to staff, and laying down punishments which would follow if they were not obeyed. In other words, authority would only take notice if things were not going well. An organisation is unlikely to be effective unless there are positive elements in the generic activity of supervision. People in organisations need to feel that the vigilance of authority, designed to prevent misdeeds, is part of a complex totality of interest which authority shows in the professional activity of the members of the organisation. Prison staff are perfectly willing to take criticism, direction and instruction from superior officers, provided they can feel that the network of activity within the organisation includes support and help. To achieve this the organisation must be respected and respectable. This is especially the case with prison staff because, like most coercive social agencies, they are vulnerable to ambivalent feelings in society. When staff feel that this supportive element is lacking, and that the negative aspect of supervision is dominant, there is talk of 'low morale'.

Du Cane sought to build up a service which could be respected, and which would induce some pride in its members. Success meant the development of a sense of group cohesion. A sense of solidarity with the organisation, with its aims and methods, makes tolerable the unpleasant aspects of prison work, and of the para-military structure which is its universal concomitant.

Quarters were built for staff especially where rents were high and where staff were 'likely to be thrown into undesirable contact with a certain class of the population in their search for lodgings'.[58] Standards of entry were raised and removed from the political arena (see pp. 38–9). The contribution of separation and silence to the development of staff cohesion has been discussed. But most important, Du Cane was ready to demonstrate that, while prisoners would be protected from staff, staff would be protected from prisoners. Staff, when in the right, would be supported. He was especially disgusted by the provision in the Act for the hearing of complaints by the Visiting Committee in private. The officer's 'character and position would thus be at the mercy of persons of lost character, with every motive to discredit their authority and weaken their position'.[59]

It must be stressed again that these features of the para-military structure are concepts against which the actual staff structure of the new prison service may be described. In summary, in respect of the uniformed officer it is probably true to say that in the period after 1877 his role was more clearly defined than at any time since.

'Militarism'

In view of what has been described, it is not surprising that ex-servicemen are attracted to prison work. The presence of large numbers of ex-servicemen in prison services is not peculiar to England, or to the nineteenth century. At the first International Congress on the Prevention and Repression of Crime, including Penal and Reformatory Treatment held in London in July 1872,[60] several European governments reported that they preferred staff with military experience. Prussia, Saxony, Württemberg and Italy were four which tried to appoint ex-servicemen exclusively.[61] In France, under a law of 18 March 1889, warders had to be selected from a list of retired non-commissioned officers prepared by the War Office.[62] At the present time, Italian prison custodial staff are members of the Corps of Custodians, a branch of the armed forces, while Austria and Luxembourg recruit their custodial staff from the military.[63]

The convict service, from its inception, had something of a martial air. Both Jebb and Du Cane continued to hold commissions for some years after their appointment as Chairmen. Du Cane, in fact, was promoted to the rank of Major-General nine years after centralisation, in 1866. The early reports of the Directors of convict prisons reflect the links with the services. Some indeed have a flavour of regimental transfers:[64]

> Captain Bramly, late Cape Mounted Rifle Corps, was appointed Deputy Governor on the 12th May, in the room of Captain Warren, who was promoted to be Governor of the *Stirling Castle* hulk, and was appointed Governor on the 1st July viceCaptain Gambier, who became one of the Directors of Convict Prisons. Captain Craig, late 1st or Royal Regiment, was appointed Deputy Governor when Captain Bramly was promoted to be Governor.

Du Cane was quite content to employ ex-servicemen as staff and indeed welcomed them:[65]

> Their [ex-soldiers] habits of order and discipline, of rendering and enforcing strict obedience and their aptitude in dealing with

large bodies of men, are unquestionably very valuable qualities for the office, and if not possessed by an officer on joining, would have to be acquired more or less perfectly afterwards.

His opinion was echoed by governors:[66]

The class of men who are the best qualified for such duties are pensioned non-commissioned officers, because from their previous habits, they not only exercise a watchful vigilance over their different gangs, but are also obedient to any instructions they may receive.

Even prisoners, apparently, thought that a military background was a prerequisite for the good governor:[67]

A few moments later the governor entered my cell. He was an exceedingly tall, fine looking man with a handsome, kindly face, and a thoroughbred look about him that stamped him at once as a gentleman. He had the unmistakable stamp of a soldier about him too, and I guessed at once that he had been in the service. I afterwards learned that he was a man of very good family, and had been in a crack regiment.

The question of 'militarism' was raised in the debates leading to the 1877 Act, with the expression of contrary views about its desirability. One Member foresaw a situation where the Home Secretary 'would be everlastingly troubled with hungry half pay officers applying for gaol appointments'.[68] Another protested 'at the introduction of military discipline into our prisons'.[69] On the other side a suggestion was made that the patronage ought to go to the Secretary of State for War. Such appointments 'would add greatly to the inducements which the recruiting sergeants had to offer'.[70]

In England reformative groups have always objected to the employment of ex-servicemen as prison staff. The objections spring from two assumptions. The first is that ex-servicemen bring to prisons attitudes which are damaging to the well-being of the prisoner. Behind this is a stereotype of the regimental idiot who becomes a governor, and the bullying martinet who becomes a uniformed officer. Secondly there has always been a belief that there are large numbers of ex-servicemen in the prison service. From time to time these numbers have been counted, and the evidence presented will be discussed.

In the early days of the convict service a complaint was made that:[71]

> Sir J. Jebb has his own crotchet on this matter and thinks that soldiers—old pensioners, smart fellows may be, but generally ill educated, wholly addicted to military, and incompetent to maintain moral discipline—are the sort of men most likely to redeem felons from the error of their ways.

Probably the most important and persistent critic of the tendency to prefer ex-servicemen, was William Tallack, who was Chairman of the Howard Association for almost the same period as Du Cane was Chairman of the Prison Commission. At the 1872 Congress he circulated his book, *Defects in the Criminal Administration and Penal Legislation of Great Britain and Ireland with Remedial Suggestions*, which pointed out 'the danger of employing ex-army men as governors, since they tended to impose a type of discipline inappropriate to prison work'.[72] The subject was raised again at the second Congress which met at Stockholm in 1878. The members spent a whole afternoon discussing 'the best means of instructing prison warders in the duties of their office'. The Governor of Rendsburg prison, Germany, emphasised the usefulness of military training as a qualification for the prison service, especially since 'a practical knowledge of most useful trades is to be found among soldiers'. *The Times* of 23 August 1878 reports that Tallack disagreed. Whilst conceding that:

> many good officers of prisons have been soldiers, [he] said that both in England and abroad there was a too exclusive selection of military men for prison duties. Such being the case it was the more important that in every prison the industrial and religious training of the officers themselves should have special attention; and that the chaplains should regularly address the warders on their present and future responsibility to God for their influence over the prisoners.

No English officials were present to comment on these remarks since:

> considerable surprise with some disappointment, is expressed at England's holding aloof, so far at least as its Government is concerned from a gathering which has excited much interest in other countries.

The Webbs say that 'as long as Sir Edmund Du Cane was in co
mand, the Home Office and the Prison Commissioners refused
take part in the International Prison Conference'.[73] Du Cane's s
cessor, Ruggles-Brise offers an explanation when he writes:[74]

> It was no doubt regarded by a section of opinion at that time
> that the movement was too idealistic in its scope—that the
> discussions were too much in abstracto, and not really helpful
> in the field of practical administration.

A hundred years of constant complaints from reformative gro
has made no real impact on the para-military structure, or
presence of ex-servicemen on prison staffs. The point has been ma
that the para-military structure is not the main blockage in
achievement of a reformative task. Nor is the presence of ex-soldi
on staffs. The assumption that their treatment of prisoners is lik
to be more severe than that of any other comparable working-cl
group, is an assertion based on distaste for militarism, which
widely felt by reformative groups, and therapeutic agencies. The r
blockage to the implementation of reform is that society has
defined this as the primary task of the prison system. Given
controlling task, it is at least arguable that people with milit
experience are likely to be capable of carrying it out. When
primary task is redefined, then perhaps the para-military structu
and the employment of ex-servicemen will no longer seem app
priate.

Notes

1 The Act came into force on 1 April 1878.
2 First Report of the Prison Commissioners 1877, p. 3. In this book,
  the Annual Reports of the Commissioners of Prisons are referred t
  as 'Local Reports' and the Annual Reports of the Directors of
  Convict Prisons are referred to as 'Convict Reports'. The Local
  Reports are noted as 'First', 'Second' and so on: the Convict Repo
  by the year—this is how they were published.
3 There is no biography of Du Cane. There are articles on him in *Th
  Dictionary of National Biography* and *The Biograph and Review*,
  vol. 3, 1880. His obituary notice in *The Times* in 1903 gives further
  information.
4 Porter, *History of the Corps of Royal Engineers*; quoted in Roberts
  Victorian Origins of the Welfare State, p. 157.

Fox, *The English Prison and Borstal Systems*, p. 51.
See Fourth Local Report, pp. 10–11; Third Local Report, p. 17;
Second Local Report, p. 11.
Gladstone Committee Evidence, question 11, 394.
Gladstone Report, para. 4.
S. and B. Webb, *English Prisons under Local Government*, p. 201.
The Times, 12 June 1878, p. 4.
Hansard, vol. 232, col. 436 et seq.
Hansard, vol. 232, col. 450.
Hansard, vol. 235, col. 24 et seq.
S. and B. Webb, op. cit., pp. 233–4.
Convict Report 1852, p. 273.
*Report of the Visitors of Her Majesty's Convict Prison at Chatham as
to the Treatment of Certain Prisoners Convicted of Treason Felony*,
1890, para. 51. See also an account of a 'knocking code' and mention
of an 'entirely original' language in Burt, *Results of the System of
Separate Confinement as Administered at the Pentonville Prison*,
p. 271.
Gladstone Evidence, questions 8493–502.
Gladstone Evidence, question 2967. The witness was The Revd
W. D. Morrison. See also the Commissioners' 'Observations' on the
Gladstone Report, p. 6, where the view is expressed that a prisoner
would 'feel aggrieved' if he was made to mix with other criminals.
Notably Du Cane (op. cit., p. 158).
Dixon, *London Prisons*, p. 154 (quoted by S. and B. Webb, op. cit.,
p. 179).
Burt, op. cit., p. 183. See also Gladstone Evidence, question 7321,
where a governor says the best way to control difficult prisoners is to
keep them apart.
Mosca, *The Ruling Class* (ed. Livingston), p. 53.
Sykes, *The Society of Captives*, p. 81.
R. H. McCleery, 'The Governmental Process and Informal Social
Control', in *The Prison: Studies in Institutional Organization and
Change*, ed. D. R. Cressey, Holt, Rinehart & Winston, 1961, p. 161.
Carnarvon Committee Report, p. XV.
Convict Report 1855, p. 155.
Convict Report 1857, p. 186.
Gladstone Evidence, questions 9665, 11208, 11209. For evidence that
they used their guns, see Convict Report 1856, p. 233, and *Penal
Servitude* by 'W.B.N.' (identified by the Webbs as Lord William
Nevill), p. 190, where he describes the shooting of a fleeing
clergyman.
Quoted in S. and B. Webb, op. cit., p. 161.
Du Cane, op. cit., p. 98.
Pugh, *Imprisonment in Medieval England*, ch. 8.
'J.H.', *Observations, Moral and Political, Particularly Respecting the
Necessity of Good Order and Religious Economy in our Prisons*, p. 13
(quoted by S. and B. Webb, op. cit., pp. 54–5).

33 S. and B. Webb, op. cit., p. 59.
34 Parliamentary Papers 1836, XXXV, 47, 817 (quoted in S. and B. Webb, op. cit., p. 120). The advantages of being a 'tower woman' in Millbank female prison are described in *Memoirs of Jane Cameron, Female Convict* by 'A Prison Matron', vol. 2.
35 Chesterton, *Revelations of Prison Life*, vol. 2, p. 3 (quoted in S. and B. Webb, op. cit., p. 104).
36 *Remarks by the County Chairman upon the Tables Published by David Ricardo Esq.* See S. and B. Webb, op. cit., p. 103, n. 2.
37 First Local Report, app. 12, p. 40.
38 'Patronage' formed another objection to centralisation and was raised in debates about other new departments of state. See Roberts, op. cit.
39 Hansard, vol. 230, col. 306.
40 Hansard, vol. 230, col. 281.
41 Gladstone Evidence, question 802.
42 Roberts, op. cit., ch. 5.
43 Fourth Local Report, p. 10.
44 First Local Report, pp. 5–6.
45 'Officers' Fees, Salaries, Emoluments', House of Correction, Coldbath Fields 1872.
46 First Local Report, app. 6, p. 30.
47 First Local Report, p. 5.
48 Du Cane, *An Account of Penal Servitude in England*, p. 80.
49 'The governor has control of the whole prison and is responsible for its management to the Commissioners and the Secretary of State.' (Standing Order 532, 1967.)
50 Banton, *Roles*, p. 29.
51 Clark, *Administrative Therapy*.
52 Banton, op. cit., p. 63.
53 Clark (op. cit., p. 125), in his brief comparison of the military and the psychiatric organisations, uses as an illustration the critical situation where a ship is near shore.
54 Convict Report 1877, p. VIII. See also Du Cane's unequivocal statements about the use of weapons and the consequences of 'any abuse of power on the part of an officer' (*The Punishment and Prevention of Crime*, pp. 165–7).
55 *HM Prisons: Their Effects and Defects* by 'One who has tried them', p. 99. See also Burt, op. cit., pp. 41–2, where it is stated that an inclination to deviate was kept in check by a sufficient number of warders. See also *Penal Servitude* by 'W.B.N.', pp. 142 and 154, where compliments are paid to the restraint of the staff and the thoroughness of investigation by governors of any complaint.
56 Du Cane, op. cit., p. 66.
57 This Order was reprinted at the end of the 'Observations' of the Commissioners on the Gladstone Report.
58 Du Cane, op. cit., p. 97.
59 Ibid., p. 72.

60 The proceedings were reprinted as *Prisons and Reformatories at Home and Abroad*, edited by Edwin Pears.

61 Pears, op. cit., pp. 124, 141, 146, 160–1.

62 *Contemporary Review*, vol. 66, October 1894, p. 550 et seq.

63 Council of Europe, *The Status, Selection and Training of Prison Staff*, pp. 54, 29, 59.

64 Convict Report 1856, p. 41.

65 Du Cane, op. cit., pp. 188–9.

66 Convict Report 1851, pp. 188–9.

67 *Her Majesty's Prisons: Their Effects and Defects* by 'One who has tried them', p. 98.

68 Hansard, vol. 230, col. 900.

69 Hansard, vol. 232, col. 1226.

70 Hansard, vol. 232, col. 1225.

71 Clay, *The Prison Chaplain*, pp. 434–5.

72 Rose, *The Struggle for Penal Reform*, pp. 33–4. Rose deals with other topics raised in the book.

73 S. and B. Webb, op. cit., p. 217, n. 1. America also declined to attend.

74 Ruggles-Brise, *Prison Reform at Home and Abroad*, p. 35.

4   1850–80: the early years

The convict service inheritance

The convict service was the model for the new local service. Not only was the style of administration and the essence of the staff structure copied, but 'a large proportion' of the Head Office staff of the local service 'was formed from that of the department of convict prisons'.[1] The local service also inherited intangible, but vital, traditions and experience from the older service, notably a growing militancy amongst sections of the staff. However, after 1877 they continued to operate independently of each other with only Du Cane as the common denominator. Each staff had different conditions of service, different pay scales, and different uniforms. Because of the convict inheritance, and because of the stresses which were engendered by the division between the two, it is necessary now to describe the development of the convict service in the twenty-seven years since it had been established.

It will be recalled that under an Act of Parliament the government prisons and hulks came under a Board of Directors in 1850. The inmates of these establishments were usually recidivists undergoing long sentences, originally of transportation, but later of penal servitude. By 1850 transportation was becoming difficult, and imprisonment in this country, sometimes followed by a 'ticket of leave' in the colonies, was becoming common practice.

The convict service inherited a troubled situation in 1850, especially on the hulks. There were several uprisings, or *émeutes* as they were called. In April the *York* had had a riot, which had only been suppressed by 'prompt and decisive conduct' on the part of Superintendent Barrow, 'an old Army officer'. He seized the ringleaders and flogged them. The same solution was used on the *Stirling Castle* at Portsmouth, and Royal Marines were called in.[2] In October some 'government' convicts escaped from local prisons, and *The Times* of 9 October 1850 expressed the hope that 'these escapes will engage the attention of some Government inspector, or other officer of the Government'. There was a mutiny on *Warrior* at Woolwich at the end of 1851 which was suppressed only by calling in the Royal Artillery and the Royal Marines to support warders who, cutlasses drawn, went below to bring up thirty-eight leaders, who were transferred.[3]

In 1852 there was trouble at Portsmouth, this time with the officers, and this was the first of a series of incidents with staff which, for some seven years, caused governors great concern.[4] In 1856 an officer helped two prisoners to escape from Pentonville,[5] while at Dartmoor in 1860 it was reported that 'among the assistant warders the changes by resignation and dismissal have been very numerous'.[6] In 1862 an officer again helped prisoners to escape, this time from Millbank.[7] It was not until 1857 that a satisfactory form of guard—the civil guard— was organised. The original military guard had been succeeded by a guard of pensioners 'who had been under the orders of the Horse Guards'.[8] They in turn were succeeded in 1856–7 by the civil guard consisting of a superintendent, sergeants, and privates. At Portsmouth there was a superintendent, two sergeants, and twenty privates,[9] while Dartmoor had twenty-seven privates:[10]

> Most of them having previously belonged to the military service, their training in their new duties was attended with less difficulty than if they had been men wholly unaccustomed to discipline.

Even so problems remained. There were several instances of disobedience in the guard, but 'peremptory dismissal' arrested any further insubordination.[11]

The hulks continued to attract attention. On the *Stirling Castle* at Portsmouth in 1856, 'no less than' eight assistant warders were dismissed, the assistant surgeon was murdered, and a warder was stabbed in the throat.[12] The surgeon was the first of the eight members of staff who have been murdered by inmates since 1850.

Several factors contributed to the unrest of the late 1850s and early 1860s. One of these was the movement of convicts to the prisons when the hulks were closed. After the licence of the hulks, both prisoners and staff seem to have found adjustment to the regime of the prisons difficult. At Chatham, which had been opened in September 1856, there were 'manifestations of discontent' which, however, passed away, drawing the comment from the Governor that the transferred hulk officers had to be taught 'their very different duties'.[13] The prisoners were insubordinate at Lewes, and the ringleaders were moved to Millbank and Pentonville.[14]

The other major contribution to the unrest was the curious operation of the Penal Servitude Acts of 1853 and 1857. Under the earlier

Act convicts got no remission, but the later Act allowed remission for those sentenced in and after July 1857; on a four-year sentence, for example, this amounted to nine months. Naturally there was much anger over this anomaly. There was a strike at Portland in 1858, and 230 convicts were transferred to Millbank and Pentonville. A hundred were put in chains at Portland, and the ringleaders were flogged. It was necessary however to call in the Wexford militia, and sailors from HMS *Argus* and HMS *Blenheim*.[15] There were mutterings at Brixton,[16] and the Governor of Chatham reported that he had failed to achieve the impossible. 'It is at all times a matter of difficulty to dissuade those sentenced under the Act of 1853 from the idea they entertain that justice has been overlooked.'[17] At Lewes the Governor noted that 'the effect of their reasoning on the subject is decidedly unfavourable to discipline and good order.'[18]

The discontent came to a head in February 1861 when there was a riot at Chatham.[19] The Governor was frank in his opinion of the causes. He had several times complained of the inefficiency of the transferred hulk officers, and he attributed to them a large share of responsibility for what happened. A 'deep laid plan' for escape was foiled, and the leader, who 'exercised the most remarkable influence over the convicts', was removed. The other ringleaders then tried to incite mutiny. They got hold of newspapers sometimes 'through the venality of officers of the prison', which alleged they were heroes. The ex-hulk prisoners were encouraged by the expressions of distaste for the regime made by ex-hulk officers. They thought the officers would 'covertly, if not openly, support them in acts of insubordination'. The riot was subdued by the civil guard who separated the ringleaders on the labour parade[20] and kept them apart 'at the point of the bayonet'.[21] The convicts were not entirely subdued. In June one of the ringleaders almost killed an officer with a shovel,[22] and in September 1862 Warder Evans was murdered at Portland.[23]

These early years were not utterly bleak. Directors, governors, and chaplains especially, worked hard to raise the standard and behaviour of staff. As early as 1856 the Chaplain of Dartmoor recommended the establishment of educational facilities for staff. After asking for an officers' library he wrote:[24]

If then an improvement in the habits of the warder can be arrived at by placing before him pursuits such as those adverted to, and by a suitable education be advancing his children's welfare, the officer will become more attached than he is at present to the service, his late unsettledness and discontent will be removed, and he becomes a more faithful servant to the Government.

This recommendation developed into a fascinating piece of pioneer staff training. Libraries and recreation rooms were set up, which seem to have been very successful in the attempt to develop a corporate spirit amongst staff. At Portland, bi-weekly lectures and bible classes were held by the Chaplain and these, it was claimed, helped warders who are 'living to (sic) God in accordance with the truths of the Gospel'.[25] At Dartmoor 'that most hardworking and enduring of men, the prison warder', together with the civil guardsmen, attended classes, one of which was conducted by the Deputy Governor. There was a winter series for warders and their families on astronomy, eclipses, tides etc.', the Chaplain commenting that the officers' reading room exerts a 'useful counter-attraction to the baneful drinking houses'.[26] Although some of the public works prisons were reporting dissatisfaction with staff, the Chaplain of Portland comments favourably on the warders' 'general habits of sobriety'[27] and in 1861 he reported:[28]

Off duty, their attention to their families, their habits of cleanliness, appearance, habits of economy, and love of their children, and the affection born by both in that mutual relation, is shown in a hundred different ways.

There was, he continued, scarcely a place in the Empire which had such a quiet Sabbath.

These attempts to develop an *esprit* amongst staff must be set against the gloomy reports of staff colluding with mutineers, and helping convicts to escape. In the same way, there is some evidence of congenial relationships which should be weighed against the evidence, already mentioned, of the crude violence of the relationship between some staff, and some convicts, in some prisons, at certain times.

At Chatham in 1860 two prisoners saved an officer from drowning, one almost being drowned himself. Another two saved a workman from drowning, whilst in a third incident an officer had a fit and was helped by two of his party who did not touch his pockets though he had 'imprudently' taken out a large sum of money.[29] At Pentonville a plan 'to open their cells by means of a picklock, murder the night

officers, and effect their escape' was discovered when one of
prisoners dropped a piece of paper with the plan on it:[30] the
ference was that this was deliberate. In 1861, the year of the r
some convicts at Chatham saved an officer from drowning.[31]

These reported episodes in the relationships between warder a
convict, highlight a universal difficulty which is encountered in
attempts to discover what actually is happening in a prison. There
several factors which militate against the discovery of accur
information. There is first of all the commonplace of sociolog
investigation that the presence of an observer alters the interperso
behaviour of the people being observed. There is also the problem
distortion in the perception of the observer, because of the latt
prejudices, definitions of normality, and value judgments about
behaviour of the group. To these well-known difficulties must
added the peculiarities of the prison situation. The widespr
inability of the prisoner to articulate well is exacerbated by a lik
reluctance to be 'observed'. If he is willing to contribute to
attempt to evaluate the quality of relationships with staff, it is v
likely that he will ascribe all the inherent unpleasantness of impris
ment to the activities of the staff, drawing attention to their coerc
role to the exclusion of almost everything else. The staff membe
aware that observers will have very definite ideas about prison,
suspect that they are hostile to staff and will respond either by
fusing to co-operate, or by deliberately trying to outrage the obser

Even if there were a vast amount of evidence in the literatur
would be difficult to be sure about the nature of staff-inmate re
tionships. The evidence from these early years of the convict serv
is slight, and I have tried to give emphasis to events which give so
objective indication of relationships, rather than placing any imp
tance on what people gave as their opinion of them. What is clea
that these early years saw the establishment of the half-friendly, h
ferocious terms on which English staff and prisoners have alw
dealt with each other.

The year 1863 was a turning point in the development of
service. Several events occurred which were to have far-reach
effects on the administration of the convict prisons. There wa
remarkable increase in crime which led Lord Carnarvon to remar
Parliament in February, that in London, 'it was dangerous to w
about after midnight'. In the Commons in March, it was stated t
garrotters had 'fortunately selected a member of that House as t

: victim', which drew from *Punch* 'the advice to garrotters to be
re cautious in future, and especially to avoid a Secretary of State
the Home Department'. The opinion was widely held that this
aviour was a consequence of the release of ticket-of-leave men
) the community. Concern eventually led to the setting up of a
ral Commission on the Penal Servitude Acts which reported, also
863. Its report expressed the view 'that the recent increase of
nces is at least partly attributable to defects in the system of
ishment now in force' and to 'the accumulation of discharged
victs at home'.[32]

he Act of 1864 which followed increased the minimum period of
al servitude. The contemporary House of Lords Committee,
er Lord Carnarvon, has already been discussed. The pressure for
re severity in the treatment of criminals seemed to be irresistible,

by coincidence, in 1863, the head of the convict service, Sir
hua Jebb, died. Jebb was a powerful figure with influential sup-
ters. He was also relatively liberal, and change would have been
cult as long as he was in charge. His death made change possible.
was succeeded by Lieutenant-Colonel E. Y. W. Henderson, RE.
: latter paid due tribute to Jebb, but said that it was not: 'our wish
any way to enter on the merits of the controversies in which the
Chairman of the Board was so prominently of late years before
public'.[33]

t was not long before the expected tightening up of convict
cipline' came. The diet was reduced on the recommendation of a
rd of Medical Officers in 1863.[34] There had been some agitation
ut the allegedly excessive amounts of food given to convicts, com-
ed with what was given to local prisoners and soldiers. The
vernor of Leicester, a local, was quoted as saying that an outbreak
diarrhoea amongst government convicts was due to 'the richness
heir food'.[35] In the separate prisons the change in food, always
most explosive area of prison administration, was effected with-
too much trouble. In the public works prisons, however, where
reduction was greater, and where, as the Directors pointed out,
convicts were more in association, the introduction of the new
e required 'more care and determination'.[36] At Portland there
a mutiny which 'threatened to be of a serious character'. The
guard, shooting at the ringleaders when they advanced armed
picks and shovels, dispersed and subdued the rioters.[37]

here were many other changes. Education was reduced[38] and

cellular teaching was started.[39] The famous 'mark system' was introduced, which meant that convicts had to earn marks, by labour, to
gain remission, or promotion to a higher class.[40] The gratuities which
they could earn were reduced.[41] Religious services were shortened[42]
and finally it was emphasised that remission would not be given to
convicts serving a second sentence of penal servitude.[43]

According to one anonymous, but apparently well-informed
correspondent to *The Times* on 2 January 1863, the staff needed as
much reorganisation as the prisoners. His letter confirms that some
people were as concerned about staff as about prisoners. The claim
was made that at Portland, Dartmoor, and Chatham, the warders
were 'more to be pitied than the prisoners'. They worked harder,
they never knew a moment free of anxiety, their pay was low, and
their numbers were not enough to secure their own safety, and the
safe custody of the convicts. Any decrease in dietary, or ticket of
leave, and 'it would be madness to keep the staff of warders at its
present weakness'. The writer concluded with some shrewd observations about the relationship between separation and control:

> You may keep up a species of separation which shall defy
> conspiracies extending to large numbers of prisoners, but the
> knowledge of their united strength, if brought to bear upon any
> one common object, is in itself a fearful element of danger.

The new Chairman was as concerned about the failure to set the
staff on a proper footing as the writer of the letter. In fact, as life for
the convicts became more disagreeable, the total staff environment
improved considerably. The new administration realised that the
standard, morale, and loyalty of the staff had to be raised, and they
used a familiar compound of encouragement and coercion to achieve
this. In the Report for 1864 they set out a statement of intent about
the kind of men they wanted:

> We have endeavoured to obtain the services of efficient men as
> warders, without reference to any particular class, but
> necessarily we are mostly dependent on the non-commissioned
> officers of the army; very few men accustomed only to civil life
> will stand the incessant watchfulness and standing duty required
> of warders, especially at the Public Works prison.

They went on to claim that 'careful selection', and 'immediate
removal' of the unfit had improved the disciplinary staff.[44]

The policy of separation was rigidly enforced in halls, school, chapel and at work so that 'communication between them is scarcely practicable'. 'The value of this . . . is very marked both for the security and the discipline of the prison and well-being of the men themselves.'[45] Whether or not the convicts were better off, the effect on the staff must have been to remove a great deal of stress, since control became easier. This was accompanied by the erection of 'penal class cells' in those prisons which did not have them, a measure which also 'greatly strengthened the hands of the officers in charge of the prison'.[46]

The Board also turned their attention to what are probably the two most highly charged problems in all prison systems—violence to staff and trafficking. Trafficking means providing prisoners with forbidden articles for some kind of reward. It is obvious that heavier punishment for assaults on staff would be welcome, but staff would applaud too the detection and punishment of staff engaged in trafficking. The existence of trafficking always causes great concern, since it lowers the status of staff in the eyes of prisoners, and it is extremely difficult to detect. The presence or absence of trafficking is a useful measure of staff integrity, or lack of it. Prison officers are conscious of this, and have no sympathy with colleagues caught committing the offence. The Directors singled out these offences for special mention: 'Every infraction of discipline, especially of violence to officers, and trafficking which at one time was very rife, has been promptly punished.'[47]

This review of the difficulties and problems of staff had its material aspects. There was an increase in staff as had been recommended by the Royal Commission in the previous year, and the Governor of Millbank was able to report that as a result every officer was able to have a half-day off during the week if he was on duty on Sunday.[48] The subordinate staff were given an increase in pay and allowances and leave and these: 'have worked very well, and have proved a great boon to them, and we believe they are now well satisfied with their condition'.[49] Compulsory dining in messes was abolished, and officers were allowed to eat at home, while at Pentonville the ground outside the prison was used for allotments for the officers which: 'afforded them healthy recreation in the summer evenings'. The standard of the schools for the officers' children was raised; at Portland it was 'rescued from the confusion and ruin in which it so long lay'.[50] In 1866 the management of the officers' libraries and reading rooms was transferred from the chaplain to a committee of warders and other discipline officers. The chaplains at Portland, Chatham, and probably elsewhere were compensated. They developed the nucleus of staff training which has been mentioned. The Convict Report for 1865 announced that all officers on joining had to be interviewed by the chaplain to receive 'godly counsel and advice'.

These several improvements in the life of the staff were introduced just in time to meet the most severe crisis which the convict service had had to deal with. In 1867 the first of many allegations were made by Irish political prisoners, most of whom were convicted of treason felony. For the next thirty years the presence of these prisoners was to be the central political problem facing the prison authorities. There were major investigations in 1867,[51] and 1870,[52] the latter involving an Irish national hero, Jeremiah O'Donovan Rossa.

In 1868 Du Cane, then a captain, became Chairman of the Directors. He had been a Director since 1863. Almost immediately the responsibilities of the Board became more onerous. The last 451 convicts had been transported to Western Australia in 1867[53] and in 1869 the Directors assumed responsibility for all the convict establishments in Australia. These were in Western Australia, Tasmania, and New South Wales. A Royal Commission on Courts Martial and Military Punishments, which had been appointed in March 1868, expressed dissatisfaction with the military prisons, and recommended that they should come under the Directors, and that there should be a central military prison.[54]

In 1870 the role of the warder was extended significantly. Two new avenues were opened to him when the Directors decided that warders could become clerks and schoolmasters:[55]

> We have proposed a change in regard to the conduct of the clerical duties of the prisons, which while it will effect an economy in administering them will be a benefit to the warders, viz., that of employing discipline officers in the place of clerks. We have reason to believe that both in trustworthiness, intelligence, and efficiency, we shall find them fully equal to these duties, and as employment of this nature is much sought after, we have no doubt that it will be found a useful stimulus and an additional attraction to induce the better educated soldiers to enter the convict service on discharge.

It is no longer the practice in the English system to employ officers as clerks, nor is this a normal promotion in the career of a uniformed officer. The Scottish prison service on the other hand, has clerical departments almost entirely staffed by 'discipline' officers, that is officers in uniform. The failure of the English system to develop and expand clerical departments staffed by warders is of great significance because the closing of this avenue limited the opportunities of uniformed staff. In addition the clerical department, not being subject to a Discipline Code, has become increasingly insular, and independent of the governor.

Warders were also to be given the opportunity to act as schoolmasters. At Dartmoor, where a new hall had been opened, the Directors: 'thought that men might be found among our warders sufficiently educated to provide a help . . . there is every prospect that the expectations of the Board will, in a great measure, be realised'.[56] It was not long before an assistant warder at Dartmoor was acting as a schoolmaster.[57]

As a result of these innovations, the bulk of the work of the convict prisons came to be performed by uniformed staff. For several years they were to be found carrying out 'discipline', clerical, educational, and instructional work. Since they were all warders, and responsible to the chief warder who was in turn accountable to the governor, there was the unity of command, and common identity, which are concomitants of the para-military structure. Specialist groups, anxiously establishing independence of the governor, who were to contribute to the organisational crises in the twentieth century, were almost entirely absent. It would appear that there was only one major conflict which, since it was concerned with security, had to be resolved.

The chief warder was responsible for security, since he was the head of the discipline staff. But the civil guard, which was concerned solely with security, had its own head, the superintendent. The intrinsic confusion in this situation was resolved by the abolition of the post of superintendent, and the guard was placed directly under the chief warder. Since he was accountable for security, it was clearly unreasonable that he should have to battle for control of part of the organisation which had security as its task. Opinions varied about the desirability of this change. The Governor of Portland, in the Convict Report for 1871, wrote that he was sorry to have lost: 'the services of an experienced and zealous officer of eleven years standing', but the Governor of Portsmouth thought the change was good:

'it places them [the guard] on the same footing as the other discipline officers, it has greatly increased their supervision and enabled the principal warders of districts to check any neglect of duty.' He was, however, concerned about the destruction of their promotional hierarchy. His discussion of the principal warders is an illustration of the organisational defect being discussed. It would have been very curious indeed, if the guard had not used the inherent confusion about spheres of authority between the chief warder and the superintendent to manipulate the principal warders. When the chief warder controlled the guard, the principal warder could give orders to the guard on the works and elsewhere. Thus the person who was accountable for effective task achievement, that is the senior uniformed officer, also had control over the resources.

The abolition of the post of superintendent consolidated the very close relationship, already established, between the governor and the chief warder. From the beginning the chief was frequently singled out for special mention in the Convict Reports. This relationship is the most important in the whole fabric of the staff structure. It always has been, and has survived even the introduction of junior members of the governor grade to the prison service. The latter are usually resentful because they are disappointed in their expectation that they will be closest to the governor. Because this relationship is so crucial, it is necessary to consider why it established itself so quickly and why it has persisted. Like many of the organisational phenomena which are being analysed, this key relationship is not confined to English prisons, or indeed to prisons at all. What follows could perhaps be said of the relationship of commanding officer and RSM, physician superintendent and chief male nurse, and many others in 'institutional' work.

The relationship of the governor and 'the chief' has always been symbiotic. Each brings expectations about the other's role to the situation. The chief, after some twenty-five years in the service, will have learned two facts about the governor's role: that through the skills of the chief, widely differing personalities can occupy it without radically affecting the routine of the prison; and that the governor will expect to rely heavily on his chief. The latter is the most experienced official in the prison, and he is thoroughly acquainted with all the idiosyncracies, interests, and weaknesses, generic and particular, of the uniformed staff. He is a master of routines, and is not prepared to buy popularity with inefficiency or corruption. He protects the governor from excesses on the part of the staff association, and identifies with the governor if there is a disagreement.[58] He is the only member of the uniformed staff that the governor can trust absolutely.

The staff, while they may sometimes feel that the chief does not support them as much as he should, nevertheless regard his position as prestigious. Most hope to be chief officers themselves, and are generally willing to defer to a man holding a position which they hope to hold. The officers are also reluctant to challenge him because of his enormous influence with the governor.[59]

It can be seen therefore that the power of the chief lies in his role as a bridge between the governor and the officers. And this power is reinforced by the control the chief has over *information*. The importance of this can be gauged from the fact that he decides which items of information shall be transmitted to and from governor and officers. An example of the exercise of this power occurs when he restrains the excesses of some zealous governor by making clear to the officers that while a weird instruction from the governor is to be carried out, it should not too easily become a part of institutional routine. By doing this, he is likely to believe that he is saving governor and officers from pointless conflict. In the other direction, the chief is able to isolate the governor from information which may be important, and thus increases the dependence of the governor on him. There is plenty of evidence that governors are content that this should be so. Two very different examples may be given. An experienced official reported to the Gladstone Committee that he had told a newly appointed governor 'to be guided very much by the chief warder'.[60] Another governor, Major Wallace Blake, reported that 'if he is fortunate enough to have a reliable chief warder—and in my whole career I have not met one who was not reliable—he has plenty of time for golf and tennis or whatever his chosen recreation may be.'[61] To all of these factors may be added the likelihood that the two men will probably have served longer than most other members of staff, and may be roughly the same age. It is probable, therefore, that they should find each other congenial professional colleagues.

From the evidence in the literature it is clear that the relationship which has been described and which can be observed in the prison service at the present day, was already established in the early years of the convict service.

In 1871 evidence of dissatisfaction with the behaviour of some staff began to reappear in the Convict Reports. At Millbank 77 assistant warders joined in the year and 38 left, resigned or were dismissed. The Governor was not too hopeful about the recruits:

> especially as the majority of the candidates for the appointment of assistant warder do not possess those suitable qualifications which they formally did, nor is there the same aptitude for acquiring, with readiness, a general knowledge of their duties.

The warders themselves gave an alternative explanation of the unrest, making it clear that an improvement in pay and conditions was the solution. Du Cane, in a minute in October 1872, whilst admitting that 'we do not now obtain the services of so good a class of men as we used to do some years ago,' put up a strong case for improving conditions,[62] both of subordinate, and of superior, officers.[63] He recommended a rise of 15 per cent for subordinate and 10 per cent for superior staff.[64] The Treasury declined to grant a percentage increase, and wanted a well-considered scheme.[65] Du Cane minuted again that governors were of the opinion that 'the new subordinate officers, as a class, fall below the requirements of the service in physique, in attainment, and special fitness for the duties of their posts'.[66] Out of 2,416 who had joined in the last ten years, 1,954 had left.

Several governors expressed concern in their reports for 1872. The Governor of Pentonville pointed out that staff were affected by the radical behaviour of the working classes:

> I regret that some mischievous persons taking advantage of the opportunity afforded by the prevalence of strikes and combinations against employers have endeavoured to create disaffection among them and to induce them to commit themselves to a course in direct contravention of standing orders. The good sense and habits of discipline however of the great majority have been proof against the attempt, and a very small number of my staff has been so misled.

Millbank was no better than in the previous year. Twenty assistant warders resigned, 15 were dismissed, and 42 new ones were appointed. Very few of the staff were competent: 'and unless some means can be devised to secure a great permanency of service, there must exist a large element of inexperience and a want of qualification among them.' One measure of the unsettled state of the staff at Millbank is the fact that during the year no fewer than 417 offences were recorded against the warders.

In August 1873 Du Cane wrote again to Liddell, the Permanent Under Secretary, urging an early settlement, otherwise the:[67]

> staff may follow advice which is urged upon them, and adopt the course which is now too common of making some public appeal or demonstration. Any concession would be attributed to this, and this would be very undesirable.

On 3 December 1873, fifteen months after Du Cane initiated the claim, the Treasury agreed to an increase of pay and allowances.[68] This sequence of events illustrates the very real difficulties facing the administrator of a department who is conscious of the justice of a claim, has to undergo considerable delays from the Treasury, and has to take the hostility for both delay and inadequacy of the awards. The public records of the period show that Du Cane, like any Chairman, was prevented from exercising real power in respect of staff unrest, because of constraints imposed by the Treasury.

The Report for 1873 notes that: 'on the whole a very substantial advantage was conferred on the subordinate officers.' The warders were not long in showing that they regarded it as very insubstantial. Chatham warders held a meeting to protest against the new rates of pay. It was claimed that the increase amounted to 5s, or 1s 8d a month, the rest of the increment being swallowed up in extra charges for meat and rations. They expressed 'great indignation' at the 'miserable conduct' of the authorities, and stated that they would try to get 'their wrongs redressed'.[69] *The Globe* on 5 November 1873 published a letter from Tallack in which he supported the warders in a very spirited fashion: 'They have long been the hardest-worked persons in Her Majesty's Service.'

In March 1874 Tallack petitioned the Home Secretary asking him to do more for the warders,[70] which drew a detailed commentary from Du Cane, in which he wrote that the statements of the warders about allowances were wrong. The ration allowance, for instance, bought more than appeared to outsiders, because staff bought food at cost price from the contractors. He concluded by stating: 'it is known that a certain secret agitation has been on foot—promoted by a few men.' It was an 'absolute necessity' that any request made by, or on behalf of, officers of a public department should be made to, or through, their superior officers.[71] Tallack persisted. He wrote again to the Home Secretary in May 1874, that the warders assured him that their complaints were accurate. They had, he reported, held public meetings at Chatham and Charing Cross Hotel, written to papers and Members of Parliament, and called on Members of Parliament.[72] The warders' efforts were rewarded by two Parliamentary questions in May. One expressed dissatisfaction at the 1874 settlement, the other asked the Home Secretary to arrange for the Commission on the Civil Service to take into account representations made by the officers of Her Majesty's Convict Service about hours of duty. To this latter question Cross gave a very evasive reply. He said that as far as he was aware no 'formal representations' had been made. Representations had been made about certain regulations laid down by the late government, 'by some association'. Despite this unhelpful reply, the complaint about hours of duty seems to have been justified, and Du Cane tried again to get a concession from the Treasury. He wrote on 4 December 1874 that: 'the officers of convict prisons having of late made some complaints of the length of their hours of duty,' these complaints were 'not without foundation'. He proposed that the working hours of convicts could be reduced on Saturdays. Although the drop in production would be slight, the new schedule would mean that warders could have a half-day.[73] Pentonville was excluded from the scheme, because the warders' work was not so hard there.

At the time of the centralisation of the local prisons in 1877, the staff situation in the convict prisons was unsettled. The governors of Millbank and Parkhurst were especially worried, whilst the Governor of Portland in his report for 1878 mentioned a new problem: 'a considerable increase in the number of officers dismissed and allowed to resign from drunkenness'. At the same time the emerging radical spirit amongst workers was affecting the attitude of some staff, and there was a new militancy in their dealings with the Directors. The experience gained in dealings between warders and Directors was being consolidated, and traditions were becoming established. But Du Cane and the Board were quite clear about the kind of officer they wanted and how standards were to be kept up:[74]

> There is perhaps no department of the public service on which the efficiency more entirely depends on the maintenance of a high tone and discipline among the staff, and a constant and effective supervision by the superiors, or on which neglect in

those points is more certain to defeat the whole object sought after, or lead to a grave class of evils.

In the Convict Report for 1877, the Directors took the opportunity to stress the high standard of officer that the service tried to get but pointed out that 'officers, while in the service, are always kept under close supervision'. Officers who do not bring forward requests of prisoners for interviews 'will be severely punished'. Nor was supervision confined to the warders. Both the governor and the deputy governor were directed to give every prisoner an opportunity, once a week, to apply personally for interview with them.

When the local service was sorting out its initial problems, the convict service was facing another critical period. During 1878–9 there was a Royal Commission on the working of the Penal Servitude Acts which made a number of important recommendations. These included the classification of first offenders which is still employed— the 'star' system—and the establishment of Boards of unofficial Visitors, on the same basis as the Visiting Committees in local prisons. On the whole the Directors felt able to report satisfaction of the Commission with the system: 'the system . . . is on the whole satisfactory; it is effective as a punishment, and free from serious abuses.'[75] The Directors were exonerated in another investigation, this time into the death of an Irish ex-prisoner.[76] At such a critical time, when there was hostility to the centralising of the local prisons, such exoneration was important. Du Cane took the opportunity to comment, in the Convict Report for 1878, that they were 'conscious of our unremitting endeavours to prevent abuses', and reminded the community that staff were vulnerable to allegations from people whose 'bitter enmity' they sometimes incur.

The early years of the local service

The passing of the 1877 Act did not end the hostility of some local authorities to the new service, and it became clear that the Commissioners would have to use great skill to reconcile the justices to the fact that they no longer ran the prisons.

As early as April 1879, the Salford magistrates convened a meeting in London to discuss the administration of the new Act. They expressed their wish to maintain the primary and fundamental links between the prison and the local community, suggesting that Prison

Commissioners and Inspectors ought to reside in the districts in which their prisons were located. (In recent years this deployment has taken place.) The meeting wanted the powers of the visiting justices extended, and advocated annual conferences between the Commissioners and district committees once a year.[77] After the meeting a deputation was assured by the Home Secretary that the local justices would have great power.[78] But in October 1879 there occurred a relatively minor, but potentially very critical, episode, when Dorchester Justices of the Peace were refused entrance to the prison by the Governor. The Commissioners apologised profusely.[79]

On 7 January 1880, in a letter to *The Times*, Tallack deplored the increasing centralisation, quoting one group as saying 'they feel their services are of small value', and emphasising the importance of the local connection. On 10 March 1880 'the electors of Hackney' met to protest against the severity of prison regulations, and the extent of the powers of the Home Secretary in the government of prisons.[80] A powerful pressure group called the Annual Conference of Visiting Committees, which included several peers, held a meeting, and saw the Home Secretary and the Prison Commissioners in 1880 and 1881. They pressed for more efficient auditing so that promises of economy could be fulfilled, and they wished to secure to prisoners the 'personal rights to which everyone is entitled under the law'. The demands made by this group were a serious threat to the new organisation, since some of the concessions they gained were not only of a generalising nature, but had to do with details of management. Some of these were that prisoners were not to be restricted to the Bible for their first month, the selection of books was to be left to the visiting justices and the chaplain, prisoners should be taught in classes, not in cells (although in fact prisoners continued to be taught in cells) and the governor's power to award restricted diet for three days was to be reduced to twenty-four hours. The Home Secretary even agreed that the visiting committees could give three days' leave of absence to superior officers, provided each case was reported on.[81]

This kind of involvement in detailed administration by a lay body was not only organisationally unsound, but militated against the primary purpose of the new Act, which was designed specifically to give the central government general and detailed control over prisons. There is little doubt that the Commissioners soon realised that the battle for control of administration was not over, and gradually this lay pressure was contained, and eventually discontinued. The reason for its demise was explained in a letter written by a visiting Justice, Henry Manton, to the Home Secretary on 11 June 1894: 'So long as Sir E. Du Cane continued Chairman of the Commissioners all efforts to amend would be useless.'[82] This struggle was important because it established the relationship of a visiting committee with its prison once and for all. Although the formal powers ascribed to them are impressive (their current terms of reference may be seen in the Detention Centre Rules 1952, the Prison Rules 1964, and the Borstal Rules 1964), in reality, for most of the time, their impact on prison regimes is very slight.

Not all the local authorities were critical of the new administration. The arguments about 'burdens on the rates' were continued in *The Times*, led by a letter from 'Ratepayer' who wrote on 17 January 1879, that the justices only 'speak for themselves'. Others pointed out the advantages of the new system,[83] and the Visiting Committee of Clerkenwell resolved that the Act had worked 'without exception most satisfactorily'. They wished to record the 'prompt attention' they always experienced from the Home Secretary and the Prison Commissioners.[84] The Prison Conference of Visiting Justices met in June 1883, and it was reported that:[85]

> The alarm (felt at the loss of prisons) had been greatly dissipated, and now they had little need to find fault because Sir William Harcourt had always given his attention to every subject that had been brought to his notice.

In 1881 the Home Secretary congratulated the Commissioners on 'very satisfactory' reports from all quarters about prisons. He also mentioned evidence of 'agreeable relationships' between the visiting committees on the one hand, and the Commissioners and the prison authorities on the other.[86]

Whether the comments on prisons were hostile or friendly, they demonstrate that many local communities continued to see the prison as part of their responsibility. Notification of intended closures for example, drew protests from Members of Parliament (such as those about the closing of Chester[87]), although to twentieth-century observers a more familiar note was struck when the Member for Dover asked on 20 April 1888, 'if it is intended to retain Dover as a convict station to the permanent injury of the borough?' And although the Commissioners may have contained resentment over the loss of the locals, it was never entirely eliminated. Indeed, in the important article, 'Are our Prisons a Failure?', by the Reverend W. D. Morrison, which has achieved such fame as a contributory factor in the establishment of the Gladstone Committee, the local administration of prisons was alleged to have been very superior.

Either because they felt attempts to intervene were useless, or because they were pleased with the new administration, the local authorities, in the early 1880s, gave up their struggle. At the same time the reformers turned their attention to 'matters other than prisons and capital punishment'.[88] The relationship between Tallack and Du Cane became relatively cordial. The Webbs noted that the post-1877 period was undramatic, but are sceptical about the reason: 'Since 1878 the prison has become "a silent world" shrouded, so far as the public is concerned, in almost complete darkness.'[89] In fact there were plenty of problems to occupy the attention of Directors and Commissioners after 1877. But since they were staff problems they have attracted no comment by writers.

The nature of the initial staffing problems in the local service has already been described. Because of closures Du Cane had to begin by discharging 41 governors, 17 deputy governors, and 143 warders and 'other sub officers' from the male prisons.[90] There were similar overall decreases in the numbers of female staff. Those who remained were deprived of a substantial and incalculable assortment of perquisites. For the most part, the remainder settled in quite well to the much more structured and supervised service. Each Local Report contains an appendix consisting of reports by the Inspectors on each of the prisons. The comments on staff are brief and usually favourable. There are exceptions; of Worcester it is reported in the Sixth Local Report, that two subordinate officers were dismissed, one resigned, and two were transferred, whilst of the remainder 'the Governor reports in an unsatisfactory manner'. At Knutsford staff conduct was described in the Ninth Local Report as 'indifferent', indifference which resulted in the chief warder being fined and severely reprimanded for letting a prisoner escape. These were minor and isolated incidents, and exceptions to the generally excellent performance of the local staff.

The smooth transition of staff from local authorities to the central government, and the enormously successful standardisation of diverse local staff structures, obscured new and more subtle divisions which could not be forecast by Du Cane, who looked at the new staff situation with some satisfaction. One of the new complications was a consequence of the policies of eliminating prisoner-clerks, and extending educational facilities for prisoners. These two developments represented the first stage in the process of 'specialisation' which has led to such conflict in the prison service. Du Cane stopped the practice of using prisoners as clerks. As a result the 97 male and 1 female clerk in post on 1 April 1878, had to be increased to 138 males, in spite of closures.[91] A Committee which was set up to inquire into the accounting system and related matters in the local prisons, recommended the introduction of a proper system of storekeeping and book-keeping, which necessitated the provision of adequate clerical staff. Consequently they drew up a scale of grades for each prison.[92] In a further report to Du Cane, the Committee pointed out that extended clerical departments, at an annual cost of £9,000, were necessary because all the financial work previously handled by the local authority had now to be undertaken by the prison.[93] To raise the standard of clerks they reported that 'certain augmentations of salary' had been approved, and that careful scrutiny of applicants culminated in a competition conducted by the Civil Service Commissioners.[94] The new clerical department soon developed a corpus which began to break away from the 'line' which constituted the main administrative chain of command in the prison. In 1881 the Committee recommended 'most strongly that the clerical staff of the entire prison service should, for purposes of promotion, be strictly treated as a whole'. Otherwise people would not be prepared to serve in minor positions. From the files which notify staff movements it can also be seen that the clerks could be transferred nationally.[95] Warders could not. Although the latter could become clerks in the convict service after 1870, local warders could not specialise in clerical work until 1895.

The extension of educational provision for prisoners led to the establishment of another important 'specialist' group—the schoolmasters. On 1 April 1878 there were 53 male schoolmasters, 3 clerk/ schoolmasters, 8 warder/schoolmasters, 25 female schoolmasters and 8 warder/schoolmistresses.[96] Under the new regime the prisons each had a school staff 'at an additional annual expense of £2,230'.[97] Since 1870 convict warders had been appointed schoolmasters,[98] and, from 1879, local schoolmasters were recruited from amongst the warders, recommended by the governor and the chaplain, and tested by an Inspector of the Education Department. They were on 'the same footing' as elementary teachers.[99]

Both the new specialisms, at different times, provided an avenue of advancement for the warders. But the development of specialisms meant that work in the prison service under the central government became more complex. This complexity, of which the two improved departments are an expression, in turn led to division of labour. Since 'division of labour creates roles of differing prestige',[100] there developed very early in the centralised service concern about prestige, and status, which was aggravated by the distinction between the convict and local services.

The problems which were posed were muted slightly by the fact that there was this mobility for the warders from discipline to clerical and teaching work. Warders could also be promoted to governor. But while these specialisms in the early years of the two services operated to the advantage of the uniform grade, the seeds were being planted of a development which was to be highly destructive of organisational cohesion in the twentieth century.

As more and more specialist work was introduced into prison, the officer was progressively excluded from it. Prestigious specialist work has been allocated to new grades appointed for the purpose, and the officer has been left with work, which, while central to the primary task requires little skill or imagination, and consequently, he suspects, has low prestige rating in the eyes of prisoners, prison service, and community. Job allocation is the test of the status of the uniformed officer, not the assertions of his importance made frequently by official and semi-official bodies. In the last sixty years this movement has gained momentum and will be a recurrent topic in this analysis.

Notes

1 First Local Report, pp. 12–13.
2 *The Times*, 12 April 1850, p. 5.
3 *The Times*, 1 January 1852, p. 5 and p. 7; Convict Report 1851, p. 220.
4 Convict Report 1852, p. 233.
5 Convict Report 1856, p. 6.
6 Convict Report 1860, p. 188.
7 Convict Report 1862, p. 46.
8 Convict Report 1857, p. 218.
9 Ibid., p. 154.
10 Ibid., p. 186.
11 Convict Report 1858, p. 221.

12 Convict Report 1856, p. 370.
13 Convict Report 1857, p. 232 and p. 230.
14 Ibid., p. 303.
15 Ibid., p. 303.
16 Convict Report 1858, p. 312.
17 Ibid., p. 285.
18 Ibid., p. 360.
19 Chatham was often in trouble. It came to be known by prisoners as 'the slaughterhouse' (*Twenty-five Years in Seventeen Prisons* by 'No. 7').
20 Trouble in English prisons has often begun on the labour parade because this is one of the few occasions when almost all the prisoners are together.
21 Convict Report 1861, p. 250 et seq.
22 Ibid., p. 255.
23 Convict Report 1862, p. 124.
24 Convict Report 1856, p. 259.
25 Convict Report 1859, p. 137.
26 Convict Report 1860, p. 228; Convict Report 1862, p. 210.
27 Convict Report 1860, p. 155.
28 Convict Report 1861, p. 156.
29 Convict Report 1860, p. 252.
30 Convict Report 1861, p. 12.
31 Ibid., p. 250.
32 Report, p. 23.
33 Convict Report 1863, p. 14.
34 Convict Report 1864, p. 11.
35 Hansard, vol. 173, col. 921, 23 February 1864.
36 Convict Report 1864, p. 11.
37 Ibid., p. 88.
38 Ibid., p. 9.
39 Ibid., p. 6. The Chaplain of Pentonville claimed responsibility for this (Convict Report 1865, p. 52).
40 Convict Report 1864, p. 21. This section of the Report describes the system.
41 Ibid., p. 8.
42 This drew complaints from chaplains—see, for example, ibid., p. 116.
43 Hansard, vol. 169, col. 222 and col. 331, 12 March 1863.
44 Convict Report 1864, p. 9.
45 Convict Report 1865, p. 8.
46 Loc. cit.
47 Ibid., p. 11.
48 Convict Report 1864, p. 50.
49 Convict Report 1865, p. 11.
50 Ibid., p. 106. This description of the school raises an interesting problem. No reference was made to 'ruin' *before* the 'rescue'. Does this mean that only laudatory remarks occur in Reports? And that

we never learn about unsatisfactory situations unless, and until, they are improved?

51 Departmental Committee on Treatment of Treason Felony Convicts in English Convict Prisons, 1867.

52 Report of the Commissioners Appointed to Inquire into the Treatment of Treason Felony Convicts in English Prisons, 1871.

53 Convict Report 1868, p. VI.

54 Ibid., p. X.

55 Convict Report 1870, p. XIII.

56 Ibid., p. 225.

57 Ibid., p. 269.

58 No chief signed the petitions of the early 1880s which will be discussed. A chief giving evidence to the De Ramsey Committee (see pp. 91 ff) said (question 2062) that 'every prison officer's hand is against the chief warder'.

59 See the *Prison Officers' Magazine*, December 1914, p. 500, where it is stated that a warder 'offended his chief, and he consequently quickly offended his Governor, and the Commission, as a matter of course.'

60 Gladstone Evidence, question 6446.

61 Blake, *Quod*, p. 24.

62 P.R.O. H.O.45/9351/16982/1.

63 P.R.O. H.O.45/9351/16982/2.

64 P.R.O. H.O.45/9351/16982/3.

65 P.R.O. H.O.45/9351/16982/6.

66 P.R.O. H.O.45/9351/16982/7, 13 June 1873.

67 P.R.O. H.O.45/9351/16982/11.

68 P.R.O. H.O.45/9351/16982/14.

69 *The Times*, 4 November 1873, p. 11.

70 P.R.O. H.O.45/9351/16982/22.

71 P.R.O. H.O.45/9351/16982/24.

72 P.R.O. H.O.45/9351/16982/25.

73 P.R.O. H.O.45/9351/16982/27.

74 Convict Report 1873, p. XI.

75 Convict Report 1878, p. V.

76 Inquiry as to the Alleged Ill-treatment of the Convict Charles M'Carthy in Chatham Convict Prison, 1878.

77 *The Times*, 17 March 1879, p. 6; 3 April 1879, p. 7.

78 *The Times*, 4 April 1879, p. 10.

79 *The Times*, 1 November 1879, p. 11.

80 *The Times*, 11 March 1880, p. 7.

81 *The Times*, 5 June 1880, p. 12; 2 June 1881, p. 6.

82 P.R.O. H.O.45/9958/V20544/20.

83 For example, Colonel Ralph, chairman of a visiting committee, *The Times*, 11 January 1879, p. 10.

84 *The Times*, 8 July 1880, p. 14.

85 *The Times*, 6 June 1883, p. 14.

86 Reprinted in Eleventh Local Report, p. 34.

87 Hansard, vol. 288, col. 1305, 26 May 1884.
88 Rose, *The Struggle for Penal Reform*, p. 46.
89 S. and B. Webb, *English Prisons under Local Government*, p. 235.
90 These figures are calculated from the table in appendix 5 to the First Local Report (p. 30).
91 Loc. cit.
92 First Local Report, app. 18, p. 30.
93 Eighth Local Report, pp. 3–4.
94 Third Local Report, app. 14, pp. 37–9.
95 P.R.O. H.O.180.
96 Third Local Report, app. 18, pp. 51–2.
97 Eighth Local Report, pp. 3–4.
98 Convict Report 1870, p. 225.
99 Departmental Committee on Education and Moral Instruction of Prisoners in Local and Convict Prisons, 1896, p. XI, paras 32 and 33.
100 Banton, *Roles*, p. 192.

5   1880–91: two major inquiries

The Rosebery Committee

The even tempo of staff life in the local service was in marked contrast to that of colleagues in the convict prisons. There was dissatisfaction in the latter in the early 1880s, mainly about pay and hours of duty. Like other manual workers at that time, the convict warders were agitating for more pay with increasing force. Unlike some other groups, they were not members of trade unions, and so had to draw attention to their grievance through anonymous letters to the press, petitions to the Home Secretary, and clandestine lobbying of Members of Parliament. The discontent betore 1900 is of special interest, since it led to two major inquiries which together are a valuable source of information about the life of the staff, and the role of the warder. They reveal that many of the features of the modern prison service were already well established before the end of the nineteenth century, and that many of the modern 'problems' had their origins in the development of the service in the early years. For these reasons, and because neither inquiry has been mentioned or discussed in any account of the prison system, they deserve a fairly detailed analysis.

The dissatisfaction of convict officers seems to have been first made known to the public in 1882, as a result of the execution of a convict called Fury. It was alleged that this man had admitted a murder so that he could be executed, and so put out of his misery. The Home Secretary, Harcourt, in answer to a Parliamentary question in May 1882 said he had inquired into the various allegations about prison life made by Fury, and he was satisfied 'that these allegations were entirely unfounded and untrue'. Tallack then wrote a long letter to *The Times* which was primarily an attack on Harcourt's reply. He wrote that an ex-warder had reported that Fury had declared in a letter, that in his eighteen years as a prisoner he had only met with: 'four or five warders and two or three chaplains whose conduct indicated humane feelings'. Tallack had questioned this ex-warder, the latter agreed with Fury, and so did Tallack from his experience.

He then launched a diatribe against staff, which must rank as one of the most vituperative to appear in a newspaper from the pen of a public figure:

> It becomes exceedingly irritating to a convict, day after day, and especially if ill or begging for medical aid to be cursed as to his eyes, cursed as to his limbs, and verbally consigned to eternal perdition, with the invocation of the Divine name and the use of ugly and filthy epithets.

Tallack finished his letter on a calmer note. He offered the answer which has become most predictable of solutions to the dilemmas of imprisonment: 'better selection and more systematic training of the warders, with more pay and fewer hours of duty for them'.[1]

On the same page as Tallack's letter, appeared a letter from 'Assistant Warder Chatham'. This man gives examples of officers being murderously assaulted by convicts, including one where an officer was nearly killed with his own sword. Such cases were dealt with leniently by the visiting Directors because the 'authorities are very chary of allowing convicts to go before the Judges, as it shows up the defects in the prison administration'. On 7 June Tallack published in *The Times* a copy of his letter to the Home Secretary, in which he wrote:

> week after week, the officers of convict prisons are, in spite of all regulations against their communicating with the press or with the public, and at their serious personal risk, in case of detection, complaining grievously of their own condition, and that of the prisoners under their care.

Newspapers for months past had had 'to narrate a series of convict outbreaks, violent assaults, and escapes which are certain proof of a very unsatisfactory state of affairs'. Although there are remarks in this letter which are supportive of staff, what was annoying Tallack were the opportunities given to convicts to communicate and combine. By 'unsatisfactory state of affairs' he meant the absence of rigidly enforced separation.

While this discussion about the behaviour of staff was being carried on in the press, more questions were asked in Parliament. Alderman R. N. Fowler, the Lord Mayor of London, who had championed the warders' cause in 1873, asked the Home Secretary in June 1882 if he would investigate the complaints against prison management which had been made in the press, and if it was true that assaults were of daily occurrence. Harcourt replied that all allegations were investigated by the visiting committees and the visitors to convict prisons. After pointing out that the International Prison Congress had spoken very favourably of management, he tried to end the matter by saying:

> I cannot entertain or give credit to anonymous charges in newspapers made by convicts who do not give their names or by warders who may or may not have been discharged, and who adduce no evidence of what they allege.

To do so would be to injure prison discipline and 'give encouragement to insubordination'. Tallack was not prepared to allow a basic error in Harcourt's statement to go unchecked. He pointed out in a letter to *The Times* on 20 June 1882, that the Prison Congress had been talking about *local* prisons; the agitation, and Fowler's question, were about *convict* prisons.

Also in 1882 Harcourt made a frank statement about the relationship between what appeared in the press, and the facts. His statement was especially important because it was supportive of the Directors. His remarks were addressed to a deputation of members of visiting committees:

> People seem to think that whatever they read in the newspapers is necessarily a complete or accurate statement of a case. My experience does not bear out that assumption. As far as I can observe, the opposite conclusion would be more correct.

He went on to repeat his unwillingness to accept allegations which were 'entirely unsubstantiated by any particular circumstances or facts'.[2]

Harcourt's attempts to dismiss the various complaints about staff conditions failed, and highly damaging statements continued to appear in the press. Francis Peek, the Chairman of the Howard Association published a letter in the *Civil Service Gazette* of 24 June 1882, which he had sent to Harcourt. Peek, like Tallack, was mainly concerned, not with staff difficulties, but with the 'opportunities for intrigue and conspiracy' which existed amongst convicts. He was in fact, demanding that greater control be exercised over the inmates. And he offered solutions to the mutinous and violent behaviour which he described. These were an end to the 'gang system', the separation of different classes, and the perennial 'intercourse with a better class of officials'. In its editorial on the same day, and again on 1 July, the newspaper supported the demands for an inquiry. Harcourt replied on 29 June that staff could be assured that any complaints which were made would be investigated and there would be no reprisals.[3]

At least one member of staff became very angry at the Home Secretary's persistent refusal to acknowledge that there was any need for alarm. 'Ten Years Assistant Warder' wrote to the *Civil Service Gazette*, and his letter was published on 1 July 1882. He wrote of 'miserable wrecks of men who a few years ago joined the Service in the full vigour of health'. He complained about short holidays, slow promotion, long hours and 'harassing with frivolous reports and vexatious fines'. He drew attention to a fundamental need of staff in a rigid structure when he appealed for 'more definite understanding as to what to do and what to leave alone'. Of assaults he wrote: 'they are of daily occurrence although it is denied. If convict were changed to warder and warder to Director the position would change.'

These were serious allegations and the Directors, in the 1881–2 annual report which was published in July, firmly denied that assaults were 'of daily occurrence'. Resistance was to be expected from a population of 10,245 convicts, but at Chatham, where it was alleged assaults were of daily occurrence, there had in fact been 'two serious assaults in the year and twelve trivial cases, consisting merely in physically resisting the officer'. The Governor in his report expands on what was meant by serious: As a result of their injuries the officers had to be retired.

The Directors' experience of inquiries of various kinds had been quite satisfactory. It was perhaps this experience, and confidence that few of the allegations could be substantiated, together with the maintenance of pressure, which led Du Cane to suggest to the Home Secretary that a Committee of Inquiry should be appointed.[4] In the same minute, dated 5 April 1882, in which he made reference to Du Cane's suggestion, Lushington expressed the view that Du Cane should not be a member but should give evidence. In fact he was appointed a member, as was his predecessor as Chairman, Sir Edmund Henderson.

Meanwhile the warders began to submit petitions to the department, and these were forwarded to the Home Secretary. Du Cane minuted to Lushington that the Directors and superior officers had never heard of any dissatisfaction, though they constantly invited complaints, and listened to any request or grievance. This is an early example of the experience of large organisations that machinery for consultation is frequently not used. He denied specifically that there were large numbers of resignations, and set out figures to prove it. Nor was there any shortage of applicants; 367 who had been selected were waiting for appointment. In 1873 convict pay was increased, in 1875 hours were decreased, and a large proportion got a half-day Saturday, without any request from officers. He warned that the local staff were likely to follow suit, since their pay was less than that of the convict officers. In spite of his suggestion that an inquiry should be instituted, Du Cane felt that 'the petitions have been put up by some individuals and the rest have blindly and ignorantly followed the lead'. He added that only a few would benefit if the suggestions about pay were accepted.[5]

The members of the Committee were the Earl of Rosebery (Chairman), Du Cane, Henderson, J. T. Hibbert MP., and R. S. Mitford (Secretary). Mitford was also a Director. The first petitions were from Wormwood Scrubs, and these were followed by petitions from Pentonville, Portsmouth, Woking, Parkhurst, Brixton, Millbank, Portland, Dartmoor and Chatham. Du Cane set out the numbers involved in one of the documents prepared for the inquiry. Out of 1,349 subordinate officers of all grades, including the civil guard, 792 signed.[6] It was not likely that any chief warder would sign, and none did. But other aspects of the petitions are puzzling. None of the staff at Borstal signed and no female staff signed. In spite of the way that Chatham had figured prominently, out of its 200 staff, only one warder signed.[7] He was not the 'Assistant Warder Chatham' who had written to *The Times*. The petitioner had been in the service nine years and had been a *warder* for one year.[8]

The petitioners all asked for:[9]

1 An eight-hour system of work.
2 An increase of annual leave.
3 A readjustment of pay and allowances.
4 Increased superannuation.

In December 1882, just before the Committee was appointed, Harcourt got a petition from the staff at Broadmoor, asking to be included in the inquiry. On 17 February 1883 they put their case in detail. They claimed, *inter alia*, that their work was much more dangerous than convict work, and that no comparison could be made, although it would be attempted, with work in the county asylums.[10] In February 1883 when the Committee had begun to take evidence, the convict schoolmasters asked to be included.[11] In spite of the employment of some warders as schoolmasters, the convict schoolmasters, unlike local schoolmasters, were usually direct entrants. There were two classes of schoolmaster, and the essence of their petition was that promotion was too slow. Both groups were included in the inquiry.

Du Cane's preparatory documentation, printed as appendices to the Report, was typically thorough. He drew up lists of staff who had petitioned with details of their backgrounds, comparisons of pay in the convict and kindred services, returns of fines imposed on staff and other information.[12] He also carried out a preliminary series of interviews with staff, which were printed. The detailed information he produced was in marked contrast to the rather wild assertions of Tallack, the 'Assistant Warders', and some other correspondents. His respect for facts also contrasted with the uncertain evidence given by the staff witnesses. He also appointed a committee of governors in December 1882, to see what adjustments could be made in the duties complained of.[13] The inquiry drew heavily on the suggestions of this group contained in their report of 20 December.[14] One of the most interesting of their proposals was that there should be a body of assistant warders under instruction at a prison in or near London or in their own locality, and from these, vacancies could be filled as they occurred. This is an early proposal for central staff training.

The Committee, which will be called the Rosebery Committee after its chairman, met for the first time on 2 February 1883, and finished hearing evidence on 20 April. The evidence given by the various grades of staff provides us with valuable information about the staff structure, the routine of the prison and the feelings of staff about their working conditions. It is thus possible to capture the atmosphere of the prison system of the period.

The witnesses started with some very indifferent evidence and some remarkably inept replies. Warder Watson, in reply to the very first question said:

The eight-hour system could not really be introduced into the convict prisons, but it was mentioned in the petition as a basis or groundwork to show that the hours at present existing are rather too long.

The second witness, Warder Alderman, agreed that the hours were too long, but when asked how they could be shortened said: 'That is a thing that I have not gone into.'[15] In spite of this kind of remark it became clear that the staff were justified in complaining about hours of duty. In particular they were irritated by a duty called 'reserve guard' which involved an officer working all day and part of the night, including stoking at some prisons, and carrying out a normal day of duty the following day. Lieutenant-Colonel Garsia, Governor of Millbank stated: 'I think the reserve guard is the greatest hardship that prison officers have to complain of.'[16]

On the subject of leave, the staff complained there was not enough, they could not get it when they wanted, and that sick leave was deducted from it. On the second point, governors giving evidence pointed out that not everybody could get leave at the same time.[17] On the third point it was claimed that sick leave was deducted (including governors') because otherwise the staff would cheat.[18] In any case, the governor could ask the Directors to restore leave which had been deducted. On pay the claim was simple: the cost of living had gone up. The question of increased superannuation raised a point which was to be raised several times in the years which followed. The staff claimed that their conditions of service were similar to those of the police. They ought therefore to enjoy the same advantages in terms of superannuation.

The evidence also provides information which, though tangential to the central issues being discussed, is interesting as a revelation of the officer's circumstances. It was stated that if an officer were transferred he lost his seniority, and therefore promotion was generally local, only 'very rarely' national.[19] Temporary officers were not employed,[20] 'promotion is very slow',[21] and there were still strongly held views about ex-service staff.[22] There was a rare account of the work of the civil guard,[23] the problem of their relationship with the warders was mentioned, and it was suggested that the two branches be amalgamated.[24] The claim was made that officers were 'harassed', in a vivid account of the problems of control,[25] and strong feelings were expressed about fining.[26] It was pointed out that staff were not allowed to hold meetings.[27] One of the most interesting facts to emerge was that although formally the grade of senior warder did not exist, informally it did. It was clear that a senior warder was recognised as a post in the service. This interesting phenomenon continued until the grade was formally established, on the recommendation of the Mountbatten Committee.

The response of the Committee to the evidence was overtly hostile. On the question of hours they considered that the Governors' Committee recommendations should be adopted. These included allowing the reserve guard to sleep, except in emergency, and employing a night stoker. With a 'moderate increase' the Committee felt that the governors could reduce the hours. They also took the civil guard one step further to amalgamation, when they recommended that they should be made available for discipline duties: 'But we are most decidedly of opinion that no important modification is required.' They suggested that leave should be more graduated, and that there should be a slight increase—two days for warders, five days for principal and acting principal warders, no extra for chief and assistant warders. Sick leave would continue to be deducted. On the third point, a readjustment of the scale of pay and allowances to make it equivalent to that of the police force: 'the complaint does appear to be general, or in any respect well founded.' In this section the Committee allowed themselves a few petulant comments:

> Warder Warren complains of his pay, as he does of most other things . . .
> If he [Warder Warren] bettered himself when he joined, and has since had a rise of 30 per cent, his complaints do not seem worth much.

They concluded: 'With one minor exception, we cannot admit that the pay is in any respect inadequate.' The exception was acting principal warders, whom the Committee recommended should get a gratuity after a time in the rank.

They drew a very curious conclusion from the evidence which was presented on superannuation: 'we are inclined to think . . . [this] is the real fountain and origin of these complaints.' They recommended compulsory retirement after twenty-five years, the addition of a 'certain number of years' in calculating pensions after twenty years' service, and also that the widow of a man who had just been pensioned should receive a gratuity if he died.

The attitude of the Committee to the petitions is clear from their final remarks. They believed that the presence of 'a sufficient supply of capable men' indicated that conditions were satisfactory, that these conditions far from being worse than before were better, and they drew attention to the increase in pay and shortening of hours in 1875. They were concerned that others, notably the local prison warders, would demand similar improvements. Above all they were against making concessions 'in deference to pressure and combination'.

> For it must be remembered that the officers have ample
> opportunities of making their grievances known to the
> Directors, but have preferred the method of public agitation.
> This is a bad precedent, bad for the service in which the
> agitation takes place, and bad as regards all kindred services.

It is not absolutely clear why the Committee was so hostile. This was the first major protest which the staff had made, and from the comments which have been quoted, it is likely that the new militancy was regarded as something which had to be quashed. At the time the growth of union activity, and the establishment of radical groups, such as H. M. Hyndman's 'Democratic Federation' in 1882 was causing great concern to the ruling classes.[28] The Committee may also have felt able to be firm because only the convict staff were affected. The employment situation was another factor which was favourable to the adoption of a strict line. 1883, for the most part, was a good year for work, but it saw the beginning of an increase in unemployment which was to reach a peak of 10·2 per cent in 1886.[29] The whole decade was one 'in which the air was full of talk about unemployment and depression'.[30]

The Convict Report for 1883–4 contained a few remarks about the outsiders, who, it was believed, fomented the agitation:

> Experience having shown us that on these occasions it was very
> common to find that some persons, who, probably from very
> excellent motives think fit to espouse the cause of the sub-
> ordinate officers of any service, do not hesitate to undermine
> their confidence in their superiors by representing them as
> hostile to or negligent of their interests, we ventured to ask that
> a special and independent committee might be appointed to
> report to you on the subject of the petition.

These 'persons' renewed their campaign when there was the seemingly inevitable delay in implementing the recommendations. Tallack wrote to *The Times* on 18 April 1884 complaining, and reporting that a warder had written to the Howard Association, in 'almost despairing terms'. Fowler raised the matter in the House in April 1884 and was told that experiments were going on to cut down night duty, that higher subordinate staff would get more leave, and that there was to be an increase in the establishment of principal warders. The proposed superannuation changes needed special legislation, and the Home Secretary was not prepared to undertake this. It was also claimed that the Home Secretary 'stated last year' that the report was a confidential document. No such statement was made in Parliament. Du Cane was against publication since employees would object to pay scales being published.[31]

While the public and Parliamentary pressure continued, Du Cane was trying to encourage the Treasury to act:[32]

> Should the agitation which has begun be allowed to continue it may attain dimensions and produce results highly detrimental to discipline.
> Concede now and they will be grateful, leave it and the sacrifice could be more costly.

The Treasury, however, seemed to be inordinately obscurantist and singularly ignorant. In their reply, they wondered if these concessions would be followed by 'local, Scotch and Irish demands'.[33] The last two were not the concern of the Home Office. They asked further, of all things, 'how the present hours compared with the night watches of a sailor in the Royal Navy'. The discussions went on for almost a year, and eventually the concessions, as described to Fowler, were implemented. There were also some administrative changes; one of the main ones was that the Pentonville warders were to get Saturday afternoon off by cutting prisoners' working hours. This system, which Du Cane had introduced, was already in force at the public works prisons.

From the agitation surrounding it, and the Rosebery Committee itself, a great deal can be learned about the problems of prison administration. It was the first major report to discuss some of the staff problems which seem generic to all prison systems. It was also the first report to indicate some of the major problems of the English system, and to furnish evidence for the study of the evolution of the officer's role within it. Some of the matters raised by the report are worth stressing, since they continued to occupy the attention of the prison service up to the present time.

One of the most disastrous is the seeming inability of the central office, and staff in the field, to communicate with each other. In the English prison service when evidence has been produced that staff will not apparently communicate with visiting Directors and Inspectors, the response of the latter is anger and bewilderment. Like many of the potential weaknesses in the organisation which have been mentioned, after 1900 it became more marked, until in the post-1945 period there was almost total breakdown.

Statements were made during the agitation leading to the Committee, that the 'authorities' were more interested in the prisoners than in the staff. The latter felt for example that the convicts could assault them with impunity. This feeling is common to prison staffs, especially where reformation is subscribed to as a prison task. This phenomenon is another example of a problem which was to become a major source of conflict in the twentieth century. Both the breakdown in communications, and the feeling of officers that they were less important than prisoners, will be constantly recurring themes in this analysis.

Other debates, later to become chronic, were raised for the first time. Three of the most important of these were: the wish of the warders to establish that their work was equal to that of the police, complaints about slowness of promotion, and demands for better staff and training. The dissatisfaction with promotion has never abated. The method, and the slowness, have been subject to relentless criticism from staff. There are several factors which contribute to this criticism. It would seem that any staff situation in which there are 'promotion prospects', raises definite expectations on the part of the individual that this applies to him. Then there is a certain frustration in a promotion system which is based on 'seniority'—that is, time served. This is heightened when the qualifying time varies according to the needs of the service. Ultimately promotion is on merit, on superior performance at work. But English prison staff have always been baffled about the criteria used to measure efficiency in a service which, since 1900, has been confused about its tasks for most of the time. Finally there is always a feeling of helplessness in the face of a selection for promotion made not by the governor, or chief, but by a group of departmental staff.

The demand for better staff and training has become one of the automatic responses to allegations or revelations of unsatisfactory staff conduct. It is never fully explained what 'better' means in this connection. If it means more educated, is this to assume that educated staff would be more humane? Or efficient? And there is a limit, in the sense that people above a given level of formal education are not likely to become prison officers.

'Training', in Victorian England, as today, is a very attractive solution to organisational problems. It tends to be regarded as almost a magical process, and the expectations of the reformers, from the early days of the prison service, about the contribution which training could make have always been unrealistic. When the task of an organisation is not clear, or is debatable, training can create more problems than it can solve. The hope that training would in some way resolve basic organisational conflicts, was to be expressed many times in the history of the service. 'Training' and 'better staff' were to become instant solutions to almost every problem which arose in the prison system.

Perhaps the most important effect of the Rosebery Committee was that its consequential discussion established the right of staff to complain and even to agitate, a result which would no doubt have startled the hostile Committee. There was an important exchange of minutes[34] between Du Cane and Lushington. Du Cane wrote on 28 January 1884 expressing concern about officers who are not promoted, and who become 'a tool of agitators':

> Or it may be that, in the course of events, the duties of an office develop or change, and their efficient performance demands qualities which the holder does not possess.

He proposed that they be paid off with a gratuity. Lushington replied briefly on 12 February, that he did not believe the prison service could be purged in the manner proposed. But Du Cane disagreed. His reply is worth quoting in full:

> I am under the impression that such movements as that which has recently occurred among the officers, which no doubt, was originated by a small number of men who found the conditions of service they had accepted and worked under were more irksome than they liked, and who believed their prospects were not good, might be easily disposed of if we were able to offer to any who were discontented a fair gratuity and discharge or even to compel them to take it.

He pointed out that a man could be discharged at the moment; the new system would allow him several months' pay.

Lushington replied at some length on 31 March. He inferred that this scheme might be used 'for the purpose of removing out of the way those who in their eyes were agitators but who by their fellow workers were regarded as leaders and champions of their class'. He could understand a governor's keenness. Such a proposal seems to offer a 'short and simple way out of his difficulties':

> 'If only', he may well be imagined to say to himself, 'if only I could get rid of these malcontents how smooth and comfortable all would be.'[35]

He asked Du Cane to consider the permanent results of such a system in the prison service.

Lushington, in effect, was talking about security of tenure. But in his concentration on the right of security of 'agitators', he failed to deal with the equally important issue of dismissing incompetent or lazy staff. Du Cane evidently believed that a man or his job could change, and he ought then to be dismissed. So that whilst Lushington established the right to complain he in fact also established the right to security of tenure, even if incompetent or lazy. Du Cane was correct when he stated that officers could be dismissed, but this has only been for criminal offences, or blatant misbehaviour, such as being drunk on duty. Lushington's decision was to have drastic repercussions on governors. Governors, who are accountable for their institutions, gradually lost the only real sanction over the staff —the power to dismiss. The modern governor has no power to transfer, and limited influence over promotion. This weakening of the governor's position had its origins in this exchange of correspondence. Governors in future were to be held accountable for their prisons, but would not be allowed crucial control over resources to achieve the task. This was the first major inroad into the autonomy of the governor. He has always been regarded as something of an autocrat, whereas in reality the process of erosion, which began with this discussion after the Rosebery Committee, has been continued. The diminution of the governor's power was a subtle process, invisible even to people outside the service who took an interest in prison affairs. It was a reality, and was yet another factor contributing to the crisis of the 1960s, which had its roots in the earliest days of the prison service.

The De Ramsey Committee

After the Rosebery Committee, there was little trouble amongst the convict staff for the rest of the decade. The Directors, after an inquiry by a Board of Visitors into some allegations, pointed out at some length in the Convict Report for 1882–3, that staff were as much entitled to a fair hearing 'and as much protection' as prisoners. The Annual Reports of 1887–8 and 1888–9 are especially distinguished by the excellence of the comments about staff performance. The Governor of Wormwood Scrubs expressed the general experience when he reported that: 'The subordinate officers have performed their duties with intelligence, zeal and fidelity, and to my entire satisfaction.'

Convict staff were once again submitted to a major investigation in 1890, and again the findings of the inquiry were favourable to them.[36] The Directors barely had time to reflect on the report when Lord De Ramsey had to be asked to investigate further complaints, but this time they were put forward by the staff.

The circumstances which preceded the De Ramsey Report, 1891, were very different from those which led up to the Rosebery Report. One signal difference was that there was very much less discussion in the press and in Parliament, and such discussion as took place was free from the rancour which heralded the earlier inquiry. Indeed, there was so little agitation, that it is difficult to be certain what the precipitating factors were. The Committee itself was not sure, and some time was spent in asking witnesses for their opinions. The Committee did not start with an assumption that the discontent had been manufactured by a handful of agitators, and there was noticeably less of the attitude that since the staff knew the conditions of service when they joined, they had little to complain about. Lord De Ramsey asked if: 'these petitions came to a head after the rise of pay to the Metropolitan Police?' Some witnesses thought this was the explanation,[37] but other disagreed.[38] Admiral Fenwick, one of the Inspectors, put forward the view that: 'these petitions were started by the spirit of insubordination and dissatisfaction which is creeping over the whole land.'[39]

Fenwick was probably correct. Since 1883 working class and trade union militancy had been increasing. Meetings organised by the Social Democratic Federation in 1886, gave London 'its first introduction to agitation with a revolutionary flavour'.[40] The famous London dock strike of 1889 had created a great stir, and perhaps of even more significance to the prison service, was the strike of London post office clerks in 1891, which was 'the first recorded strike of civil servants'.[41]

Another important difference between the two inquiries was that the local prisons were involved, and furthermore the initiative had come from them: 'I think that at Stafford the complaints were first set afoot by the officers of Newcastle prison, at least I have heard so.'[42]

This was accurate. In the Appendix to the Report there are printed copies of letters sent by each subordinate officer at Newcastle, a local prison, to the Governor asking for permission to petition, the Commissioner's reply, and a copy of the petition. These documents were circulated to other prisons from Newcastle on 16 October 1890.[43] There had also been allegations in the Newcastle newspapers that the officers were afraid to complain to the Governor.[44] The Governor of Newcastle was the only governor to be criticised quite heavily by a witness.[45] Garsia said of Newcastle, in his evidence to the Gladstone Committee, 'It is the worst prison I have ever seen.'[46]

It is not clear how many local staff petitioned, since Du Cane does not give a total in the usual thorough documentation he had prepared, and which was published as an appendix. The Fourteenth Local Report shows that there were 59 locals. It can be calculated from the report itself that 23 petitioned. Some of the local chief warders appeared to have signed, since several witnesses claimed to be representing them in general and specific terms.[47] The female officers from two local prisons petitioned,[48] and a representative was called to give evidence.[49] Of the 855 convict officers, 685 petitioned.[50] As in 1882, no convict chief warders or female officers signed. And, as in 1883, the Broadmoor staff were included in the inquiry.

The lack of acrimony before the inquiry was no doubt due in part to the very different response of the Home Secretary and the Commissioners to the unrest, as may be gauged from the documentation reproduced in the Report. To the request from Newcastle for permission to petition they replied: 'The Commissioners will be most happy to receive any application the officers may wish to make.' Furthermore, less than two months later, Du Cane suggested to the Under Secretary of State that a committee should report on those matters which are 'beyond the Commissioners' power'. Du Cane also made the annual leave in the locals the same as in the convict prisons, arranged more time off at weekends, and made 'some small modification' in the routine to limit the hours spent on duty. Finally he had instructed the five Inspectors, before the petitions were submitted, to ensure that officers had every opportunity to bring forward complaints, and 'to report whether officers appear to believe that they will suffer from making their wishes known to the Commissioners.' The replies varied considerably.

On 5 February 1891 the Member for Rochester asked the Home Secretary if he knew that a petition had been addressed to him by the warders at Borstal. Henry Matthews replied that a departmental committee had been appointed. But Matthews did not write to Lushington, the Under Secretary, until 28 February, saying that he was going to set up a committee to look into the representations.[51] The letter of appointment was sent out on 2 March.[52] On 10 March the Home Secretary was asked if the inquiry would include warder/ schoolmasters, to which the answer was that it would.

The Chairman of the Committee was William Henry, Lord De Ramsey, and the members were Sir Robert Fowler MP, Walter Long MP, Francis Mowatt, and Du Cane. Du Cane resigned at some point between 5 April, when the last witness gave evidence, and 14 July, when W. J. Stopford, one of the Commissioners, was appointed in his place.[53] This was just a week before the Report was submitted on 21 July. There is no evidence which might explain Du Cane's resignation. It is arguable that a resignation immediately before printing would indicate that he disagreed with some of the recommendations, although it is highly unlikely that he would. Careful reading of his questions, analysis of how the Committee dealt with those topics which were most threatening (such as the claim that promises made to staff at the time of centralisation had not been honoured), seems to suggest that the recommendations were likely to be acceptable to him.

The Committee was asked to report:

Whether any, and, if so, what changes should be made in the conditions of service of the subordinate officers in the Convict and Local Prison Services, and of the officials of the Broadmoor Criminal Lunatic Asylum, with regard to the points mentioned in the representations in question.

Both local and convict officers had petitioned for:

1 An increase of pay and allowances.
2 A change in the conditions of promotion.
3 An increase of annual leave.
4 A reduction in the hours of duty.
5 An increase in the scale of superannuation.

But in detail their demands differed from each other. The local officers wanted to be 'put on the same footing' as the convict staff, which meant a 20 per cent rise in pay—the differential between the two staffs. Convict staff asked for a 10 per cent rise. They both wanted automatic promotion from assistant warder to warder, the local men after seven years, the convict officers after ten. Local staff were asking for fourteen days leave for the warders and assistant warders, whereas the convict staff wanted sixteen days. The hours of duty, it was asked, should not be more than twelve hours inclusive of meals in the locals, ten hours including meals in the convict establishments. On superannuation their demands were the same.

The attitude of the Committee was entirely different from that of the Rosebery inquiry. That they were much more tolerant of staff discontent, is apparent from the tone of their questions to the witnesses, and their approach to the inquiry as expressed in their Report:

> The petitioners have, doubtless been encouraged by the concessions obtained by other public servants at the time to urge their claims to consideration, but they have done so in a strictly orderly and proper manner, without interruption of their important duties and these are circumstances which we think well deserving of notice.

The tone of the exchanges during the giving of evidence may be illustrated by Du Cane's answer to Warder Baggott, when the latter said he had been as truthful as he possibly could: 'No doubt of it, very straightforwardly and properly done.'[54]

The Committee had had the experience in the late 1880s of seeing how angry, and militant, frustrated workers could become, and they were no doubt genuine in their approval of the restrained behaviour of the staff. There were other factors present which may have made the Committee much more conciliatory than their predecessors in 1883. An improved economic situation had led to a decrease in unemployment from 10·2 per cent in 1886 to 3·5 per cent, although it was soon to rise again to 6·3 per cent in 1892.[55] Finally *both* services, and hence many more staff, were involved in the 'unrest', so the threat was obviously much greater.

The witnesses were very much better prepared than they had been in 1883. They even went so far as to submit suggestions and proposals about schedules of work and so on.[56] Most of the evidence which was given was quite ordinary. There was discussion about the cost of living, analogies with other services were claimed and denied, and the members of the Committee learnt a great deal about the English prison service. But certain points emerged, which help to give an understanding of the important issues which dominated the professional lives of staff at the time. The first of these was central to the discontent of the local staff. This was the division between the convict and local services,[57] which the latter resented. The convict warders' pay was much higher, and they had a free issue of boots.[58] This last was not as mundane as it might appear, since this was an extra expense of some importance to the local staffs. The first local witness's evidence[59] was representative. He put forward the claim that their duties were as arduous and dangerous as those of the convict staff, and that the local staff had to handle the convicts for the first nine months after sentence when 'they are more careless of their own lives and other people's'.[60] The practice of confining convicts in local prisons to undergo their nine months separate confinement was introduced in 1886–7. Other prisoners come into prison:

> mad with drink . . . and we have as much danger, or more,
> with these men than we should have with convicts . . .[61]
> They could not see why there should be a difference between
> the two services.[62]

The difference was acceptable to the convict staff.[63] Justification lay in the fact that work in the convict prisons was much more difficult and dangerous, because the men worked in association, and were in possession of tools which could be used, indeed had been used, as weapons. Furthermore convict officers frequently had to work in the open air. Du Cane apparently regarded the differential as fair.[64]

Another issue which had been simmering for some fourteen years was the change in conditions of service which had followed central-isation. There was great resentment about this. It was claimed that the assurances about superannuation, which had been given at the time, had not been honoured: 'that is a very sore point, sir, that affects us.'[65] The essence of this complaint was that staff who were in the local service at the time of centralisation, understood that their superannuation would be calculated at the rate of two-thirds of their salary by the new service, since this was their entitlement under the local authority. The government rate was, roughly, at the rate of one-sixtieth for each year of service, up to a maximum of forty-sixtieths. The portion of service which the old local authority officers completed under the centralised service was calculated in sixtieths, which they considered a breach of agreement. This complex matter was discussed in detail.[66]

This was not all that the local staff felt they had lost because of the Act of 1877. Some felt they would have been promoted and: 'receiving pay for years past' if they had 'remained under the county'.[67] It was said too that leave was shorter in the new service,[68] and there was a lot of bad feeling about the reduction of perquisites, especially tailoring. It was said that in the old service, staff could have old uniforms turned into clothes for children 'at cost price',[69] and that warders' clothes and boots could be repaired.[70] Faced with this recital of so much that had appalled him, Du Cane could only ask: 'Are you aware that this is strictly contrary to the statute?'[71] Even more extraordinary was the statement that one governor had had a carriage made in the prison![72] Older local officers complained about allowances for escort duties. Under the local authorities the allowance of time and money was so generous that an officer, having handed over his prisoner, 'travelled in the country and enjoyed himself at the expense of the county'.[73] Escort duty, it seemed, 'was a great holiday to an officer in those days'.[74] If an officer had a higher allowance than he needed, Du Cane wondered, did he put 'something in his pocket?' He was told that he did, 'and perhaps something more in his inside'.[75] 'All these little indulgences', one witness said, 'sweetened the service and made officers satisfied.'[76] But Wilson, one of the Inspectors, wanted no resurrection of 'indulgences'. He was even: 'Very much against mending boots or uniforms at all inside the prison; it would lead to jobbery.'[77] When it was suggested that their current perquisites were really very good, most of the witnesses did not agree. One said that if he asked for a piece of meat at contract price: 'He would tell me I could have it if I took half a bullock.'[78] The meat was of poor quality, contract coal was dear, and inferior, and flour could only be bought in bulk.[79]

The Inspectors qualified the eulogy of the old service. Wilson said that some were better off, but that conditions varied.[80] The other Inspector, Fenwick, considered that they were much better off than they had been in the old days,[81] except for superannuation.[82] Long, who seemed especially sympathetic to staff complaints, obviously thought that Fenwick had overstated his case. He asked him how it was 'that your opinion differs so entirely from the opinions of the men themselves which have been represented to us?' Fenwick replied that the staff to whom he had spoken agreed with him, except for the Stafford officers.[83]

The truth seems to have been that many of the lamented 'emoluments' were unspecified, as Du Cane had discovered in 1877. Even the regulations about superannuation seemed, in at least one case, to be only an 'implied understanding',[84] which, as Du Cane pointed out, left staff in a vulnerable position when they were trying to prove that 'those conditions of two-thirds pensions were part of their original service'.[85]

One meeting point of the two services, local and convict, was the dissatisfaction about the serious blockage in the promotion structure. One witness said that the prospect of promotion to principal or chief warder was 'very remote—very remote'.[86] At Dartmoor there had been no new staff appointed, and no promotions from assistant warder to warder since 1884.[87] At Portland there were assistant warders with sixteen to seventeen years' service, whereas some years before assistant warders were promoted to warder after eight or nine years.[88] In the civil guard it was claimed: 'there is no promotion at all.'[89] The guardsman went on to say that the rank of sergeant was to be abolished[90] and in reply to Du Cane he said that there was little realistic chance of guardsmen being promoted to assistant warder.[91] There was no dispute about the causes of the blockage. There had been so many closures, that vacancies for senior ranks had been drastically cut. This was the price paid by staff for the much vaunted 'economies' which are described in many of the annual reports. It emerged from the discussion that at that time chief and principal warders were transferred on a national basis,[92] whilst others were generally promoted within a single prison. Because of closures, staff were being moved to fill vacant senior positions, which annoyed assistant warders who expected to be promoted *in situ*.[93] The petitioners offered several solutions, notably the abolition of the assistant warder grade, and automatic promotion from assistant warder to warder.[94] A highly progressive proposal was made by one assistant warder:[95]

> have a roll kept at the Home Office, and have every officer promoted according to seniority in the service, and then a man would have no cause for grumbling.

This is precisely what is done at the present day.

Everyone seemed to agree too, that the housing position was not good. Du Cane's admirable intentions in respect of quarters had never really come to fruition:[96]

> The Commissioners soon observed the necessity for providing quarters for the warders etc., in proximity to the prison, and especially the necessity of doing so in towns where the rents are high, and the officers likely to be thrown into undesirable contact with a certain class of the population in their search for lodgings within their means. Considerable progress has already been made in this direction.

Unfortunately this progress had not been kept up. In the Thirteenth Local Report there is a list of quarters, purchased, rented, or built. There were ten quarters for superior officers, ten for chief warders, nine for principal warders, and 136 for warders.[97] This provision was clearly inadequate for the staff of fifty-nine prisons. The situation varied a great deal from place to place. At Bodmin all the staff had quarters,[98] but at Newcastle only the chief warder had a quarter.[99] There were complaints that the quarters were too small, as the entitlement for a warder was two bedrooms.[100] The staff pointed out further, that the rent allowance was quite insufficient to get a house away from the 'certain class'.[101] Newcastle, as in all other respects, seemed to suffer as much as any: 'in the vicinity of the prison it literally swarms with brothels.'[102] This problem of accommodation raised another question of universal relevance to prison staffs, which is their relationship with the total culture from which both they, and prisoners, tend to be drawn. One witness said that he had never known of a warder belonging to working men's clubs, or institutions 'of that kind' in the neighbourhood of the prison because they were fatigued.[103] One of the warder/schoolmasters offered another explanation in the following exchange:[104]

> And from what class do warders come chiefly. Are there many of the labouring class?—No sir.
> What is it?—Rather more learned, because they have to pass an examination which most of the labouring class could not pass.

Two subjects, now familiar, which were raised, were the validity of the analogy with the police service, and the presence of ex-servicemen on the staff. The same claims about the similarity between prison and police work were put forward as had been advanced to the Rosebery Committee, and just as firmly resisted.[105] On the 'ex-service' issue, the chief warder in charge of Carmarthen was sure that 'men who have belonged to the Army or Navy make good warders'[106] while the Governor of Pentonville said, with some pride, 'I have non-commissioned officers who have served in the Guards, here now serving at Pentonville Prison.'[107]

The only group who were subjected to open hostility were the warder/schoolmasters. At the root of this hostility was the feeling, expressed by discipline staff and Inspectors, that they had an easy job. The schoolmasters wanted equality with the convict schoolmasters in respect of pay, hours, leave and promotion.[108] They were especially incensed because their exemption from sleeping-in duty, granted in 1883, had been revoked.[109] They had even managed to have a question raised in Parliament in February 1891, when the Home Secretary pointed out that although that privilege had been withdrawn, they were still exempt from night duty.

The warders were equally angry that the schoolmasters had avoided this duty.[110] One of the Inspectors made his view quite plain: 'not the slightest grievance under the sun, he has got uncommonly little to do, and is very well paid for what he does.'[111] He went further. He believed that education was 'quite unnecessary in our prisons'.[112] This was a feeling which had been expressed by the Commissioners:[113]

> the general educational system in operation throughout the country is very much diminishing the number of prisoners who require the assistance of the prison schoolmaster or are likely to profit by the educational advantage which can be accorded to them during the period of a short sentence of imprisonment.

Fenwick, the other Inspector, expressed positive distaste for warder/schoolmaster Bodinner, perhaps because the latter had claimed that an Inspector[114] had promised him an improvement in his position:[115]

> I have a very lively recollection that he was so bumptious and self asserting in his speech, and 'up and dressed' in his manner, and so very careless in the performance of his duty, that he would be the last man in the prison service to whom I would promise promotion.

There was a certain amount of strain, and the Chairman twice reprimanded Bodinner, telling him to answer the question[116] and to 'please confine yourself to facts'.[117] In spite of their reception, the schoolmasters managed to put forward their grievances, not the least of which was that the schoolmasters in the local prisons who had been appointed by the local authorities before 1877, and were still employed as schoolmasters, were paid more.[118]

On the whole the recommendations of the Committee were favourable to the local staff. But they did not agree that local and convict work were analogous. Local staff:

> deal with prisoners singly i.e. those who are undergoing separate confinement, and are therefore less dangerous than convicts working on gangs in the open. Moreover their duty is all performed under cover, whilst the convict officer is exposed to bad weather, his hours are longer, and his work generally is more exhausting.

They did recommend that local staff should get a rise in pay, free quarters, and an issue of boots. Du Cane had already asked for an increase in pay for chief warders in charge, and this was supported.[119] They did not recommend a change in the rank structure, but suggested that assistant warders who had completed eleven years' service should get two further increments. Leave should be increased slightly for warders and assistant warders. With regard to hours of duty, they made administrative history by introducing a phenomenon which has been a constant worry to senior staff ever since—overtime! They were not sympathetic to the grievances of the 'former County Officers', since any rights which they may have had, and which were specified, before centralisation, had been respected. They had also benefited, it was claimed, from access to a larger field of promotion.

The convict officers were not as fortunate. There was to be no general increase in pay, but the Committee did make a recommendation which would offset a Treasury ruling, disadvantageous to staff, about the point at which a newly promoted officer entered the pay scale. The pay of the civil guard was to be increased. On promotion, they proposed the same solution, with variation, as for the local officers, together with the same slight increase in leave. As in 1883, it was recommended that sick leave should continue to be deducted from annual leave. Finally the Committee considered that the average ten hours worked was fair, especially since they were off on alternate Sundays, and alternate Saturday afternoons. No mention was made of overtime, presumably because the situation did not arise where it might have to be worked. They were not prepared to alter the superannuation arrangements for either group.

The petitions of the female officers about pay, promotion, and superannuation were dismissed totally, as were the grievances of the warder/schoolmasters: 'who do not possess any special qualifications or perform any amount of duty which would justify an increase of their emoluments.' They went further and asked 'whether the system, which is now carried on at very considerable expense, should be longer maintained—at all events on its present lines.' Treasury approval for the changes was given in November and December 1891.[120]

An extremely important problem, which had been raised in 1883, was raised again. This was the breakdown of communication between the staff in the field, and the Head Office, personified by the Inspectors. Almost all the subordinate staff were questioned very closely as to the reasons why they had not put their complaints about the service to either the governor, or the Inspector on one of his regular visits.[121] The Committee were clearly fascinated by the almost universal failure to do so, and it is indeed a fascinating question. Most of the staff who were questioned assured the Committee that they were not afraid to speak to the Inspector, but the first witness, Warder Ling, went on to say that there was a fear 'something might occur'.[122] Another witness went into more detail: 'if an officer makes a complaint he is in dread of being looked down upon by his superiors.'[123] Other witnesses said that their complaints had achieved nothing. One said:[124]

> it is not received exactly in the right spirit, in the spirit that a complaint should be received in, I think, the officer seems to be set to one side instead of listening in the proper manner to his complaint.

He went on to claim that this was the officers' experience in dealing with the chief warder and the governor. Asked if he had complained to the Inspector, he said he had, but 'he did not make any alterations',[125] nor was he very optimistic that they would.[126] There were, then, two reasons apparently why 'all these years something was not said'.[127] The first was a fear that people who grumbled would be penalised, although no one could cite an instance of that happening.[128] This fear is not by any means confined to the prison service, although the 'discipline' overtones of the organisation, and the fact that, in a sense, its 'business is conformity', perhaps heightens it. Nor can the apprehension about being 'difficult' be dismissed as a product of fantasy. It is a commonplace of experience in organisations where people depend on others for promotion, congenial postings and so on, that the troublemaker is likely to suffer. Documentary evidence of this was produced in the discussion of the aftermath of the Rosebery Report (see pp. 89–90). Although Du Cane did not have his way, there were plenty of other ways in which the value of 'loyalty' could be stressed.

The second reason why staff were reluctant to complain, is perhaps unique to the English prison service. Ever since 1877, the main link between the Home Office and the prisons has been the periodic visits of the Inspectors, the Commissioners and, currently, the Assistant Directors. These visits are basically intended for the purposes of inspection, but complaints have been solicited and from such evidence as there is, including that of the De Ramsey Report, interviews have been readily given. What staff quickly learned, it seems, was that little action came out of this process, not because the visitor did not want to act or because 'he is entitled to form his own opinion',[129] but because he did not have the executive authority to act. And staff have never been consoled by the fact that 'he listened to what you had to say'.[130]

During the period before 1900 governors became less and less able to deal with staff problems. More and more officers had to rely on visiting Inspectors and Commissioners to help them with personal problems about pay, postings, quarters and so forth. The inability of governors to help with these problems, except marginally, has been accelerated since 1900. The Rosebery and De Ramsey Reports show that the visiting official from the central office was becoming powerless himself. The officers therefore, from very early days, could not establish contact with the people who really exercised executive power—the civil servants. The officers who gave evidence to the De Ramsey Committee knew that Fenwick, as an example, was unsympathetic to their case. But even if he had been sympathetic, he was powerless, and there was nothing to be gained, but a great deal to be lost, from discussing anything with him. The powerlessness of the visiting official was discussed by the Gladstone Committee. The statement made by an Inspector on that occasion is relevant to almost the whole history of the prison service in England:[131]

They have no executive power, but to what extent do you think they could be said to have actual authority and practical power?—They have absolutely none.

Notes

1 *The Times*, 31 May 1882, p. 4. For a contrary view expressing great admiration of the warders, see *The Times*, 13 June 1882, p. 5.
2 Reprinted in Eleventh Local Report, p. 34 et seq.
3 P.R.O. H.O.45/9625/A20355.
4 P.R.O. H.O.45/9625/A20355/5.
5 P.R.O. H.O.45/9625/A20355.
6 P.R.O. H.O.45/9625/A20355/7 and the Rosebery Report, 1883, p. 85.
7 This may be deduced from the details on p. 85 of the Rosebery Report.
8 Rosebery Report, p. 77. It is possible that the assistant warder who gave evidence, Thomas James Stevenson, was the author of the letter, since he said in evidence that he was party to a 'memorial' (question 580).
9 Rosebery Report, p. 9.
10 P.R.O. H.O.45/9625/A20355/11.
11 P.R.O. H.O.45/9625/A20355/12.
12 The complete list is on pp. 4, 5 and 6 of the Report.
13 P.R.O. H.O.45/9625/A20355/9 and Rosebery Report, p. 106. They were the Governors of Wormwood Scrubs and Chatham, and the Deputy Governor in charge of Millbank.
14 Rosebery Report, pp. 107–8.
15 Ibid., questions 124 and 125.
16 Ibid., question 347.
17 Ibid., questions 311 and 377.
18 See, for example, ibid., questions 108–11, questions 267 and 268 (where a governor agrees) and questions 327–9 (where a governor disagrees).
19 Ibid., questions 34–43 and 806.
20 Ibid., question 374.
21 Ibid., question 257.
22 Ibid., questions 407–13, 557, 727, 368.
23 Ibid., questions 657–68.
24 Ibid., questions 656 and 901.
25 Ibid., questions 900 and 922.
26 Ibid., questions 162–71 and 367.
27 Ibid., question 549.
28 Slater, *The Growth of Modern England*, p. 522.

29 Labor Information M.S.A., *Economic Development in the United Kingdom 1850–1950*, p. 27.
30 Clapham, *An Economic History of Modern Britain*, III, p. 455.
31 P.R.O. H.O.45/9625/A20355/16.
32 P.R.O. H.O.45/9717/51528/1.
33 P.R.O. H.O.45/9717/51528/3.
34 P.R.O. H.O.45/9717/A51528/10.
35 Lord Rosebery had used the term 'ingenious malcontent' in the Report, question 707.
36 *Report of the Visitors of Her Majesty's Convict Prison at Chatham*, 1890.
37 For example, De Ramsey Report, questions 2542, 4057 and 1922–5.
38 For example, ibid., questions 3622 and 4370.
39 Ibid., question 573.
40 Williams, *The Main Currents of Social and Industrial Change 1870–1924*, p. 112.
41 Clapham, op. cit., p. 485.
42 De Ramsey Report, question 3463.
43 Ibid., p. 163.
44 Ibid., question 1912.
45 Ibid., questions 1912–19.
46 Gladstone Evidence, question 6727.
47 See, for example, De Ramsey Report, questions 583, 594 and 636.
48 Ibid., p. XIV.
49 Ibid., p. 149.
50 Ibid., p. 174.
51 P.R.O. H.O.45/9717/A51528/17.
52 De Ramsey Report, p. IX.
53 Ibid., p. X.
54 Ibid., question 580.
55 Labor Information M.S.A., op. cit., pp. 26–7.
56 De Ramsey Report, pp. 192–4.
57 If a prison was reclassified, the entire staff was normally transferred. See Fourteenth Local Report, p. 2 and Convict Report 1886–7.
58 De Ramsey Report, question 418.
59 Ibid., questions 87–110.
60 Ibid., question 89.
61 Ibid., question 110.
62 Ibid., question 108.
63 Ibid., questions 3639–40.
64 Ibid., question 95–102.
65 Ibid., question 645.
66 See, for example, questions 645–718 and 3109 (where an Inspector said that he was under the impression that the two-thirds figure would be maintained). See also p. 172 of the Report for an account of the Civil Service rates.
67 De Ramsey Report, question 1374.
68 Ibid., questions 1404–5.

69 Ibid., question 2370.
70 Ibid., question 2376.
71 Ibid., question 2406.
72 Ibid., question 3525.
73 Ibid., question 2383.
74 Ibid., question 2494.
75 Ibid., question 2521.
76 Ibid., question 2388.
77 Ibid., question 3081.
78 Ibid., question 4818.
79 Ibid., questions 3880–5, 3995–4004 and 4553.
80 Ibid., question 3087.
81 Ibid., question 3438.
82 Ibid., questions 3461–2.
83 Ibid., question 3520.
84 Ibid., question 680.
85 Ibid., question 714.
86 Ibid., question 124.
87 Ibid., question 4412.
88 Ibid., question 3672.
89 Ibid., question 4771.
90 In any case there were only ten sergeants to 158 privates (ibid., p. 189).
91 Ibid., question 4778.
92 Ibid., questions 3176–80.
93 Ibid., questions 1246 and 3855.
94 Ibid., pp. 161–2 and p. 174, enclosure I.
95 Ibid., question 4322.
96 Du Cane, *The Punishment and Prevention of Crime*, pp. 97–8.
97 Thirteenth Local Report, p. 53.
98 De Ramsey Report, question 1970.
99 Ibid., questions 1660–1.
100 Ibid., questions 3729–36.
101 Ibid., questions 991–8.
102 Ibid., question 1688.
103 Ibid., question 2098.
104 Ibid., questions 1741–2.
105 Ibid., questions 296, 1229–31, 1498–1502, 1689–92, 1771–80, 2396, 3540–1.
106 Ibid., question 2636. Another chief warder agreed, but wanted a 'good proportion of the civil element' (ibid., questions 2526–8).
107 Ibid., question 2754.
108 For details, see ibid., p. 164.
109 Ibid., question 3006.
110 Ibid., questions 1437, 1444–8.
111 Ibid., question 3137.
112 Ibid., question 3142.
113 Thirteenth Local Report, p. 13, para. 71.

114 Probably Fenwick himself. Du Cane thought so—see questions 2898–901.
115 Ibid., question 3484.
116 Ibid., question 2880.
117 Ibid., question 2856.
118 Ibid., questions 2839–45.
119 Ibid., p. XII. Du Cane's letter to the Under Secretary is printed on p. 164 of the Report.
120 Fifteenth Local Report, p. 9.
121 Both Inspectors were insistent that they gave staff every opportunity (ibid., questions 3131–5, 3571–2). There were rare exceptions (see question 558).
122 Ibid., questions 331–46.
123 Ibid., question 1433.
124 Ibid., question 1149.
125 Ibid., questions 1153–60.
126 Ibid., questions 1178–9.
127 Ibid., question 573 (by Du Cane).
128 See, for example, ibid., question 969.
129 Ibid., question 1161.
130 Ibid., question 1162.
131 Ibid., question 6402.

6   1892–5: the Gladstone Committee

Events leading to the Gladstone Committee

Implementation of the changes advocated by the De Ramsey Report did not put an end to complaints from uniformed staff. During 1892, 1893, and 1894, pressure was kept up in Parliament to improve superannuation and promotion prospects, and to reduce hours. The analogy with the police was argued on several occasions, and was always denied. To all the questions in Parliament, Asquith, the Home Secretary, gave standard answers: the De Ramsey Report had much improved the situation, he was not going to publish it or make it generally available, and no further investigation was justified.

All of these events were overshadowed by the best known investigation in the history of the English prison system—the Gladstone Committee.[1] The reasons for Asquith's decision to initiate an inquiry are obscure. There seem to have been two precipitating factors. The first was the conduct of the Reverend W. D. Morrison, Assistant Chaplain at Wandsworth, and the second was a discussion about prison accommodation in the Metropolis, which was carried on by A. C. Morton and the Home Secretary in Parliament. It is generally held that Morrison was largely responsible[2] because he was the author of several critical articles about prisons (see Bibliography). He was also the author, or instigator, of a series of articles in the *Daily Chronicle* which comprised a serious attack on the prison system.[3] The newspaper also took up the question of prison accommodation in London. Morton had raised this question several times,[4] but the *Chronicle* claimed that the information which was given to Morton was inaccurate, that there *was* overcrowding and (on 25 July 1893) that: 'At present our local prisons are controlled by men at the Home Office who have not had a week's practical experience of these establishments.' This lack of practical experience was one of the complaints made by Morrison when he deplored 'dilletantism', and he included the Secretary of the Howard Association as an example (see 'Are our Prisons a Failure?', p. 467). Du Cane explained to the Under Secretary of State that the *Chronicle* was wrong, since it counted only 'certified cells', not, for example, hospital accommodation. So that on 3 July 1891, an article had said that at Pentonville there were 1,185 prisoners and only 1,174 cells; but 43 cells in the hospital had been left out of account.[5]

It seems clear that the contribution of the press to the controversy was very important. This was the view of the Committee, since its Report (p. 14, para. 5) mentioned that: 'In magazines and in the newspapers, a sweeping indictment had been laid against the whole of the prison administration.' Nothing, it appeared, could stem the flow of fact and fantasy, allegation and denial, other than an investigation.

The first mention of the Committee was in Parliament on 19 April 1894 when Asquith replied to Morton, who had asked if a commission was to be appointed to consider the question of prison accommodation in London:

> It is my intention to appoint a Departmental Committee to consider several questions, one of which is the subject of prison accommodation in the metropolis.

Five weeks later, in May 1894, the House was given more details. The Chairman was to be Herbert John Gladstone MP. Asquith refused at first to include an Irishman, but later because of pressure from his countrymen, the Member for East Donegal was appointed. The Committee were to be instructed to examine:

1 Accommodation.
2 The treatment of young prisoners.
3 Prison labour.
4 Visits and communication with prisoners.
5 Prison offences.

Asquith added that there was no want of confidence or censure on the prison administration. When the Warrant was issued on 5 June 1894, there was a significant addition to the terms of reference:[6]

> 6 the arrangements by which the appointment of a deputy governor is limited to prisons with more than 700 prisoners; and a warder in charge acts as governor in prisons with not more than 100 prisoners.

Later, at the request of the Committee, two further matters were included, the prison treatment of habitual criminals, and the classification of prisoners generally.[7] Finally, when they came to take evidence they: 'felt it [their] duty to enter upon a comprehensive examination of the conditions under which prisoners are confined'.[8] This breaking of the boundaries set out by their terms of reference, meant that there is rather more discussion about staff affairs than there might otherwise have been. But although the press had mentioned the staff occasionally, there was no reappraisal in the Report of the material conditions of service, which some of the staff had hoped for.

That the Committee was only really concerned with the treatment of prisoners is clear from the almost incredible fact that no warders were invited to give evidence. Ostensibly this was because of 'limits of time'. The best that the Committee could do was to chat to them when they visited prisons.[9]

Since the general outline of the recommendations of the Committee in respect of prisons is well known,[10] this account will deal with the sections about staff, which have never been discussed. Questions affecting prison staff as dealt with by the Committee, may be divided in six parts:

1 The 'chief warder in charge'.
2 Appointment of deputy governors.
3 The numbers, and desirability, of ex-servicemen on the staff —'militarism' again.
4 The training of staff.
5 The warder/schoolmaster.
6 The behaviour of staff generally.

Each of these topics will be examined in turn. The first two were specified in the Committee's terms of reference.

The evidence and background to it

The decision to establish the grade of 'chief warder in charge' was taken in 1885. As on other occasions, 'economy' seemed to be the agent of change. It was stated in the Eighth Local Report that governors of prisons with a very small population were being paid at rates 'disproportionate to their duties'. These posts were to be filled instead by an officer who had been a chief warder in a large prison. By this means:

we shall obtain the services of one who will be well suited for the duties to be done, and a very desirable stimulus will be given to the subordinate grades by putting before them the opportunities of suitable promotion which will result from faithful and intelligent service.

The Howard Association objected strongly to this innovation, and in a letter to the Home Secretary, which invited him to consider some 'abuses and defects', Peek and Tallack explained their objection, which had nothing at all to do with the treatment of prisoners. They wrote that the chief warder in charge could not deal with chaplains and surgeons who: 'are really his superiors, both by reason of their higher social position and by their more secure tenure of office'.[11] In November 1893 the matter was raised in the House of Commons, when the Home Secretary was asked how many prisons were in the charge of chief warders, whether they were superior staff, and what the relationship was between deputy governors and chief warders.

The usual reaction of the Gladstone witnesses who were asked about the subject, was that it was undesirable, but only for the 'social' reasons advanced by Tallack and Peek. The Governor of Liverpool was one of several who expressed views to the effect that 'The Chaplain is a gentleman; the chief is not, probably',[12] and in this he was supported by his colleague at Leeds: 'I think it is the most retrograde movement that ever was done.'[13] The matron of Strangeways objected to being subordinate to the chief warder, adding that 'it would be quite different if there were a deputy governor'.[14] But the most significant witness who expressed dislike of the scheme was Ruggles-Brise, soon to be the most powerful man in the service. Asked if he was in favour he replied: 'No, I do not think I am; in fact I may say emphatically, I am not.'[15] Tallack was not asked. There were a few who thought the scheme was good, notably Morrison,[16] Stopford,[17] who was both a Commissioner and a Director, and of course, Du Cane himself.[18] He took the opportunity to correct Morrison, who had alleged that the 'in charge' posts went to convict staff in preference to local men.[19] Another group were content to see the posts kept, but wished the men in charge to be called governors,[20] while others discussed whether or not uniform should be worn.[21] But no complaint was made about the administrative competence of the chief warders. The Deputy Governor of York was asked specifically if the feeling against them was because of inability to manage, or because there were difficulties in relation to other staff. He said that the latter was the problem.[22]

The origins of the objections to restricting the establishment of a deputy governor to prisons with more than 700, are obscure. One of the best-informed witnesses, Morrison, when asked his opinion could only reply: 'Yes, I did not quite see the drift of that reference, I did not quite understand what it was about.'[23] Nor was much said in evidence on the subject. Such discussion as there was, and the line of questioning by the Committee, served to show that there were two reasons why this item was included. The first was the 'social' problem again:[24]

> It may be a matter you think which is raised by the visiting justices?
> Yes, it may be. It may be a matter of feeling with the officials. Of course some may prefer to deal with a deputy governor rather than with the chief warder, and perhaps friction may sometimes arise because you only have a chief warder.

The second reason was that some people apparently felt that a governor needed the assistance of a deputy to help him, where he had a lot of prisoners to get to know. This is a subject which will be dealt with more fully at a later stage.

The origins of the objections to 'militarism', by which was meant numbers of ex-servicemen in the prison service, were discussed in an earlier chapter. The critics had continually voiced their objections since 1877, and such was their pressure that this subject, although not within the terms of reference, was discussed at some length, and was supplemented with substantial amounts of documentary evidence. Some representative comments will indicate that the objections were continually being expressed. The Governor of Maidstone in 'Some Notes on Prison Discipline' in *The Times*, 24 December 1874:

> agrees with Mr. Tallack of the Howard Society that selections from the Army, Navy or Militia are not always the best . . . some warders have a mistaken idea that the highest merit can only be gained by extreme severity.

Next month a ticket-of-leave convict, charged with theft, wrote in a letter to a Recorder (*The Times*, 7 January 1875):

> I could speak of bad example set to prisoners by the subordinate officers of the prison whose only qualification for their offices consists in their having been in the Army or Navy a number of years with good characters for martial discipline.

In August 1879 Parnell expressed the opinion that 'military men ought not to be employed as governors of prisons'. There was a very angry outburst from another MP in March 1884, who asked if a military prisoner in Durham had hanged himself and 'is the Governor of Durham Prison a military gentleman?' He also wanted to know whether a large proportion of the prison officers were ex-soldiers or ex-policemen and 'has the Colonel Governor presided on any Sunday afternoon at as many as three courts martial upon as many prisoners?'

Some of the Gladstone Committee witnesses were asked about the assertions that ex-service staff predominated, and that they were unsuitable for prison work. As in other discussion, opinions varied. The Governor of Pentonville said he preferred ex-servicemen 'because we get the pick of military men for the service'.[25] The Deputy Governor of Wandsworth believed that military applicants were better educated. Current civilian applicants were 'illiterate and inclined to be rough'.[26] Stopford stated that there were more applications from ex-servicemen, that there was no preference for either group, and that there were good and bad in each.[27] Tallack's views were well known. He thought that although military warders 'are better for discipline',[28] 'civilians have a higher moral character than the soldiers'[29] and 'a larger proportion should be civilians'.[30] Some of the governor grades agreed with him,[31] as did Michael Davitt, a well-known Irish Nationalist.[32] The Governor of Leeds clearly felt that the transition from the Army to prison service was very natural. When asked to say something about himself, he replied 'I am a major in the Army.'[33]

Documentary evidence was furnished to test the assertions which had been made frequently, and were made again to the Committee, about the prevalence of ex-servicemen. Morrison, for instance, said that governors were selected entirely from the Army.[34] Appendix VIII to the Evidence contains details of the occupations followed by the senior staff before joining, the numbers of ex-servicemen amongst subordinate staff, the numbers of governors with a service background who worked for the local authority service, and a comparison of the backgrounds of applicants for the service. This information is summarised in Table 1.

In respect of the local authority figures it was claimed that the numbers of ex-servicemen were likely to be higher than the figures given. In many cases where the information had not been documented

Table 1 Ex-servicemen in the prison services in 1877 and 1894

Service	Grade	Number	Ex-service	Ex-civilian	Date
Local	Governor	55	34	21	31 March 1894
	Deputy governor	3	3	—	31 March 1894
	Subordinate	1,269	556	713	28 June 1894
Convict	Governor*	8	7	1	31 March 1894
	Deputy governor	3	3	—	31 March 1894
	Subordinate	690	431	259	31 March 1894
Local authority (local prison)	Governor	110	40	70	1877
	Deputy governor	33	12	21	1877

* The exception was a governor/medical officer.

by the local authority, and present governors were asked, it was found that some were ex-servicemen.

Figures were also drawn up to compare the applications and nominations of the two groups. 1893 is a typical year: the following figures are for local, subordinate staff:

Applications received   Army or Navy 614 (66%)
                          Civilian   317 (34%)
                          Total   931

Candidates nominated Army or Navy 129 (61%)
                          Civilian   83 (39%)
                          Total   212

Of the local governors, it was said that since centralisation there had been 20 appointments as governors and deputy governors, and 20 as chief warders in charge. Of the former, six had been civilians, and of the latter, twelve.

Staff training was another subject which had been discussed before. The International Congress of 1872 had debated it,[35] and the committee of governors which had made recommendations at the time of the Rosebery Committee had suggested that training should be carried out in a special prison. The trainees, it was suggested, would be supernumerary, and could be dispersed as vacancies occurred. Garsia, the Secretary to the Commissioners, had been a member of that committee, and he was the first to raise the question of training in evidence. From his evidence it can be learnt that officers were given 'on-the-job' training. This lasted for three months and until the end of that time they were not allowed to take charge of prisoners. This was the situation in the convict service, but in the locals a trainee might be needed to help in the event of a shortage, and so would have to carry out a trained officer's job. There was also a problem of local staff who may 'not themselves be qualified to instruct'. Garsia also said that there had been a training school for deputy governors at Millbank, but because the number of appointments was small, it had been discontinued.[36]

Tallack was very much in favour of training, and no doubt would have suggested it if Garsia had not done so.[37] Most other witnesses were in favour, including the Governor of Strangeways[38] and Ruggles-Brise who reported that in Rome 'they teach the warders in ambulance classes and so on'.[39] Du Cane said that he had 'often thought that it would be a good thing'[40] but that the concomitant mobility to and from the training centres was the difficulty. The Governor of Leeds was against the idea, but he admitted that he had not thought about it.[41]

There was not a lot of discussion about warder/schoolmasters. Morrison considered their position 'most unsatisfactory',[42] was against the wearing of uniform, and said that they ought not to do disciplinary duty.[43] The Deputy Governor of York[44] and Du Cane,[45] however, felt that they should be uniformed officers.

Several witnesses were asked for their assessment of staff conduct and standards, and most made complimentary remarks. The Governor of Dartmoor, asked if he was satisfied with the class of men he got as warder, replied: 'Yes—as a whole they are very good.'[46] The Deputy Governor of York believed their conduct was better than it had been under the local authorities[47] and the Governor of Wandsworth commented: 'I think I have got a very fair set of men.'[48] Similar remarks were made by the Governors of Leeds[49] and Strangeways,[50] and by Garsia.[51]

One ex-prisoner said that the officers were well chosen[52] but others were not as euphoric. One, 'Mr E.', stated that some were good and others bad, and went on to make very serious allegations[53] which drew a reply from the prison authorities.[54] Davitt also alleged violence by the staff, but he seemed especially angry that he had been treated more severely because he was a Fenian.[55] Morrison was generally critical of the staff, claiming that 'many officers are not very discreet or very sensible people'.[56] Apart from 'Mr E.', the strongest anti-staff language was used by Tallack. He said that amongst warders he had found 'some of the best men' but 'there were also some great brutes'.[57] The use of this term was challenged at length, but Tallack could not justify it.[58]

The Committee's recommendations

The conclusions of the Committee on all these subjects were brief. They recommended in their Report, that there ought to be a deputy governor in all prisons with a total population of 600, male or female. They considered that the chief warder in charge ought to be replaced by a new rank, a class V governor. These would not necessarily be recruited from the chief warder and clerical ranks.

With regard to 'militarism' they reported that 'excepting the convict prisons, the military element does not predominate', although since 1877 the numbers of military and naval officers appointed to deputy governor and governor 'largely exceeds the numbers of civilians'. They concluded:

> Military and naval training undoubtedly develops capacities for organisation and the maintenance of discipline, but we do not consider it to be by any means essential to the qualifications of a prison governor.

On the other hand:

> under the present system, in regard to warders there is [not] any appreciable difference in the merits of those who before entering the prison service were in the Army and Navy and of those who were civilians.

The Committee apparently had become very interested in staff training, and reported on this question at some length. Their proposals on this subject were the most radical and far reaching of all. They proposed that some of the systems in other countries be emulated. They recommended that two or more prisons should be set aside as training schools for all grades, that there should be 'systematic and scientific instruction', that deputy governors and others nominated for promotion to governor should be trained at the schools, and that 'present members of the staff should undergo a certain amount of training in them', a process later to be called 'in-service training'. Throughout the service there should be lectures to staff and 'the offering of prizes for the best papers by the officers on various branches of prison management'. The schools could be used as well for training 'discipline staff in various branches of industry'. They foresaw a commonplace of organisational experience when they stated that with the 'considerably higher qualifications . . . an increase of pay would be necessary'. Less inevitable was their speculation that younger, unmarried men would have to be employed, because married men could not be expected to move frequently.

In respect of the warder/schoolmasters they expressed themselves as against uniform, and very much against cellular teaching. They were 'inclined to think that they should not be discipline officers at all'.

On the general behaviour and standard of staff their views were summarised as follows:

> We think that the members of the general prison staff have discharged their duties consistently and well, and that since 1877 a more uniform standard of efficiency has been maintained.

They were 'satisfied that the cases of gross ill-treatment by warders which have occurred are very few in number' and 'as a body they discharge their most difficult and responsible duties with forbearance and kindness'. Tallack was singled out for special mention as being:

> unable to show that there was any ground for the charge other than the general *a priori* argument that in a large body of men there must be some black sheep.

Finally they considered that 'the whole staff is somewhat under-manned', that hours of duty were optimum and that the system of employing temporary officers should be stopped. The only material recommendation was that staff ought to be paid for 'sleeping-in duty'.

In their 'Observations' on these staff matters, the Commissioners seemed willing to accept the recommendations. They agreed that fifth-class governors need not be drawn from only warder and clerical grades, but said that some chief warders in charge were not fit to be promoted to governor. They also pointed out that a governor grade would have to be paid more, but that his duties could be combined with that of a storekeeper and thus some money could be saved. The idea of training schools was accepted enthusiastically. The proposal to appoint a deputy governor to prisons with a roll of between 600 and 700 was irrelevant, since there were no such prisons.

On numbers of staff the Commissioners observed that the situation was satisfactory. There was a difference of 24 between the numbers approved in the Estimates, and the number in post. These would be appointed as supernumerary, would undergo training and would be posted as vacancies occurred. With regard to education they observed: 'we cannot say the existing system is a failure', and announced their intention of setting up a departmental committee to examine the whole subject.[59]

The effects of the Gladstone Report

The Gladstone Committee Report set forces in motion which were to have profound effects on the prison service, and the role of the officer within it. The most important recommendation was about the purposes of imprisonment. Up to 1895 the 'manifest' task of the prison system was deterrence. In reality, at an 'extant' level, the task was control. Either because the latter was a limited and somewhat negative goal, or, as is more likely, because it was taken for granted, it was rarely discussed. Nor did a conflict between the manifest and extant tasks appear, because the methods of achieving both are compatible. Organisational devices which are introduced into prisons for the purposes of control may appear deterrent in aim, and certainly may be so in effect. The policy of separation is the best example of a method which contributed to both punishment and control.

The Report introduced confusion with its definition of 'reformation' as a 'manifest' task. The situation was made worse by its advocacy of *two* primary tasks, in the most frequently quoted statement in prison literature:

> we start from the principle that prison treatment should have as its primary and concurrent objects deterrence, and reformation.

These proposals meant that somehow the prison service had to cope with two mutually exclusive tasks. Different tasks call for different structures, which in turn call for different communication patterns. The confusion with which the service had to cope can be demonstrated by some of the more obvious and major differences between regimes which have deterrence, and those which have reformation, as their respective manifest tasks.

In a reformative regime, decisions are made on the basis of the needs of the individual, not on the need of the community to restrict him. In a prison system committed to reformation, a decision, for example, on whether a prisoner should be put in open conditions, sent on home leave or given parole, would take into account only the needs of the man: risk to the community would rate very low. This was the crucial conflict which was to haunt the prison system until the post-Mountbatten developments established that the wishes of the community were to be paramount.

Clearly, the role of the officer would be very different in a reformative regime. There would be a substantial increase in the discretionary part of the officer's role, with much more independence of action on his part. The classical fear that the officer might abuse this flexibility would be removed, because in a reformative regime physical coercion would be unnecessary. A different pattern of communications would be established, the keynote of which would be an emphasis on discussion about cases and problems which would be quite alien to the deterrent regime. Junior staff, for instance, would be able to argue and disagree with senior staff, because knowledge and expertise would not be synonymous with time-serving.

These were the main organisational facts which the prison service came to identify, and to ponder on, in the post-1900 period. The Committee, with its contradictory proposals, sowed the seeds of the organisational confusion which has dogged the twentieth-century prison service. The Committee went on to recommend two changes which were to add to the confusion. These were concerned with association, and the role of the governor.

Since the Committee was determined to cause the introduction of reformative methods, it was natural that they should make recommendations in the Report about the central debate concerning the life of a prisoner, the question of association. The Committee saw separation and silence as being intended to prevent contamination, and to deter. They felt that the dangers of contamination were exaggerated, and naturally wishing to diminish deterrence, recommended reconsideration of the silence rule, the initial period of cellular confinement, and the cellular work system in the locals. The Committee said that the advantages of association outweighed the disadvantages. They rejected the 'meditation' concept, said that it was impossible to control all communication, and the failure to do so merely brought authority into disrepute. Nevertheless they approved of the principle of the separate system, but felt that associated work would be satisfactory if there was 'careful supervision' and 'proper classification'. With these precautions:

> The fears expressed by some witnesses that freer association might lead to combinations and risings, would under such precautions be groundless.

They pointed to the working parties in the convict prisons as examples of the validity of their premise. They had, however, taken no account of the civil guard who, in a very stark fashion, ensured control by killing prisoners. Remarkably enough, the Committee seemed to ignore the guard. Out of 11,815 questions, only three were about this group of staff.

While the Commissioners at first resisted[60] most of the demands for more association (except for associated labour), the advocacy of a policy of increased association was to undermine the basic device for control in the local prison. Although a gradual process, as association was extended, staff control correspondingly, diminished. It was inevitable therefore that the uniformed officer's job would become more difficult, and his approach to it less certain.

The definition of reformation as a manifest task raised the question of organisational resources to achieve it. The Committee put forward novel ideas about the contribution of the governor to this aim:

> we consider that a governor or his deputy should be brought into close personal relations with prisoners . . . this is the aim of all governors who take an interest in their work.

This aim was the premise which lay behind the wish for more deputy governors, and it coloured the questioning of the witnesses about the role of the governor.[61] Du Cane realised that such a role for a governor of a prison was highly optimistic:[62]

> I should imagine that it was almost impossible for him to attempt to know personally and exercise a personal influence on a great many.

This change of role for the governor has had two significant effects on the development of the prison service. First there developed what is called within the service a 'gold dust' theory. By this is meant faith in the therapeutic effect of the mere presence of a member of the governing grade, or his casual contact with a large number of inmates. At a 'manifest' level, it was to be alleged that the impact of senior staff is the crucial experience for inmates. At an 'extant' level, such contact is slight, usually of little importance, and overshadowed by the much more significant contact with the uniformed staff. The 'gold dust' theory was to have devastating repercussions in the service. In the 1920s and 1930s many governors were to be chosen because it was believed that, in some way, their personal virtues could be communicated in an almost mystical sense to the inmates. The ability to administer a complex organisation was rarely considered to be relevant. It may be noted too that the 'gold dust' theory, in spite of its assumptions, *inhibits* the development of really reformative regimes, since reformative groups in the community, like the Committee, are consoled by the prospect of an articulate, warm and apparently devoted governor generally exercising a reformative influence.

The Committee did ask, occasionally, about the role of the junior staff in the context of the new tasks. The outcome did not augur well for the warders. Some witnesses were optimistic. Du Cane said that some of the witnesses who had come forward proved his point that there were men in the ranks who could become very able governors.[63] The Governor of Strangeways described the warders as a reformatory influence, and insisted that, with training, they could develop.[64] The Committee itself stated that 'the warders could be trained to do some of this work'. But these views were not as influential or as decisive as those of the most important witnesses, Lushington and Ruggles-Brise. From the point of view of the warders, the latter's opposition to the 'chief warder in charge' and his proposal to make clerks eligible for promotion to the governor grades were ominous: 'Yes, I think they have, perhaps, stronger claims than the disciplinary officers.'[65]

The second effect of the proposed change of role for the governor was even more serious. The generic apprehension of prison staff that the prisoners are more important than officers was expressed in the discussion leading to the Rosebery Inquiry. The definition of the reformative task, and the involvement of governors in it was to convince the officers that their suspicions were correct. As the reformative movement gathered momentum, so did the certainty among staff that the bonds between officers and governors were being weakened, because of a strengthening relationship between governor grades and prisoners. The officers resented this bitterly, and frequently expressed their anger about it. An example of the conflict between the prisoners and junior staff, and the need of the latter to be supported by governors, occurred in the evidence. It was said that the Deputy Governor of Wandsworth, whenever a prisoner was reported, took the part of the prisoner against the officer with a resultant 'utter state of discontent'.[66] Lushington saw the officers as 'persons whose main duty is the custody of prisoners'.[67] Their contribution about the working of the Acts and so on was limited. Head Office could learn little 'from the warders, who are mere subordinates, who have strictly to obey orders'.[68] Lushington it appears, knew little about the staff. He did not know, for example, the difference between a principal warder and a chief warder.[69]

These momentous changes were proposed against a background of continuing poor communications between Head Office and the institutions. This problem had been discussed in both the Rosebery and the De Ramsey Inquiries. Ruggles-Brise gave evidence that the root of the trouble lay in the Head Office. He described how 'departments' had evolved, in which the real power and authority resided. These were controlled by civil servants who were independent of Commissioners and Inspectors.

Three such independent departments had grown up 'owing to the power of the Chairman'.[70] Ruggles-Brise discussed one of these in some detail. Du Cane's 'confidential clerk or private secretary, whatever he is called',[71] 'is really practically constituted the head of the patronage department.'[72] The work of 'this large department . . . does not necessarily come under the knowledge of the Commissioners.'[73] In fact:[74]

> in regard to the patronage of the lower ranks we are not necessarily consulted. We are not consulted as to the appointment of a medical officer or a chaplain; we are not consulted at all as to the appointment of warders and subordinate officers.

It also appeared that the Commissioners had almost nothing to do with the preparation of the Annual Report.[75]

The discussion about prison industries is a good example of this gradual erosion of Commissioners' and Inspectors' power, which in turn led to a diminution of governors' authority. A clerical witness pointed out that the needs of 'discipline' clashed with the needs of work.[76] Out of this came three dramatic recommendations: that a 'manufacturer' should be appointed to take charge of prison indus-tries, that there should be a distinction between industrial instructors and warders, and that the Store Accountant should be elevated to the rank of Prison Inspector to superintend all prison industries, accounts and manufactures. The first of these suggestions was resisted, the second was ignored, and the third was accepted. In fact he was appointed 'Comptroller of Prison Industries'.[77] Thus another civil servant gained authority in an important part of institutional activity, and in time would ensure that he had a representative in each prison. The governor slowly lost control over the prison work programme.

Over the years the transfer of power from the Commissioners and Inspectors who were in touch with the institutions, to civil servants who rarely left London, was to prove disastrous in a highly centralised organisation. The evidence to the Committee showed that relation-ships between centre and field were no better than they had been in 1883. They were to become a good deal worse.

In the formative years of the prison service, the clarity of task and role, together with the personal influence of Du Cane, created a situation in which the uniformed staff could identify with the service. In the prisons, the closest bond in the social triangle was between senior and junior staff. Du Cane, and his predecessor in the convict service, had substantially increased the range of opportunities open to the warders both for promotion, and for specialist appointments. There had indeed been problems and crises. Where these centred round the treatment of prisoners, the service had usually been exonerated. Investigations are not inherently damaging, and where allegations are unproven staff morale is higher afterwards than it was before. Where staff had voiced discontent, this was almost always because of some defect in material conditions. It was obvious that Du Cane and the Directors and Commissioners had little control over these conditions, but they had a good record for advancing staff claims to a reluctant and generally ignorant Treasury.

As far as the uniformed staff were concerned therefore, the Gladstone Report had four far reaching effects. Reformation was introduced as a manifest task, control was undermined, governors and prisoners were drawn together, and participation of the warders in the new developments was restricted. These effects make up the substance of an overall change in the operation of the prison service, which was to create a profound sense of alienation on the part of the officers.

Notes

1 The Committee's Report is in two volumes: *Minutes of Evidence taken by the Departmental Committee on Prisons with Appendices and Index*, C. 7702–1 (referred to in this book as 'Evidence') and *Report from the Departmental Committee on Prisons*, C. 7702 (referred to as 'Report'). Both were published by HMSO in 1895. There was also printed *Observations of Prison Commissioners on Recommendations of Departmental Committee*, P.R.O. H.O.45/10025/A56902/4, which is referred to as 'Observations'.

2 See, for example, Rose, *The Struggle for Penal Reform*, p. 49; Leslie, *Sir Evelyn Ruggles-Brise*, p. 88 and S. and B. Webb, *English Prisons under Local Government*, p. 219, n.4. For a short biography of Morrison, see Rose, op. cit., p. 57 and his obituary in *The Times*, 15 December 1943. The story, often repeated (see Fox, *The English Prison and Borstal Systems*, p. 53), that Du Cane 'sacked him' is without evidence.

3 Rose, op. cit., pp. 58–60.

4 See, for example, Hansard, vol. 14, col. 1703 (17 July 1893); vol. 16, col. 860 (22 April 1893).

5 P.R.O. H.O. 45/9958/V20544/4.

6 Gladstone Report, p. A, para. 2.

7 Loc. cit.

8 Ibid., p. A, para. 6.

9 Ibid., p. 6.

10 See Rose, op. cit., pp. 61–4; S. and B. Webb, op. cit., pp. 219 31; Fox, op. cit., pp. 53–6.

11 *The Times*, 10 February 1891, p. 10.

12 Gladstone Evidence, question 1832.

13 Ibid., question 7993.

14 Ibid., question 5233.

15 Ibid., question 10344.

16 Ibid., question 2958.

17 Ibid., question 83.

18 Ibid., questions 10803–4.

19 Ibid., question 10808.

20 Ibid., question 9852.

21 Ibid., question 6516.

22 Ibid., question 9395.

23 Ibid., question 2951.

24 Ibid., question 2957.

25 Ibid., question 798.

26 Ibid., question 2601.

27 Ibid., questions 258–9.

28 Ibid., question 6955.

29 Ibid., question 6957.

30 Ibid., question 6958.

31 Ibid., questions 9527 and 1888–93.

32 Ibid., question 11207.

33 Ibid., question 7867.
34 Ibid., question 3375.
35 Pears (ed.), *Prisons and Reformatories at Home and Abroad*, p. 33.
36 Gladstone Evidence, questions 6460, 6463.
37 Ibid., question 6899.
38 Ibid., questions 7467–71.
39 Ibid., question 10351.
40 Ibid., question 10797.
41 Ibid., questions 7999–8003.
42 Ibid., question 3051.
43 Ibid., question 3052.
44 Ibid., question 9455.
45 Ibid., question 11016.
46 Ibid., question 8782.
47 Ibid., question 9465.
48 Ibid., question 4148.
49 Ibid., question 7961.
50 Ibid., question 7446.
51 Ibid., question 6474.
52 Ibid., question 8543.
53 Ibid., question 9649 et seq.
54 Ibid., p. 617.
55 Ibid., question 11203.
56 Ibid., question 3078.
57 Ibid., question 6898.
58 Ibid., questions 6912–20.
59 This was done. Departmental Committee on Education and
   Moral Instruction of Prisoners in Local and Convict Prisons, 1896.
   P.R.O. H.O./45/10025/A56902/B.
60 See Observations, pp. 8–9 (abolition of separate confinement),
   pp. 5–6 (associated labour) and 7–8 (abolition of silence rules).
61 See, for instance, Gladstone Evidence, questions 89, 6926 and 7325.
62 Ibid., question 10786.
63 Ibid., question 10803.
64 Ibid., questions 7367–72.
65 Ibid., questions 10347–8.
66 Ibid., question 6446.
67 Ibid., question 11398.
68 Ibid., question 11397.
69 Ibid., question 11417.
70 Ibid., question 9993.
71 Ibid., question 9997.
72 Ibid., question 9998.
73 Loc. cit.
74 Ibid., question 9996.
75 Ibid., question 10006.
76 Ibid., questions 4784–8.
77 Annual Report 1895–6, p. 9.

7   1895–1921: a change of direction

Introduction

Du Cane, who had been ill and had reached superannuation age, retired at the same time as the Gladstone Report was published, an event which his implacable enemy, the *Daily Chronicle*, described as 'the inevitable end of a discredited system'.[1] *The Times* was more generous.[2] It quoted at some length the remarks about his achievements which appeared in the Eighteenth Local Report, including the summary given by Lushington to the Gladstone Committee (see p. 28). Du Cane wrote an article in the *Nineteenth Century* in August 1895 in which he expressed disagreement with the Committee's conclusions, but *The Times* was more approving, emphasising, however, that the prisoner should not be pampered, or 'let out too long before he has served his time'.[3] The Du Cane regime was over.

The new Chairman was Evelyn John Ruggles-Brise—'an Amurath to Amurath succeeding'.[4] His background was very different from Du Cane's. Born into a prominent Essex family in 1857, he went to Eton and Oxford, and then joined the civil service, after an impressive performance in the entrance examinations. He was one of the new breed of professional civil servants, limited in practical experience, intelligent, conscientious, and possessed of understanding of the politician's need to arrive at decisions which were politically expedient. His father was a Member of Parliament and was friendly with Sir William Harcourt, Home Secretary in the early 1880s. This friendship resulted in the son's appointment to the Home Office, where he became Private Secretary to four Home Secretaries.

Ruggles-Brise's style of life was also very different from his predecessor's. He was a close personal friend of many important and influential people, and spent his free time at Dunrobin, Blenheim, Warwick Castle and other centres of political power in late Victorian England. Not the least significant of his friendships was that with Herbert Gladstone, Chairman of the 1895 Committee, and Home Secretary in the Liberal government in 1908. They had been at Eton together. Ruggles-Brise used these aristocratic contacts to build up sympathy for the prison system, especially for the changes in the methods of dealing with juveniles which were starting to be introduced.

He was appointed Prison Commissioner in 1892, and so came into contact with Du Cane. The latter wrote to welcome him, but very soon Ruggles-Brise began to resent the autocracy of the Chairman. The problem was resolved by the Gladstone Report and Du Cane's retirement. It is largely from the comments of Ruggles-Brise about Du Cane, that the picture of the latter as the embodiment of despotic bureaucracy has been built up. In fact, Ruggles-Brise had a great deal of respect for his chief. He admired the latter's courtesy, and his exceptional ability, and he felt that the press campaign was 'largely dictated by personal motives', and 'much malice'.[5] It was Ruggles-Brise's biographer who created the terrifying picture of Du Cane which is perpetuated by writers. Shane Leslie wrote, for example, of Sir Edmund's 'barbaric philosophy' which 'pervaded the whole system'.[6] Later writers have been careful to select from Ruggles-Brise's account only the least commendable of Du Cane's characteristics.

As far as attitudes to prisoners and to staff were concerned, there was little difference between the two Chairmen. Du Cane's overall contribution was greater, since he was the architect of the system. Ruggles-Brise established the borstal system, which in his day, in fact, amounted to separation of young people from the general prison population and a successful attempt to interest influential people in their welfare. But generally Ruggles-Brise put the purposes of imprisonment in the same order of priority as Du Cane, 'retributory, deterrent, and reformatory'.[7] With regard to staff, Du Cane was probably more sympathetic than his successor, who resisted their attempts to form an association, and called the Prison Officers' Representative Board 'the Soviet'. Both were angered by 'outside' interference. Ruggles-Brise's over-sympathetic biographer approvingly quotes a summary of him, which would have been appropriate to Du Cane:[8]

> an absolute sahib, yet clever and autocrat (sic), accustomed to make up his mind and then sweep all obstacles out of the way of his will.

Their final experience was very similar. Both men, Ruggles-Brise, the

country gentleman as he regarded himself, and Du Cane, the techno-
crat, finished their careers in a flurry of severe criticism.

The Home Secretary's instructions to Ruggles-Brise when he
appointed him Chairman were, 'the views of the Committee should,
as far as practicable, be carried into execution'.[9] The changes which
were introduced into prison during this period, were made within the
context of important developments in the administration of criminal
justice, external to the prison system. These developments were part
of the Liberal programme of 1906–13, and were cumulatively
designed to reduce the numbers of people who were needlessly, or
erroneously, sent to prison. The most important pieces of legislation
passed for this purpose were: the Probation of Offenders Act 1907,
the Children Act and the Prevention of Crime Act both of 1908, the
Mental Deficiency and Lunacy Act 1913 and the Criminal Justice
Administration Act 1914. These, respectively, authorised probation
as a statutory method of dealing with offenders, established juvenile
courts, removed some offenders under 21 and recidivists from the
normal prison system, gave the courts power to certify instead of
committing to prison, and compelled magistrates to allow time for
payment of fines.[10]

The major piece of legislation affecting the prison system was the
Prison Act of 1898. It was introduced by the Conservative government, which had been returned in the election of 1895. The Liberals,
including Herbert Gladstone himself, generally approved of the
measure and supported it. The debate would have been fairly restrained had it not been for the Irish Members, who took the opportunity to launch a lengthy, violent, attack on the prison system,
and on the timidity of the measures proposed in the Bill. As they had
done before, they raised the level of the debate, because of their
detailed personal knowledge of prisons. Both major parties, in the
face of this attack, joined together to deny the allegations which
were made.

One of the most important provisions of the Act was that which
drew the convict and local services together, although their pay scales
remained different. From 1895–6, the Annual Report described the
work of both services. Other provisions allowed local prisoners to
earn remission, limited the use of corporal punishment in prison,
allowed a part of payment of a fine to be accepted in lieu of imprisonment, gave the courts authority to classify prisoners into three
divisions, and gave the Home Secretary the power to make Rules for

administration.[11] But the most important developments which followed Gladstone, centred round the removal of barriers to communication between prisoners.

The end of the separate system

It has been shown that although there were extensive discussions about the punitive effects of the separate system, its main structural function was to facilitate control. The Gladstone Committee attacked the separate system, construing it as the main tool of punishment, and the core of the deterrent regime. It was apparent to staff that an end to separation, while it could lead to a more congenial life for prisoners, would pose radical problems for them.

The Committee had recommended three changes, all of which, if implemented, would undermine the separate system. These were that talking should be allowed, that the period of separate confinement should be reconsidered, and that there should be work in association. In their 'Observations' the Commissioners disagreed with the first two. They were more sympathetic to the third, but pointed out that there would have to be substantial increases in staff. The Commissioners resisted the assaults on the silence rule, and on separate confinement for as long as possible, but the purity of the separate system was breached principally through the introduction of associated labour.

The fact that local prisons had been intended for cellular employment posed real difficulties, which Commissioners and staff tried hard to overcome.[12] The extent of the new association ranged from situations where cell work was continued but all the doors were open, to purpose-built workshops.[13] The approval of the Commissioners and staff of this development at first sight appears odd, since they were very conscious of the potential dangers in any kind of association. There were, however, several features of the new system which counteracted the possible danger of collaboration between prisoners.

In the first place, association for work did not mean the ending of the silence rule, a fact made clear by the Commissioners in the Report for 1898–9:

A strict and effective superintendence will, of course, be necessary to enforce order and discipline and prevent communication.

Next, the staff was not large enough to ensure this 'superintendence' and had to be increased, a point which was stressed by the governors in their reports: 'Now that prisoners are so much out of their cells the necessity for more officers is absolute.'[14] Increase in the numbers of staff is always welcome, and, provided there were enough, super-vision of the activities of prisoners could be more effective if they were in groups, than if they were in individual cells, as long as there was no talking.

The third feature of the new association rule which made it palat-able to staff was that it was not allowed to all prisoners indiscrimin-ately. In 1898–9, it was reported that a hard labour term in a local prison still began with a period of 'strict separation' for the first month, while the convict serving a term of penal servitude still under-went a period of six months' separate confinement. This was a reduction from the traditional nine months. Also in the 1898–9 Report it is pointed out that in the local a prisoner was 'eligible', after a month, for associated labour, but this was a privilege, not a right. Associated labour was therefore one of a complex of privileges which were to distinguish the period, and which were to be such powerful aids to control. The governors realised this very quickly, as was reported in 1905–6:

> The effect of associated labour is good from a discipline point
> of view—the possibility of its suspension tends to keep the
> prisoner quiet.

Finally, and most happily, it appeared that the prisoners worked harder in association.[15] This highly satisfactory state of affairs was certain to please reformers and reactionaries alike. There could, after all, be little dispute about the desirability of hard, productive work. From the point of view of prison staff, the implementation of this section of the Gladstone Report did not undermine control and, in some ways, fortified it.

The silence rule was a different matter. There was almost universal resistance from Commissioners and governors to the idea that prisoners ought to be allowed to talk. The pressure from Parliament was great, however, and eventually, in 1899, the rule was altered, although the concessions were minimal and grudgingly made in the convict and local prison codes: 'The privilege of talking may be given after a certain period as a reward for good conduct.' This privilege, which applied only to long-sentence prisoners, and could be indulged in for only short periods, was given at the discretion of the governors, was disliked by them, and was sparingly awarded. Most governors disapproved strongly, and many flatly refused to allow it: for example the Governor of Knutsford in the 1901–2 Annual Report said:

> Talking at exercise . . . is only a fruitful source of mischief . . . I have only once been asked for this indulgence, and that by an old convict, whom, in the interest of discipline, I refused.

In the 1902–3 Report, the Governor of Dartmoor was one of a very few who felt that, used with discretion, 'association of selected prisoners does not lead to harm in the prison itself'. Dartmoor, in spite of this small concession, did not lose sight of the supremacy of security. In the same Report the Governor reported that each work party was to be kept together in the same hall in the prison. Thus a member of one party could not contact a prisoner from another party and so 'opportunities for clandestine communication were greatly diminished'. At the same time the telephone helped to tighten security, as did the establishment of the famous pony patrol.

The governors claimed in the 1899–1900 Annual Report that their views about the undesirability of conversation happily coincided with those of the prisoners, very few of whom, it appeared, wanted the privilege anyway.[16] Whether or not this was so, in the local prisons the practice was effectively stopped. The qualifying period was raised from six months to twelve months in 1902, and by 1907 only one governor allowed it. In the convict prisons it was rather more successful, and in 1905 was extended (but only for prisoners in the 'long-sentence division', see pp. 133–4), being allowed every day. This difference was no doubt due largely to the different systems of supervision in the two services.

Evidence of the structural function of silence, and the relationship between communication and loss of control, is furnished by crises which arose as a result of the presence of some political groups during the 1914–18 War. These groups were given privileges under the 'Churchill Rule'[17] designed to lessen the various deprivations of prison life. These privileges included associating and talking at exercise. The result, the Commissioners reported, was disastrous, and led 'to mischief and combination to resist authority'. There was 'considerable disorder' at Wandsworth amongst conscientious objectors which led to an investigation[18] and at Lewes[19] which housed Irish prisoners. Both incidents show that prisoners have to be able to communicate relatively freely, before they can effectively break the control of the staff. Had these prisoners been kept separately, each may well have been troublesome, as Irish prisoners had been in the past, but there would have been no opportunity for concerted action. Realisation of this fact lay behind the resistance of staffs to 'conversational exercise'. And while Ruggles-Brise was Chairman, all attempts to extend such communication were firmly resisted.

New methods of control

A prison staff can only control the inmate community in one of two ways. They can either exercise legitimated, relentless coercion, or they can demonstrate to prisoners that good behaviour is more profitable than bad behaviour. The first alternative is only feasible if the system authorises it, and if there is considerable control over the movement of inmates, in the way that the separate system makes possible. When prisoners are allowed association the staff have to use some other method of control, a task which is difficult because of the refusal of the inmate community to recognise the legitimacy of staff rule. The absence of such recognition is a very serious matter, since the staff are outnumbered most of the time.

One way of ensuring control is to punish wrongdoing. But this is only slightly effective, first because it can anger other prisoners, and second because the effect is generally short lived. Another way is to institute a system of rewards for good behaviour, rewards which are sought after by the prisoners. If no meaningful rewards can be offered, then control is almost impossible.

Sykes describes this problem in his study of Trenton Prison, New Jersey.[20] The experience there was different in degree from the experience in the English system. The American situation is complicated by forms of association which amaze the English prison official. Enormous mess halls, catering for the entire prison at one time, pose insoluble problems of control. Again, for decades the American prison officer has dealt with the prisoner who is a novelty in England, the 'lifer' who will probably never be released, and has little interest in incentives to good behaviour. But, in essence, Sykes's description is applicable to the English system. He stresses the futility of punishment as a means of 'moving more than one thousand two hundred inmates through the messhall in a routine and orderly fashion',[21] and describes the transition from a situation where rewards are awarded for effort, to one where they are regarded as a right. Eventually the staff cannot control any more, and are 'corrupted', in the sense that they have to come to terms with the prisoners.

In outline this was the development of the English system after 1895. The demands for greater freedom for inmates, which had been expressed before the Gladstone Report, were sustained afterwards. The prison system had to adapt, since the absolute power of staff was eroded when association, and communication between prisoners, were introduced.

And so there was set in motion the process of control which has been used in the English prison system since 1898—the promise of privilege. The flowering of an elaborate system of rewards has been generally approved. Prisoners have welcomed the opportunity to earn concessions which make life rather more bearable, reformers have applauded the flexibility of the borstal sentence, or the parole system, removed as those are from the doom-like certainty of the 'fixed' sentence, and society has looked with approval on a system which rewards good effort, rather than penalises lack of it. These attributes were incidental. The main function of a reward system in prison then, as now, is to maintain order.

The earliest of these substantial rewards for the bulk of prisoners was remission, the system whereby for good conduct part of the sentence is waived. This important change in the prison system was welcomed by Commissioners and governors alike. While occasionally its value is discussed as an encouragement to a man to work hard, and therefore be better prepared for release, it is more usual to find emphasis given to its excellence as a tool for control. Ruggles-Brise wrote:[22]

> Moreover, the risk or fear of losing remission marks operates as a powerful deterrent against idleness or misconduct, and it has been found, generally, that under the influence of this salutory provision there has been a marked improvement in the tone and demeanour of the prisoners, while, at the same time, an aid has been furnished to those responsible for maintaining order and discipline.

The Governor of Northampton, like his colleagues, was frankly relieved. His report in 1907–8 notes that remission:

tends to strengthen a Governor's hand in maintaining discipline,
and gives him an alternative punishment to the 'well worn'
bread and water diet, for which I am thankful.

The new system of rewards, replacing as they did the more visible
controlling methods of the earlier period, made possible the development of two new kinds of regimes which have achieved some fame—
the systems of preventive detention, and borstal.

Preventive detention, as a penal measure dealing with recidivists,
was introduced in the Prevention of Crime Act 1908 (and abolished
by the Criminal Justice Act 1967). Broadly, preventive detention
allowed the courts to award two sentences to the proved habitual
offender, one for the particular offence, and one because he was a
recidivist. The second sentence would be for a period of between five
and ten years.[23] In 1908–9 it was reported that a 'special place of
detention', was set up at Camp Hill on the Isle of Wight, and there
was a bold attempt to organise a regime which would be tolerable,
and where the 'conditions of detention' would be 'less onerous in
some respects than those of ordinary penal servitude'. This relaxation
inevitably brought a risk of loss of control. Promptly, if briefly,
control was lost. The prison opened in March 1912 and in August
there was a mutiny. The leaders were removed, and the prison settled
down to implement the complex system of privileges which the
Commissioners and staff saw as the main method of control. In the
Annual Report 1911–12 (part I, p. 23) it was stated:

> There are already signs that the fear of losing the many
> privileges, given contingently on good conduct, is a most potent
> aid to discipline, and it is on this principle that the establish-
> ment will be administered.

And in the Annual Report for 1913–14 (part II, p. 127):

> So much time is spent in association, with ample opportunities
> for arranging combinations against discipline, that it would not
> be a cause for wonder if the statistics as regards misconduct
> were much less satisfactory. The antidote to this is contained in
> the extensive privileges which preventive detention prisoners
> enjoy. There is so much to lose!

As well as this special regime for preventive detainees, the Annual
Report for 1904–5 reported the establishment of a 'long-sentence

division', for ordinary prisoners. Men who had served more than seven and a half years of a sentence of at least ten years could obtain privileges, including conversation, through hard work.

The introduction of incentives enabled the Commissioners to cope with the long-standing demands for a reformative regime for young prisoners. These were met by the introduction of the borstal system. The borstal institution then, as now, depended for its stability entirely on a system of rewards. The preliminary efforts to set aside a special regime for lads aged between 16 and 21 were consolidated in the Prevention of Crime Act 1908. The borstal sentence was for a period of between one and three years, the time of release depending on conduct. Progress through the system was marked by a series of grades, each of which carried extra privileges, all of which could be withheld if there was any deterioration in behaviour. The culmination was selection for discharge.[24]

The inmate society was thus controlled by new, less visible devices, and by the development of these devices, the prison service was able to cope with change. For although critics were later to deplore the lack of really fundamental change, this *was* nevertheless a period of change.

The staff in a changing situation

The staff during the period 1895–1921, continued to spend the bulk of their time coping with the universal, irreducible tasks which are the kernel of the routine of prisons. There was a crop of violent assaults, which, in 1903, led a meeting of Birmingham magistrates to observe that:

> in addition to violent assaults upon officers, other acts of gross insubordination by prisoners had been steadily on the increase.

They claimed other magistrates agreed with them (*The Times*, 8 January 1903).

There were some very nasty assaults at Dartmoor, and in 1901 the Commissioners reported that, as a result of thirteen escapes and attempted escapes of a 'sensational character' from Borstal:

> The idea of trying to escape seems to have seized the imagination of prisoners throughout the country . . .

The Royal West Kents had to be sent for because of trouble at Maidstone in 1906, and there was a mutiny and escape at Gloucester in the same year. If uniformed staff needed a reminder of their primary role, in 1907 at Wormwood Scrubs they received it. The Commissioners reported that insubordination there amongst prisoners made it 'necessary to deal with several officers for improperly discharging their duties'.

The staff had also to cope with some new problems. The last years of the nineteenth century saw an economic boom, unemployment sank to 2 per cent in 1899—the lowest figure since 1874. The boom came to an end when the Boer War finished in May 1902.[25] Unemployment began to rise, and wages to fall. In 1904, 6 per cent were out of work, and although the figure dropped slightly in 1906–7, by 1909 it stood at 7·7 per cent. The beginning of increasing government intervention came in 1903–4 with the 'colony scheme' whereby applicants for relief were sent to work in farm colonies while their families stayed in London.[26]

The effect of the economic situation on the prisons was dramatic. The position is described in the 1912–13 Annual Report. The numbers of people committed rose steadily, from 153,460 receptions in 1899–1900, to a peak of 184,901 in 1908–9. Thereafter the numbers decreased, especially after the outbreak of war. Not only was the increase in numbers a matter of concern, but the quality of the prisoners drew regular criticism from the governors. As could be expected in a time of economic depression, tramps presented the greatest problem, numerically and qualitatively. They were sent to prison in huge numbers for various offences of vagrancy, and for workhouse offences, such as refusing to work. The Governor of Lincoln in his Report for 1907–8 expressed a common opinion: 'There seems to be an army of tramps marching up and down Lincolnshire year after year.' Nor were they easy to control. Since as a rule they served between seven and fourteen days, they did not qualify for remission. Predictably therefore, many governors reported that they refused to work. As economic prosperity returned, their numbers fell from 27,000 in 1909–10 to 1,612 in 1919–20.

There were also large numbers of people committed for offences of drunkenness, and most governors, in most reports, express doubts about the suitability of prison for this class of offender. In 1913–14, out of 136,424 total receptions, no fewer than 51,851 were for 'drunkenness etc.' And this represented a decrease from previous years. By 1918–19 this figure had dropped to 1,670.

Another difficult problem of the period was the political prisoner.

There were three main groups: the Irish, the Suffragettes and the conscientious objectors. All three were the subject of confused and ambivalent feelings on the part of the public and Parliament, and all three presented prison staff with very difficult problems of control, problems which were exacerbated by the depletion of prison staffs, to some extent in the Boer War, and to a much greater extent in the Great War.

The Commissioners described the response of the uniformed staff to these problems in glowing terms. In their 1911–12 Report, for example, they wrote:

> The many administrative changes introduced during recent years . . . have undoubtedly added to the duties and responsibilities of all ranks, superior and subordinate, disciplinary and clerical. We desire to take this opportunity of recognising the admirable spirit with which new and more exacting duties have been undertaken.

This is the usual tone to be found in the reports, and, to the end of the period they maintained an unswerving belief that the staff were contented and co-operative. Towards the latter half of the period, when it is clear staff were dissatisfied, the persistent refusal of the Commissioners and the Home Secretary to accept evidence of discontent is ludicrous. There was discontent, and this sprang from the new reformative task, and from the desire to help prisoners which was central to it. These new emphases can best be studied through an examination of the changed role of the governor, since much of the growing confusion among staff, sprang from this change.

The role of the governor

We have seen that in the Du Cane regime the governor was expected to bear responsibility for what happened in the prison, and had to be able to command and control. He was expected to ensure that rules were obeyed, that staff exerted coercive measures of control within clearly defined bounds, and that prisoners were not ill-treated. It was a role which called for firmness, experience, and judgment.

Although the governor in the Ruggles-Brise regime was still expected to exert control, the Gladstone Report introduced some expectations of governors which, in the long run, were perhaps to have more effect on staff than they were to have on inmates. The

Gladstone Committee was anxious to establish the governor as a reformative agent. The Ruggles-Brise regime, carried along by commitment to reform, produced governors who interested themselves in reformation, sometimes becoming very involved in the various agencies called into being for that purpose. *The Times* was soon confused by the new system. In a leading article on 14 March 1898, the tone of the governor's role was described as follows:

> it is not the sole duty of the governor to be able to produce 'the body of AB' at any time he is called upon. He is a schoolmaster and a practical moralist rather than a gaoler; he has charge of a sort of polytechnic; every prison is a reformatory.

However, in the next month, on 5 April, angered by Irish, 'truly Hibernian notions of evidence', and radical opposition to the Prison Bill, the newspaper expressed the opinion that:

> Philanthropic people however, must bear in mind that no legislation, however liberal, can turn a prison into a paradise, and that, as far as they tend to do so, measures of prison reform are destructive of the objects—disagreeable, but indispensable— for which prisons themselves exist.

While not all governors accepted the new role, there is evidence that some certainly did. In 1906–7 the Governor of Stafford sent in a rather startling report:

> When opportunities present themselves, I have visited cases of juvenile-adults who are resident in Wolverhampton, Newcastle-under-Lyme, Walsall, Hanley and Stoke, in order to encourage them.

Other governors found work for lads on discharge, made provision for the homeless and destitute, sat on committees to supervise Police Court Missions, and were members of Borstal Committees.

The contribution of borstal to the developing conflict of the dual role of the governor deserves special discussion. Borstal has always, at a manifest level, proclaimed reformation as its task. It originated as an expression of the belief that delinquents, if dealt with early enough, can be deflected from a life of crime. As a result, the borstal governor has always been regarded as a reformer. But there was as much confusion about the meaning of the term 'reform' in 1900, as there is today. What early borstal governors seem to have felt was that it stood in some kind of polar relationship to deterrence, which in turn was equated with repression. In the view of some, reformation began to be seen as allowing people to do as they wished, so that punitive treatment could be demonstrably absent. The result at Borstal, according to Deputy Governor Blake, was 'a state of constant insubordination'.[27] Borstal, even today, continues to wrestle with the problem of what is meant by reformation and training. The point is that during the period 1898–1921, one part of the prison system, borstal, began to accrue high status in the eyes of the community, status which was to be raised even more after 1921, and for the first time the Commissioners, at least in theory, began to look for different qualities in its governors. The 'reformer' had arrived.

Very significant too was the introduction of a new grade. In 1912–13 four 'tutors' were appointed with administrative responsibility, and a clearly defined reformative role—two at Borstal, two at Feltham. This innovation was significant because it was likely to attract a different kind of senior member of staff from the traditional, tutors would eventually become governors, and logically, to some degree at least, would retain some of the reformative impetus which had propelled them into the service in the first place. In time this grade, renamed assistant governor, was to be universal in the prison system. The last respect in which borstal was to herald future changes concerned titles. The tutors were also to be deputy governors, and took charge in the absence of the governor. The chief warder was to be known as the 'chief of staff', principal warders were to be known as 'principal officers', and warders as 'officers'.[28]

While these major changes were confined to the institutions set apart as borstals, all prisons felt the impact of the new 'training' in some degree. Every prison had a section of prisoners between 16 and 21 who had a special regime, and a Borstal Committee to look after them on release. This system was set up in 1905–6.[29] The 'modified' borstal system, as it was called, introduced a reformative note into all the locals.

The introduction of a reformative element into the role of the governor, had important consequences for the uniformed staff. To understand these it is necessary to stress the power which officers have always believed that the governor wields. Much of this power has always been illusory. He cannot change policy, nor set up a regime totally unlike every other prison in the system. But until recently subordinate staff would have agreed, at least as far as their careers were concerned, that he was 'absolute master'.[30] To some he may have been a 'paper tiger', but to staff he had 'real teeth'[31] and they looked to him for guidance and approval.

It follows, therefore, that the staff would try to please the governor. This in itself is difficult, but could be achieved in the Victorian system, where the primary task was clear. The governor regarded a good warder as one who could control a group of men, using legally approved means. In the post-Gladstone era, it was very much more difficult. It must have been almost impossible for uniformed officers to know what was expected of them. How could a satisfactory performance at work be evaluated when the objectives of the work became so confused? What, for example, was expected of the borstal warder? Some idea of the confusion in which staff must have found themselves can be gained from the contradictory statements made by the Governor of Borstal in 1905—Major Blake. In his Annual Report for 1905–6, he writes:

> I cannot speak too highly of the conduct of the subordinate staff. The schoolmasters, instructors, and all officers seem to be fully imbued with the spirit of the Borstal scheme, and do all in their power to promote its success.

At the same time:

> The strictest discipline is maintained. I have impressed upon all officers that, while every encouragement is to be shown the lads to improve themselves, they are not to overlook the slightest breach of the Prison Regulations.

In *Quod*, discussing the same period, he expresses some distaste for Borstal, and for the 'very ragged staff' (ibid., p. 112) he had. Under his predecessor, so that the return of punishments would be 'nil', 'it was tacitly forbidden for a warder either to reprimand or to report a boy' (ibid., p. 85). This odd, but by no means incredible, situation would result in the Commissioners assuming that the Governor knew 'how to 'andle the lads' (ibid., p. 87).

Nor was the new confusion confined to borstal. In 1910 a series of 'anonymous' articles appeared in *The Times*. The new emphasis on the prisoner is demonstrated by some of the statements made. It is reported that warders who are judged for the 'plums': 'must improve the moral (sic) of the parties in their charge, which means more than being constantly on the alert.' Further, it is claimed that governors are suspicious of warders who bring too many complaints against prisoners. The warders who will get on are those who:

> having troublesome prisoners thrust into their hands, so deal with them that they cease to be rebellious and insubordinate.

Except for criminal conduct against prisoners, the Du Cane regime was unequivocally supportive of staff. A radical change after 1900 is indicated by the statement that if prisoners constantly complain against an officer he 'would presently be watched without his knowledge and quietly tested, and dealt with accordingly'. This description of the assessment of work performance was all the more ominous, because, it transpired, it was written by Alexander Paterson, the most influential and important Prison Commissioner of the century.[32]

The confusion about task, present to some degree in all penal establishments during those years, was especially visible in those which had a regime where traditional controlling devices were being dramatically undermined. Borstal and the Preventive Detention Prison at Camp Hill are examples. At Camp Hill, it was alleged, warders were discontented because they had to discharge duties rigorously controlled by the old convict regulations, which were unsuited to the Camp Hill regime. The Commissioners replied that there were no differences between their duties and those of other prison staff.[33]

Although there was clearly still a demand for the traditional skills of the prison warder, skills of control which could curb incipient or actual riot or escape, these were devalued in the Ruggles-Brise era. They became less relevant because of the new reformative orientation, and this was highlighted by the pattern of promotion. The Commissioners had agreed to the Gladstone Committee's suggestion that the title 'chief warder in charge', should be varied to Governor Class V. In 1893 there had been twenty-two chief warders in charge[34] as well as an undisclosed number of governors who had been warders. The change of title underlined the feeling that socially, emotionally, and intellectually, warders could not be effective governors, if the reformative theories were to be translated into practice. The 1903 Departmental Committee's Report disclosed (p. V) that out of eighteen Class V governors then serving 'no less than fifteen were formerly members of the clerical staff': furthermore the clerks wanted more governor posts to be given to them. This pressure was unsuccessful, although in 1922 there was still a larger number of ex-clerks than ex-warders amongst governors.[35] Since the total number of clerks was much lower than that of warders, the chances of a clerk being promoted to governor were clearly much greater. Nor was the introduction in 1896 of a new grade of 'clerk and schoolmaster warder' (reported in 1895–6) of much advantage to the uniformed staff. They were promoted to principal warder, not to governor,[36] and were paid much less than the 'civilian' clerks.[37] And while it was felt that warder clerks would take on more of the work done by civilian clerks, the possibility of *all* clerical work being done by warders was regarded by the 1903 Departmental Committee as:[38]

> injurious to the interests of the service. Some of the duties which fall to the clerks require a higher degree of intelligence and education than can reasonably be expected of an officer drawn from the subordinate discipline staff; and—a matter to which we attach much importance—it is necessary to provide for the training of officers for the post of storekeeper, a post which, for many reasons, we think ought to be held by a man with qualifications which could not ordinarily be looked for in a prison warder.

Prisoners and uniformed staff—situations compared

The period was notable for decided improvements in the treatment of prisoners, some of which have already been described. Borstal and Camp Hill were a kind of 'new deal' for prisoners, and special conditions were introduced for the political prisoners. From 1903 to 1911 impressive efforts were made to establish after-care facilities, educational provision was improved, diet was changed, and on the lighter side, concerts and lectures were introduced into both convict and local prisons.

The pressure to go further, and give prisoners more freedom, was barely diminished by these changes. A considerable boost to demands for an end to 'separation' and silence, was given by the production of John Galsworthy's *Justice* in 1910. The play was a story of an ordinary man who was convicted and sent to Dartmoor. Much stress is laid on the devastating effects of his separate confinement. Ruggles-Brise was annoyed by Galsworthy's campaign, of which the play was a part, and asked Winston Churchill, then Home Secretary, to try to stop it. Galsworthy replied that if Ruggles-Brise was trying to introduce reforms, he should recognise that Galsworthy was on his side.[39] The reaction to Galsworthy's 'revelation' that for thirty-five years prisoners had undergone separate confinement, was considerable. The Commissioners discussed the separate system in their 1909–10 Report, and there was a renewal of Parliamentary demands to abolish it completely, and to allow talking.

There was noticeably less increase in the freedom given to staff. While the 1911–12 Annual Report could state that 'it has been found possible to go further in the way of relaxation of prison discipline', the 'discipline' affecting staff was as rigorous as ever. Attempts by Members of Parliament to abolish fining of officers failed, as did the attempt to end the system of confidential reports. The failure to improve material conditions was abysmal. The quarters situation was unsatisfactory, while complaints about pay and conditions were raised persistently in Parliament. To most of these complaints the respective Home Secretaries replied either that there was no dissatisfaction, or that if there was, there was no justification for it.

Very occasionally some concessions were made to staff demands. Night duty, which the new regime introduced in 1896–7, was abolished in 1911–12. After a long struggle, in 1918–19, local officers were paid the same as convict colleagues, and there were some important changes in the pension scheme. Increases in pay, when they were eventually given, were quite inadequate to meet rising costs, especially during and after the Great War.

The uniformed staff soon realised that no reformative zeal was being directed at improving their situation. They watched with alarm as governors, and later 'tutors', drew closer to the inmate community, leaving staff confused and suspicious. As far as the warders were concerned, this new alliance between governors and prisoners was the most obvious, and the most threatening, expression of society's desire to give more attention to the needs of the prisoners. It was not long before the officers' alarm turned to anger at this unequal distribution of freedom and sympathy, and they began a protest which was to last sixty years.

'Put your trust in the magazine and all will be well'[40]—officers and trade unions

The petitions which led to the appointment of the Rosebery and De Ramsey Committees, bore evidence of communication between staffs in different prisons. The demands which were made were identical, and clearly the product of discussion. But the first real attempt by the uniformed staff to set up machinery for the expression of discontent occurred in 1895 with the publication of a magazine. It collapsed after six months and no copies have survived.[41]

The early 1900s were not conducive to the establishment of any kind of trade union or staff association. The Taff Vale case of 1901, and the Osborne decision of 1909 had damaged the union movement.[42] Unemployment during the decade meant that jobs were difficult to get, and those who got them were not likely to risk losing them by joining unions and thus incurring the displeasure of their employers.

The question of a union for prison officers was mentioned for the first time, in Parliament, on 15 March 1906. The Home Secretary was asked about alleged grievances of warders, and whether he would allow them the right to 'federation' which postal employees enjoyed. As was usual with the Home Secretaries of the period he did not know of any grievances, and he deferred a decision on federation. On 5 April he announced a new Standing Order, whereby with the sanction of the governor, or of a Commissioner, or on appeal to the Home Secretary, staff were to be allowed to 'meet and discuss among themselves questions relating to their duties and position in the prison service'. Two years later, on 28 May 1908, the question as to whether that ruling meant that prison staff had the same rights of association as other workmen, went unanswered.

In spite of this discouragement, in 1910 the *Prison Officers' Magazine* was founded. It was edited from outside the service by Frederick Ludlow (see the issue of October 1914 for a biography) and was called 'the red 'un', ostensibly because of its colour, but also because of its radical views. In fact, in its early years it was studiously restrained in tone. Nevertheless, it was an 'underground' publication, and officers took good care not to display it openly.

Churchill's reformative enthusiasm on behalf of the prisoners had no counterpart in his handling of staff affairs. His wish to improve the conditions of the one, and his refusal to do the same for the other was, for staff, the most typical and most depressing feature of Home Office rule after 1906. The difference in approach can be seen by a comparison of his famous speech on 20 July 1910 which is frequently quoted, and his less notable speeches about the staff. On 16 February 1911 Churchill made a definitive statement about unions which remained the official response for many years. Asked if Standing Orders could be modified to allow prison officers to hold one general meeting a year, and also to give more opportunity to the subordinate staff to present grievances, he replied that they had ample opportunity to do so. Prison officers, he ruled, were like policemen, soldiers and sailors. It was inappropriate for them to form unions. They could meet in individual prisons to discuss grievances, but the proposed meeting in a London hotel was contrary to Standing Orders. He was warned that they would organise secretly. On 2 December 1915 the Home Secretary was asked again if the warders could meet. He refused, and in the same year the underground 'Prison Officer's Federation' was formed.

The intention to form a Federation was announced in the *Magazine* in May 1915. Reference was made to an abortive attempt to form a Federation three years before, which had lacked support, and had been overtaken by the National Union of Police and Prison Officers (NUPPO) which was formed in 1913.[43] But, it was suggested, prison officers had never favoured association with the police, and wanted their own organisation. In spite of what the magazine said, there was a certain amount of support among officers for the NUPPO especially at Pentonville, where one of the officers, clerk and schoolmaster/warder Renshaw, was on the executive committee.[44] The new Federation hoped for harmonious relations with the older union.

The President of the Federation was J. Gilbert Dale,[45] who was the first chairman of NUPPO, had twice been an Independent Labour Party candidate, and was chairman of the Colston Publishing Company, which published the *Prison Officers' Magazine*. In 1916 the Federation was affiliated to the Labour Party.[46] The new organisation declared eleven aims: to maintain contact with Parliament; to throw more light on prison affairs through the press; to improve pensions; to abolish long hours in the convict service; to increase pay; to improve conditions in the Irish service; to raise the level of pay in the local service to that of the convict service; to fight for preference for civil guardsmen over outsiders for appointments to the warder grade; to vigorously resist the appointment of Army and Navy officers to superior posts; to abolish the confidential report; and to afford a permanent means of protection for officers.[47]

The very unsatisfactory situation in the Irish prisons figured prominently in the magazine. The last contribution from prisons in Eire was in January 1929. Army and Navy officers were singled out because they were the commonest, but the intention was to stop *all* direct entry.

This bold attempt to organise the staff was only modestly successful. 1916 was a very uncertain time, both for the Federation and the magazine. Many officers had gone to the war, several prisons withdrew their support, and when the petition for a war bonus failed, many officers refused to subscribe.[48] The editor was very worried, and asked in the May issue, why there was a reluctance to join. He believed that it was 'fear of the consequences', even though the membership list was secret. This was not an adequate explanation. Part of the failure to join can be ascribed to the customary reluctance of people to support staff associations, especially if, as was the case with the Federation, the association is entirely unofficial, and is not recognised by employers. But some of the unwillingness arose from the peculiarities of the prison service. Many officers supported the view that the service was a 'discipline' service, and were hesitant about going 'behind the backs of superior officers' not through fear, but because they believed it was underhand.[49] There was discussion in the *Magazine* in October 1914 about 'a furious fight going on' over unionism, which was not simply a struggle between old officers and young officers.

Detailed information about recruitment, understandably, was withheld. By July 1915 it was reported that 'about 500' had joined out of a staff of about 4,000 in England, Wales, Scotland, Ireland and the colonies. In December 1916 the editor claimed that 'almost every prison' was represented from 90 per cent in two or three, to about a dozen in one or two. It became increasingly obvious that the Federation was not going to flourish.

Then, in 1918 the NUPPO called a strike. The NUPPO committee was received by Lloyd George, who later stated that the country 'was nearer to Bolshevism that day than at any time since'.[50] The outcome of the meeting was confused, but the strikers believed that they had established the right to form a union. There was great excitement, and 96 per cent of all the London prison officers attended a meeting in Holborn Town Hall.[51] In the face of this success the Federation announced in the *Magazine* for November 1918, that it would amalgamate with the NUPPO, and 'the red 'un' stopped publication.

The success of the NUPPO was short lived. In 1919 the Police Act was passed, which forbade police officers to join a union. The NUPPO responded by calling a strike in August. Everybody who took part was instantly dismissed, including sixty-eight officers from Wormwood Scrubs, and six from Birmingham. All attempts to have the men reinstated over the ensuing years failed, and their treatment is one of the blackest episodes in English trade union history. Expectations that a Labour government would reinstate them were not realised, which was the final touch of irony in a situation of unrelieved treachery. The attitude of the Labour party disgusted and alienated the magazine, which had been very closely associated with it. Each time the question of reinstatement was raised the Home Secretary was adamant, and was warmly supported by the Prison Commissioners in their Report for 1919–20. A Departmental Committee closed the matter finally in 1925.

The government tried to placate the anger of both police and prison officers, by setting up consultative machinery in the form of a Police Federation, and a Prison Officers' Representative Board (PORB).[52] But in 1920 the *Prison Officers' Magazine* began publishing again, edited by 'E. R. Ramsay'. The latter, whose real name was Hubert Witchard, had been a prison officer, had contributed to the *Magazine* from 1914, and had taken over as editor in January 1917 when Ludlow, worn out with worry and overwork, had to retire.

When the *Magazine* ceased publication in 1918, Ramsay had become editor of the *Police and Prison Officers' Magazine*. When 'the red 'un' restarted publication, he had to defend himself frequently against the charge that he had advocated that the Wormwood Scrubs officers should strike. The officers who had been prominent in the NUPPO, now leaders in the PORB, disliked him, disapproved of the magazine, and discouraged colleagues from taking it whenever possible. Ramsay tried to encourage officers to take an active part in the PORB so that the Board would not continue to be 'dominated by a few who lack ordinary intelligence'.[53] He was condescending about the Board's achievements, including their success in changing the name 'warder' to 'officer'.[54]

Ramsay became a folk hero to an earlier generation of English prison officers. His influence on them, and ultimately on the prison system, was enormous. His early articles were highly critical, and when he became editor, the caution of the early years was completely abandoned. He became the mouthpiece of staff discontent, and built their grievances into a staff culture. He set the tone of the *Prison Officers' Magazine* for all time.

Ramsay was violently antagonistic to the Commissioners, to

governors, and to those senior uniformed staff who were unduly autocratic in their dealings with warders. In the *Magazine* for November 1914 he wrote that the Head Office was antiquated, and out of touch and sympathy with the feelings of officers. In December 1918, he referred to the 'inglorious gang of autocrats and parasites that control the prisons of the United Kingdom.' He launched personal attacks on individuals in the service, one of the most vitriolic being on the Deputy Governor of Dartmoor in the issue of January 1921.

The warders, like other working class groups at the time, were becoming increasingly impatient of the equation of ability with 'class'. They had a long history of being regarded as inferior, and their status and prospects had suffered because of the assumption that men of their 'class' could not be relied upon to take on responsible jobs. Thus, after the Gladstone Report the chief warder in charge of posts had been abolished, and since 1900 they were being squeezed out of clerical work because they were not considered intelligent or educated enough to perform it. Ramsay expressed all the smouldering anger of the uniformed staff about 'class', making the abolition of direct entry to the governor grades the spearhead of his attack.

But he was at his most venomous when he wrote about the inmates. Ramsay despised prisoners. He called them 'the scum of the earth and a pest to society',[55] 'gutter snipes',[56] and jeered at governors who were frightened by prisoners' petitions.[57] The anxiety which these created could be relieved, he suggested, by the establishment of an aeroplane service which could fly the petitions to the Home Secretary. Alternatively each prisoner could be given a telephone, and when he had 'important information' about an officer it could be transmitted quickly.[58] Article after article, cartoon after cartoon, had as their themes the contrast between the increasing freedom of the prisoners, and the continued restriction on the staff—the 'Slaves of Siberia'.[59] The post-Gladstone developments, and the Liberal reforms, by-passed the officers. In all of these views and opinions, especially of the changes in the treatment of prisoners, Ramsay received a great deal of support. As the reformative movement developed, officers increasingly agreed that their situation was becoming more and more unfavourable, and joined in his denunciation.

Because of the treatment of the 1919 strikers, relationship with the Labour Party were very frail. The inevitable break with the Howard

League and other reformative groups left the officers with very little contact with any important body. In the early days of the magazine relationships with the reformers had been good. Even as late as 1922 they were reasonable.[60] The situation had recovered from the damage done by Tallack's attacks. But as the officers reflected on the interest shown in prisoners, so the rift between them and the reformers grew. One unnamed society 'has committed the almost unpardonable error of liberating the prisoner and chaining up the officer'.[61] The break came finally in 1924 when Ramsay announced his resignation from the executive committee of the Howard League, and from the League itself because 'reform had been too one-sided'. Thereafter the League's activities were regarded with contempt.[62]

For twenty years the PORB was the official channel of communication between officers and Commissioners. It was attacked persistently by the magazine, which criticised the way it operated, and the indifference of staff to it. It was widely criticised too because it was too closely identified with the Commissioners. This was inevitable, since the officials were all serving officers, and had to consider their future in the service. It obviously lacked independence of action without a full-time official to organise it. As an example of the PORB's conservatism, it was pointed out in the *Magazine* for January 1922, that the representative from Wormwood Scrubs *opposed* the reinstatement of the strikers. In 1938 the officers were given permission to form the 'Prison Officers' Association', and the magazine became its 'official organ'.

The end of the Ruggles-Brise regime

The period finished, as it began, with an inquiry. This was carried out and published by 'The Prison System Inquiry Committee' as *English Prisons Today*. Its authors were Stephen Hobhouse and A. Fenner Brockway. It was quite different from the Gladstone Report, mainly because it was unofficial. Its origins are described in the book's Foreword. The Prison System Inquiry Committee had originally been set up by the Executive of the Labour Research Department, but in 1921 it became independent. The bulk of the book was written by Hobhouse and Brockway, who had both served sentences of imprisonment for conscientious objection, although they were helped by many people including Howard League officials, and the Reverend W. D. Morrison.

Because it was unofficial the Commissioners refused to co-operate, or to allow staff to give information, although some in fact did. Indeed the authors managed to get some views from warders, which was more than the Gladstone Committee had done. *English Prisons Today* is different from the Gladstone Report too because it is more thorough in its description of the system.

The account is, of course, highly critical of prisons. Chapter 14, on staff, is devoted mainly to proving the existence and undesirability of militarism. There are moments of shrewd objective assessment. At the beginning of the chapter there is a profound observation about the distinction between role and personality:

> It will be clear to those who have followed what has been written that even if the officers who operate the system were people of the higher type they would be able to do little to humanise it.

Later, in discussing the chief warder, it is reported that the coming of a new chief had entirely changed the discipline of the prison, although there had been no change in the governor.

English Prisons Today is in the mainstream of the reformative tradition. It strikes a blow for a change of task, declaring reformation to be the desired aim. As in other reformative literature, the prison system is heavily attacked because its structure militates against this reformative task.[63] The Report made a strong impact, and it no doubt added to the Parliamentary demands for an official investigation into prisons which had been voiced since 1918. The investigation never took place. Ruggles-Brise retired in 1921 (he died in 1935) and a substantial programme of reforms was mounted. This programme forestalled the critics, and successfully conveyed the impression that Hobhouse and Brockway were describing a historical situation which no longer existed.

Notes

1   *Daily Chronicle*, 15 April 1895 (quoted in Rose, *The Struggle for Penal Reform*, p. 64).
2   *The Times*, 14 October 1895, p. 6.
3   *The Times*, 24 April 1895, p. 9.
4   Fox, *The English Prison and Borstal Systems*, p. 57. Ruggles-Brise was knighted in 1902. The only biography of him is that by Shane Leslie, from which most of this information is drawn. Leslie made much use of his subject's unpublished autobiography.

5 Leslie, op. cit., pp. 86–7.

6 Ibid., p. 90.

7 Ibid., p. 163.

8 Ibid., p. 158.

9 Ruggles-Brise, *The English Prison System*, p. 77.

10 For discussion of this legislation, see Rose, op. cit., chs 5, 6 and 7; Fox, op. cit., pp. 56–66 and 34–5.

11 For a full account, see Ruggles-Brise, op. cit., pp. 78–82.

12 Annual Report 1898–9, pp. 7–8.

13 The variety of situations is described in the 1901–2 Annual Report, p. 447 and the 1904–5 Annual Report, p. 290. Detailed accounts of associated labour appear in most Annual Reports.

14 Annual Report 1900–1, p. 261; see also p. 525 and Annual Report 1901–2, p. 428.

15 See, for example, Annual Report 1900–1, p. 243 and p. 441.

16 Annual Report 1899–1900, pp. 198, 210, 224, 338, 399, 486. At a few prisons the prisoners did want the privilege—see pp. 301 and 405 of the same Report. For a discussion by an ex-prisoner of the bad effects of talking, see *Twenty-five Years in Seventeen Prisons* by 'No. 7', p. 215.

17 For a discussion of this, see Hobhouse and Brockway, *English Prisons Today*, p. 222 et seq.

18 Annual Report 1918–19, p. 222; *Report of Allegations against the Acting Governor of Wandsworth Prison*. See also *Quod* by Major W. Blake (the Acting Governor concerned), pp. 173–82.

19 Annual Report 1916–17, pp. 11–12.

20 Sykes, *The Society of Captives*, especially ch. 3.

21 Ibid., p. 49.

22 Ruggles-Brise, op. cit., p. 81.

23 For details of preventive detention, see relevant sections of Annual Reports, beginning with that for 1908–9, p. 23; Ruggles-Brise, op. cit., ch. 5; Fox, op. cit., p. 315 and the report, *Preventive Detention*, by the Advisory Council on the Treatment of Offenders. For an account of what it was hoped the regime would achieve, see Annual Report 1911–12, p. 198.

24 For an account of borstal, see the appropriate sections of the Annual Reports, especially 1908–9, pp. 13–16. For a modern review, see Hood, *Borstal Reassessed*. For a description of the first-grade system, see Annual Report 1908–9, app. 17 and Ruggles-Brise, op. cit., pp. 249–64.

25 Labor Information M.S.A., *Economic Development in the United Kingdom 1850–1950*, pp. 27–8.

26 For a brief account, see Williams, *The Main Currents of Social and Industrial Change 1870–1924*, p. 123 et seq.

27 Blake, op. cit., p. 88.

28 A memorandum to governors setting up the borstal organisation virtually as it is today is reprinted in Ruggles-Brise, op. cit., p. 247.

29 See Annual Report 1905–6, p. 19 and app. 17; Annual Report 1907–8, p. 19 and app. 17.
30 *The Times*, 21 June 1910, p. 4.
31 Gladstone Evidence, question 7620.
32 The articles appeared on 1, 3, 7, 10, 15, 21, 27 and 30 June and 4 July 1910: they were collected in Paterson's book, *Our Prisons*, which Hobhouse and Brockway describe as 'a kind of semi-official apologia for our prison system' (op. cit., p. 65).
33 Hansard, vol. 58, col. 1967–8, 28 February 1914.
34 Hansard, vol. 18, col. 1795, 27 November 1893.
35 Hansard, vol. 152, col. 695, 23 March 1922.
36 The promotion to principal warder was conceded only after a battle between Ruggles-Brise and the Treasury—see P.R.O. H.O.45/10025/A56902/31–33.
37 Report of the Departmental Committee, 1903, p. VII.
38 Loc. cit.
39 Leslie, op. cit., pp. 150–1.
40 Several of the prison staffs had mottoes; this was Lincoln's (*Prison Officers' Magazine*, June 1914, p. 251).
41 *Prison Officers' Magazine*, August 1920, p. 4.
42 For an outline of these events, see Slater, *The Growth of Modern England*, pp. 528–31.
43 See Reynolds and Judge, *The Night the Police went on Strike*, pp. 18–19.
44 Ibid., p. 89. Renshaw later became first Chairman of the Prison Officers' Representative Board.
45 *Prison Officers' Magazine*, November 1916, p. 314.
46 *Prison Officers' Magazine*, December 1916, p. 351.
47 *Prison Officers' Magazine*, May 1915, p. 173.
48 *Prison Officers' Magazine*, January 1916, p. 1 et seq.
49 *Prison Officers' Magazine*, July 1914, p. 274.
50 Reynolds and Judge, op. cit., p. 70.
51 *Prison Officers' Magazine*, October 1918, p. 290 et seq.
52 The Annual Report for 1918–19, pp. 28–30, gives an account of how the Board was to be organised.
53 *Prison Officers' Magazine*, November 1923, p. 281.
54 *Prison Officers' Magazine*, January 1922, p. 4.
55 *Prison Officers' Magazine*, January 1915, p. 3.
56 *Prison Officers' Magazine*, November 1914, p. 451.
57 Loc. cit.
58 *Prison Officers' Magazine*, February 1915, p. 47.
59 *Prison Officers' Magazine*, November 1914, p. 493.
60 See, for example, *Prison Officers' Magazine*, April 1922, p. 85.
61 *Prison Officers' Magazine*, February 1915, p. 44.
62 See, for example, the remarks about the *Howard League Journal* in *Prison Officers' Magazine*, December 1930, p. 355.
63 For other criticisms, see Rose, op. cit., pp. 109–10.

8   1922–45: the Paterson initiative

The golden age of prison reform

The last years of the Ruggles-Brise regime coincided with the 'Geddes Axe', and resultant drastic cuts in expenditure. Nevertheless the impetus to remove restrictions on prisoners was sustained. The new 'stage' system for convicts allowed extra privileges consequent upon promotion, the most significant of which was an increase in association. Others included activities such as chess, music, shaving, and walking in the grounds of the prison. In August 1921, Ruggles-Brise retired. During the next twenty years there was a succession of Chairmen, all of whom were career civil servants. They were M. L. Waller (1922–7), A. Maxwell (1927–32), H. Scott (1932–8), and C. D. C. Robinson (1938–42). In 1942 L. W. Fox became Chairman. None of these had the personality or ability of either Du Cane or Ruggles-Brise, and all were eclipsed by Alexander Paterson, a Commissioner, and one of the giants of prison reform.

Paterson was born in 1884 into an upper middle class family in Cheshire.[1] While at Oxford he developed a lifelong concern about poverty in London, and in 1911 wrote a very influential book on the subject called *Across the Bridges*.[2] In 1908 he became assistant director of the Borstal Association, which organised after-care. In 1909 Churchill asked him to begin the first experiment in after-care for convicts. When war broke out he led a group of Bermondsey men to join the Army, for some time refused commissioned rank, was wounded, and decorated for bravery.

His personal influence was enormous. As early as 1908 Herbert Samuel sought his advice, and as a result Paterson is said to have been responsible for some thirty amendments to the Children Act of that year. Between the wars he became the most famous prison reformer of all time. He and Waller drafted the 'Minimum Rules for the Treatment of Prisoners' of the League of Nations,[3] he spoke out against Nazi ideology in Berlin in 1935,[4] and it was to Paterson that the French appealed for support at an International Prison Commission meeting in 1937 when they wished to close the penal settlements in Guiana, which included the infamous Devil's Island.[5]

In this age of the 'anti-hero' it is difficult to understand, or envisage, the very real veneration in which Paterson was held by Chairmen of the Commissioners, governors and borstal boys. He was the product of a society which acknowledged charisma, and created popular heroes. In recent years a prevailing mood of cynicism, fathered by an obsessive interest in 'motives', has altered this. The mood of the 1950s and 1960s has been destructive of heroic images, especially those which have been erected within traditional value systems which themselves are under attack. But in the inter-war years, considerable numbers of people believed Paterson to be a great man because of his rare ability to translate penal theory into practice on a grand scale, and acclaimed him for it.

Within the prison service assessments of Paterson are varied. Most of the older senior staff subscribe to the heroic image, but some who worked under him were never sure of his sincerity. It should be added however that there is a tendency among prison staff to ascribe dubious motives to the reformer, whether in or out of the service. Certainly in the light of the changes that he introduced, it would be strange if all prison staff approved either of him or his ideas. Most officers decidedly did not. In its issue for April 1922, the *Prison Officers' Magazine* objected to his appointment.

Although he was never Chairman—he was 'a missionary not an administrator'[6]—he set the pattern for borstal which still survives. He was persistent in his efforts to introduce change, and it is probably a measure of his status, personality and knowledge that the reform programme survived the events of 1932 (see pages 157 ff). It was written of him, and quoted in the 1947 Annual Report, after his death in that year:

> One may well ask whether any one man had had knowledge at once so deep and so wide of the condition of man in captivity.

This then was the man who was appointed a Prison Commissioner in 1922 at the age of thirty-eight. He was younger than any governor in the service.

The first report after Paterson's appointment, for 1921–2, demonstrated that the reforms, already begun, were to be extended. The convict stage system was further modified, the convict 'crop' was abolished, prisoners were to be transferred in civilian clothes, the broad arrows were removed, visiting conditions were improved, talking was allowed at work, and the system of prison visitors was developed. Lady visitors were invited to visit male prisoners under twenty-one while male prisoners over twenty-one were allowed to have a male visitor. This last-named innovation has always been regarded with the utmost suspicion by the uniformed officer. These changes heralded the golden age of prison reform. The 'object in view' was defined clearly in the 1922–3 Report as 'a system of training such as will fit the prisoner to re-enter the world as a citizen'.

Borstal was to be the avenue through which change was to be introduced into the prisons. Special treatment for the young offender had become a rallying point in the reform programme in Victorian times. The Gladstone Committee stressed the need for a review of methods of dealing with young offenders, giving impetus to the faith in the 'reclamation' of the young. Borstal rose from this faith, and consequently, from its inception had always been committed to reformation. Borstal was, by definition, not prison, and it was in the borstal service that Paterson, with the support of sympathetic Chairmen, began his work.

Paterson wanted to give to the borstal boy something of the happiness and pride which, he believed, characterised the experience of the public school boy. The basic structure was the house system, headed by a housemaster, supported by a matron and officers. On this public school model, staffed by housemasters many of whom wanted to help boys whom they genuinely believed to be deprived through society's failure, there developed the most famous method of dealing with young offenders which the world has ever seen. Its ingredients were singularly English and middle class, and substantially pre-war in emphasis. Attempts to transplant the system to other countries, and to perpetuate the original system in the 1960s, have been generally unsuccessful.

Once again it is important to try to recapture the spirit of the times in which borstal was developed. The paternalism which underlay the system, and the readiness of large numbers of borstal boys to accept this paternalism, are very much out of tune with the distrust of authority, and the comparative sophistication, of the post-war teenager. Today the middle class housemaster trying to help 'lads', is viewed with a mixture of derision and suspicion. But in the 1930s many inmates were impressed by the fact that people from upper classes were anxious to teach and train them. Interested people in society were impressed as well. Of W. W. Llewellin it was said that he did not have to march to Lowdham (see below); he was a wealthy man and 'could have been on the golf course'.[7]

By 1930 the borstal system was well established and highly regarded by those interested in reform. The officers no longer wore uniforms and some at least had entered into the spirit of the venture, by giving up spare time for teaching boys. In May 1930 one of the most remarkable events in English penal history took place. A group of staff and boys marched in stages from Feltham Borstal in Middlesex, to Lowdham Grange in Nottinghamshire, and set about building an open borstal, the first open penal establishment in England. The march was led by W. W. Llewellin, who has the unique distinction amongst English governors of being described as a 'twentieth-century saint'.[8] Paterson's calm assumption that this revolutionary idea would be acceptable, is illustrated by the style of the first announcement that Lowdham was to be built. It is by no means clear that this was to be an open institution, nor are any potential problems even mentioned.[9] In 1935 Llewellin led a similar march from Stafford, to Freiston near Boston in Lincolnshire. A second open borstal, North Sea Camp, was built there. The rigours of life there, and especially the very heavy work, made the Camp at the time a symbol of all that was challenging in borstal. It was a symbol of the rejection of the torpor and misery of the treadwheel. On 1 April 1938 yet another open borstal was started, Hollesley Bay in Suffolk.

In many respects the innovations in prison were even more spectacular because the traditional faith in the reclamation of the young, central in the English attitude to offenders, did not extend to adults. Some of the most notable reforms in the 1920s and 1930s were the consolidation of after-care arrangements, the institution of a prison newspaper, the introduction of an earnings scheme, and 'accumulated visits'. Pictures, wireless and the cinema added to a growing complex of facilities. Of great significance was the removal of the vestiges of the pivot of the Victorian system. The period of separate confinement was abolished in the Prison Rules of 1930.

Reformative zeal reached a new peak on 27 May 1936. It was on that day, for the first time, English adult prisoners slept in open conditions. This was at New Hall Camp near Wakefield. The site had been acquired in 1933, and had been prepared by a daily working party. It was reported in the 1936 Annual Report that on 27 May 1936 twenty prisoners, two officers, and a housemaster slept there from

Monday to Friday, and from January 1937 stayed there all the time.

The response of the prison governors to these developments was predictable. Like other employees, they were anxious to please their employers, and, except on rare occasions, they tended to react to the power and the influence of Paterson and his disciples with applause. Consequently it is not at all uncommon to find in the Annual Reports statements about the improved behaviour of prisoners which are ridiculous, like this from the 1924–5 Report (p. 26):

> The prisoner understands that while discipline is fully main-
> tained, he is being subjected to a scheme of training which has
> been devised for his benefit; and that the Governors and
> officers with whom he has to deal, though firm in their control,
> are friends and not enemies. It continues to be true that most
> prisoners now consider the man who misconducts himself, and
> resists authority, as a nuisance; instead of regarding him as a
> hero, as used to be the case.

In the same Report it was recorded that at one of the earliest governors' conferences which was convened, governors asked that prisoners should be broken up into parties of about fifty, each under a housemaster.

This welter of reforms made England a world centre of the prison reform movement. English staff were detached for periods of duty to many different countries, and in 1936 the practice began, which is still continued, of holding courses for overseas prison staff.

Although the period under discussion is so recent, it is very difficult to gauge the attitude of the community to these radical changes in the prison system. There was little expressed criticism in Parliament. On the contrary, while some Members praised the system, others criticised it for not having gone far enough. There were still occasional demands for an inquiry, and for a Royal Commission. Correspondents to *The Times*, similarly, welcomed the changes or claimed that they had not gone far enough. The organised reform groups were by no means satisfied.[10]

Sir Harold Scott, the Chairman in the 1930s, was very conscious of an anti-reform lobby. Although Sir John Gilmour, the Home Secretary, told the Commons in December 1932 that he was not aware that disturbances were increasing in prisons, in fact he was very worried. Scott recounts how Sir John 'had evidently come to the

Home Office well primed by critics of prison reform.[11] Scott also detected, in 1932, a 'noticeable reaction against the last ten years of Paterson's regime'.[12] Paterson himself spoke at the Annual Borstal Dinner in 1930 of a 'tremendous lot of criticism'.[13] But with the exception of the views in the *Prison Officers' Magazine*, very little of this criticism was expressed openly.

A unique event in English prison history was to test the relative strengths of the opposing factions. This was the Dartmoor mutiny of 1932, the greatest crisis which the Commissioners, staff, and reformers had ever faced. Amazingly, the reformative movement survived it, together with a number of unpleasant incidents in other prisons, and contained the pressure to revert to the old regime. Their success in doing so is a useful measure of the sympathy of the community for prison reform at the time.

The mutiny is worthy of detailed discussion not only because it was an important event, but because it was, in a sense, a dress rehearsal for the much less serious, but in effect much more devastating, Mountbatten Inquiry.

The Dartmoor mutiny

During the last months of 1931, the Governor of Dartmoor became apprehensive about behaviour in the prison. Many ominous items had been found, including home-made keys, 'coshes', ropes, and hacksaw blades. In January 1932 there were complaints about the porridge, in England the most important physical symbol of the experience of imprisonment. Tension increased on the 22nd, when a prisoner severely wounded an officer with a razor blade fastened to a piece of wood. The next day the prisoners were assembled, as usual, in the chapel to hear the week's news. They were abusive, and it was only with difficulty that the Governor got a hearing. He apologised about the porridge, explaining that he was arranging for an extra issue of food, and that in future the cook would himself prepare the porridge. The Governor then informed the Commissioners, and an Assistant Commissioner went to the prison. The local police were also alerted.

On Sunday 24 January all the staff were called in. The day began with a series of incidents, reports of which were confused. Since the prisoners could not be sure of what was happening, this stage in the proceedings provides a profitable case study of the fantasies which develop in prison where information is restricted, and often un-reliable. In spite of the obvious restlessness in the prison, it was decided that the normal routine should be followed, which included a parade for chapel. It was on the parade ground that the riot began.

Channels of communication between prisoners had been open for some years, and preparation had been reasonably thorough. A ringleader gave the order 'Draw your sticks,' a significant remark more appropriate to a senior officer, and there occurred:[14]

> the first English prison mutiny within living memory where the convicts have through violent action obtained control of a prison for some hours.

Naturally the staff, being heavily outnumbered, failed to control them. The situation became extremely dangerous, a police official remarking that if the mutiny had succeeded 'it would have meant the sack of Princetown'.[15] In fact no prisoners escaped. They were pre-vented from doing so partly because of police help, but mainly because of the use of firearms. The police, already standing by in Plymouth and in the county, were called in by a resourceful gate officer when the Governor was cut off inside the prison. They helped to drive the prisoners back to their cells. The staff surrounding the perimeter wall were issued with firearms, which were in common use on outside working parties. When prisoners tried to scale the walls, the pointing of revolvers was followed by the firing of carbines. Two prisoners were wounded, one seriously, and this both angered and deterred the mutineers. Eventually they were contained.

An inquiry was held after the mutiny by Mr Herbert du Parcq, KC. His account and conclusions, but not the evidence, were published in 1932. In his conclusions, Du Parcq dismissed suggestions that the mutiny was due to 'humane' treatment, changes in administration in the prison, or the sinister activities of prison visitors. Nor did the grievances of the prisoners justify the riot. A small number of officers were guilty of 'irregularities and worse', but this fact may have aided some of the mutineers, not caused the mutiny itself. Once the trouble had started, Du Parcq believed, the Governor had made an error in addressing the men in the chapel, and it had been a mistake to allow the prisoners out for exercise on the parade ground.

Du Parcq offers no explanation for the mutiny. He was sure that the 'humane' treatment of prisoners, of which he approved, had not contributed to the disorder. He was wrong. Dartmoor prison in 1932 was a very different place from what it had been thirty years before. The reforms which had been introduced had created an inmate community, able to communicate, and thus able to organise. The origins of the mutiny lay in the social dynamics which association initiates. New stresses arise among prisoners, and between prisoners and staff, which are difficult to ease in the secure prison. There has to be an outlet.

The fact that association creates as much stress and dissatisfaction as it removes, is confirmed by prisoners' accounts of their experiences. The prisoner who is propelled into an inmate society which can be only loosely supervised by staff, is likely to find himself from time to time in a situation which may be intolerable, and from which he must find relief. At the same time, with the greater freedom which association brings he is probably going to reflect on the increased feasibility of escape. And finally, much to the dismay of liberal administrators, as more restrictions are removed, those which remain become more intolerable. Days when hair was cropped, food was meagre, silence was imposed, and officers carried guns are soon forgotten, and eventually it becomes apparent that reformation, which means something more than the issue of extra letters, logically demands the removal of all restrictions. At last the community of inmates is left with only one major restriction, the wall, which is the most intolerable of all.

To the pressures inherent in the experience of imprisonment then are added the pressures of intra-group life consequent upon association, and increased, rather than reduced, resentment at being confined. Under the separate system relief could be found by attempts to escape, which were rare, 'smashing up' cell furniture, attempts at suicide, and so on. While such events were disturbing for staff they could be dealt with. In a regime which allows association, new social and psychological pressures are relieved in new ways. The position in such a regime is that a majority group of prisoners confronts a minority group of staff. Physical control is no longer possible, and different techniques have to be applied. It has been shown that the main one is the promise of reward. In this changed situation it is obvious that the staff cannot know what is going on. Inmates are encouraged to report possible trouble, but this all. The inter-group, and intra-group, culture and relations in the inmate community which necessarily develop, do not concern staff. The 'contamination' issue which is so real is ignored, and concealed by claims about the success of classification.

The pressures which develop in such a community are considerable. When there is a community of prisoners serving fairly long sentences, who have little interest in the reward system, and enjoy communication with each other, there is likely to be trouble unless there is a 'safety valve'. If perimeter security is firm—that is, reinforced with firearms—then there is likely to be a riot. This is the situation in the United States. In England the riot is rare, partly because of the reward system, partly because very long sentences are unusual, but mainly because as the regime allowed more association, escape became easier. Not only did it become easier, but it was condoned and, at an 'assumed' level accepted as a price which had to be paid for giving prisoners more freedom. Escapes thus relieved stress, and obviated the need for more staff to cope with the changed situation. In a sense the Governor of Dartmoor precipitated the mutiny. He tightened up security. He would not condone escaping and it was reported in *The Times* on 27 January 1932 that the real grievance of the convicts was that: 'the Governor has repeatedly frustrated efforts to escape'. This frustration was the catalyst which touched off the mutiny, the ingredients for which are present in every prison where the inmates are allowed the freedom to associate. Had the Governor condoned escaping, it is highly unlikely that there would have been any mutiny.

The *Prison Officers' Magazine*, discussing the mutiny, eulogised the Dartmoor staff. Ignoring Du Parcq's adverse remarks (the Commissioners ignored them as well: no action was taken) it was suggested that a roll of honour be set up with all the names of the staff inscribed on it. The lessons which had to be learnt from the mutiny were, according to the March 1932 issue of the *Magazine*, simple and to the point. Adequate arms were required since:

'Personality' does not count where communists and bandits are concerned. The only 'personality' they respect is lead or cold steel.

Further there was a need to curb the:

so-called reformer type, most of whose followers are of the conscientious objector type who sees red in any man in blue whether he is a prison or a police officer. Borstalizing in prisons will not do.

In a later article in the June issue, the Commissioners were held responsible because they had reduced the numbers of staff.

An angry outburst from the community would have been a normal reaction to these events. In fact such comment as there was, expressed the view that Dartmoor contained a special kind of prisoner. Dartmoor was different from the rest of the system. *The Times*, although commenting that these events 'seem to belong to another age, or at least to some other country',[16] nevertheless considered that:[17]

> there will be no question of reversing the humane tendencies in prison administration because of these events at Dartmoor.

Comment in Parliament was surprisingly slight. There was a demand, in February 1932, which was refused, for the Du Parcq evidence to be published, and questions were asked in May about the prosecution of those officers who had allegedly committed offences at Dartmoor.

From the point of view of both the reformers and the prison service, however, the situation in 1932 was grave. Gilmour was very worried both about Dartmoor, and other troubles which attracted adverse publicity. There were disturbances at Chelmsford which prevented local people sleeping,[18] and the suicide of a prisoner at Birmingham excited discussion in Parliament and drew criticism of the staff. After the Dartmoor mutiny, as after the escapes of Blake and Mitchell in 1966, the press were zealous in the reporting of escapes, trouble, and even rumours of trouble. The situation worsened later in 1932, when two prisoners got a ladder and scaled the wall at Dartmoor, one for the second time.[19] This event attracted some attention, as did an assault on the Governor, rumours of insubordination, and the news that there were mounted guards outside the walls, and armed guards inside.[20] There was a change of governor and further changes in a staff which was already very different from that at the time of the mutiny.[21]

Scott, who was Chairman at the time, writes of 'frequent interviews' with Gilmour 'since it was quite on the cards that he might decide to make a drastic change in the control of HM Prisons'. Eventually Scott told his wife: 'We keep our governors, and I think I've won the Home Secretary to our point of view.'[22] The Home Secretary's intentions were not made clear by Scott, but it is evident that some kind of drastic action was being contemplated. Yet the unseen, unarticulated pressures on Gilmour were resisted. The impetus of the reformers was barely touched, and their victory was completed when Gilmour, approached about the North Sea Camp project, 'entered into it with gusto'.[23]

There were two principal factors at work which restrained the anger of the community. The first was the weight of opinion supporting reform. The second was undoubtedly the personal influence of Paterson. Scott was himself a confirmed disciple, which must have influenced the advice which he gave Gilmour. Paterson assisted Du Parcq in the inquiry. Now while the latter emphasised in his Report, that Paterson 'scrupulously abstained' from any attempt to influence him, Du Parcq was in the situation in which outsiders always find themselves when they try to discover what is going on in a prison. They are unable to do so. In this very vulnerable situation it would be very strange if a personality as powerful as that of Paterson made no impact on Du Parcq.

Reformation and the officer. I: crystallising a conflict

The total effect of the changes in the regimes, and of the establishment of open institutions, was to increase physical freedom of prisoners, to allow them much more association, and to make the physical restraints of the individual cell ineffective. By 1945 the majority of prisoners were held only by the perimeter wall.

It has already been shown that, because of the primary controlling task, there is a simple, inescapable and irreducible conflict between the staff, especially the uniformed officer, and the prisoner. The latter is not usually willing to accept the justice of his position, resents being dependent on people who cannot put his interests first, and will not enter into the observance of rules dictated by a regime which is alien and repugnant to him. The perennial and universal central fact of prison life, compared with which everything else is incidental, is that the officer must contain, restrict, and reduce the movement and initiative of prisoners, and that the latter seek to increase it. As the reformative movement gained impetus, and prisoners were allowed to talk, to associate, and to live in open conditions, the task of control became more difficult. Where a group of prisoners could not be enticed by the promise of reward, control was impossible. On one page of the Annual Report for 1922–3, three changes are announced which reduced supervision; unsupervised work parties—the 'honour parties'—abolition of officers on raised platforms in workshops, and removal of officers from the front of the chapel to the side and the back. New dangers were created, of assault, and of condemnation when custody was breached. And gradually there came to fruition that incipient feeling which had been noted in the period up to 1921, that all the organisational resources at a time of great stringency, all the articulated sympathy of the community, were addressed to the prisoner. This feeling on the part of officers is clearly justified by the evidence. Once this basic clash of interests is appreciated, it is easy to see how inevitable was the development of the schism with the reforming groups which has already been mentioned. On one occasion the Prison Officers' Association discussed a resolution that all assaults by prisoners upon officers should be tried by the civil authorities and not by the Prison Commissioners. One officer:[24]

> stated that the biggest argument against the resolution was that it would have the support of the Howard League for Penal Reform.

There were real practical difficulties under the new regime. Ruggles-Brise had understood something of the relationship between regime and staff structure. He had asked for more staff. The greatly increased freedom under the new regime meant that the numbers of staff were quite insufficient to exert any meaningful control over the prisoners. Although there was some increase, the ratio remained low. And so there was talk of understaffing. An example occurs in the trial of the Dartmoor mutineers. An officer was asked if 'When a riot of this kind occurs the prison officials are helpless?', to which he replied that the prison was understaffed.[25] The authorities claimed frequently that there was no shortage of staff. But the Commissioners and the staff were talking about two different situations. Statements about the adequacy or inadequacy of staff are meaningless without a clear definition of what the organisation is trying to do, and what the role of any section of the staff is to be. When, in a prison or mental hospital, inmates are secured by locks, few staff are needed to look after them. Under such conditions a prison wing of sixty inmates can be manned by four officers. If, on the other hand, there is association, with activities that staff are not only supposed to supervise, but are encouraged to join in, then very many more staff are needed. They are needed both to control in a very much more volatile situation, and to 'train', 'treat' or 'reform' the inmates.

Basic questions about the effect of changes in organisational goals are rarely asked, which is hardly surprising, since to adjust staff numbers realistically in prisons during this period would have meant doubling the establishment of officers. The latter, in the changed situation, were never able to communicate adequately with the Home Office and the Treasury about the problem, and so numbers of staff continued to be calculated to deal with a historical situation which no longer existed.

Although the Commissioners were not quite devoid of awareness of the strain on the staff, they would not, and financially could not, cope with the rather startling implications of the changed situation. They noted blithely in the 1932 Annual Report that:

> the development of the employment and educational side of prison work continues to make increasing demands on the energies and intelligence of the staff.

In 1927 an increase in educational and training work is reported in spite of overcrowding and strain. Borstal was especially busy. In the 1934 Report it was stated that the increase in the number of committals 'strained the accommodation of the six existing Institutions to the utmost'. The Commissioners developed two means of avoiding the question of the strain imposed on the officer. The first was usually a variant of what came to be known in the prison service as 'kiddology'—that is, the meeting of every expression of concern with bland assurances of admiration for the way staff are coping, as in the 1921–2 Report (p. 28):

> We thank the prison staffs for their willing co-operation in progressive measures . . .

And the 1932 Report (p. 30):

> To all these demands there has been a praiseworthy response.

The second sprang from the mood of total commitment to the new measures on the part of the Commissioners. It was to regard talk of personal difficulty, demands for assistance, or improved conditions, as demonstrating lack of initiative, unwillingness to co-operate, or a display of undesirable self-interest. This was well known as Paterson's attitude,[26] and Watson gives an example. On one occasion Watson pointed out to Paterson that some assistant housemasters, whose posts were non-pensionable, unestablished, and ill paid, were anxious to be promoted to housemaster. Paterson's reply was:[27]

I don't want to attract to this service young men who are concerned about their pay, or their careers, or their prospects of marriage. I only want those who are so keen about this job that *nothing else matters.*

This attitude is still common in the borstal service.

As far as the uniformed staff were concerned, all that mattered during the period was that the status of the prisoners was being elevated at their expense. The *Prison Officers' Magazine* continued its opposition to this trend with increasing force. As early as October 1923 the complaint was made that the 'borstal game is being carried a bit too far', and later, in December, that when officers were assaulted the latter were expected to accept that 'the dear prisoners did not mean it'. In March 1923 there appeared the first of many hundreds of letters which complained of discipline being weakened due to 'so-called reform, in which prisoners are humoured and "coddled" and made heroes of'.

It is a common experience in organisations that, given time, changes are accepted by the staff. It is a measure of the deep-seatedness of the officers' objections that they never accepted the reformative changes. In August 1941, twenty years after the new policies were introduced, a letter appeared in the *Prison Officers' Magazine* which summarised the experience of the English prison officer since 1921:[28]

Under cover of the staff reform methods during the last five years and more have moved to a high degree, comparable only with the best humanitarian methods of the social standards in this country. During the same period, five years and more, especially prior to the forming of the Prison Officers' Association, how much had been done for the staffs? *The reply must inevitably be—very little indeed.*

The borstal housemaster

One of the unique features of the English prison system is the borstal housemaster. It is necessary now to consider the development of this position because he personified the reformative mood, and influenced the development of the role of the uniformed officer. Originally introduced as a 'tutor', his role was partly disciplinary and partly teaching. One of Paterson's first acts was to increase the establishment of tutors. In 1921–2, it was reported that four assistant tutors were added to the established six. Their appointment enabled the development of the house system complete with housemasters 'monitors, house colours, cricket and football teams'.[29] Soon the housemasters, as they came to be known, had assistants to help: 'so much is his absence felt during leave, sickness, and even short intervals of necessary rest.'[30] Paterson saw these housemasters as the people who would individualise the treatment and training of the boys, induce a sense of community, and generally foster the corporate spirit which, allegedly, was a precious hallmark of the public school. Housemasters were usually well educated, often drawn from upper middle class families, and reformative in intent. Of thirty-nine governors and housemasters appointed in the years 1931 and 1932, eleven were ex-service officers and ten had been to public school.[31] As well as coping with the hurly-burly of sports days, they carried out relatively sophisticated work such as vocational testing, for which they were trained by the National Institute of Industrial Psychologists.[32] Although often described as the head of a house team their work was obviously with the inmates. The role was regarded as an excellent innovation by people sympathetic to reform, about which only good could be said.

The uniformed officer held a different view about the housemasters. Their appointment provided yet another piece of evidence that more resources were being deployed to meet the needs of inmates. In addition their method of work, which involved privacy in their dealings with lads, heightened the officers' apprehension that they were becoming excluded from an increasingly close relationship between the superior grades and the inmate.

The officers soon realised too that the introduction of the 'tutor' was going to reduce their chances of promotion.[33] The Commissioners looked for qualities for this grade which officers did not have. The recruitment of 'tutors' led to a raising of the standard of the governor grades. The idea of recruiting university graduates, the *Magazine* believed to be of very dubious value.[34] The campaign which had begun in 1915 against direct entry was maintained, and in March 1924 the subject was raised in Parliament for the first time.

The officers were right to be apprehensive. The view, which had been expressed in the Gladstone Evidence, that officers would not make good governors was being translated into administrative action. During the years 1927–32 no discipline officer was promoted to governor or deputy governor,[35] although out of thirty-nine people appointed to governor, housemaster, and assistant housemaster in 1931 and 1932, four of the twelve housemasters and one of the nineteen assistants were discipline officers.[36]

On the surface the establishment of a 'Staff Course' at Wakefield Prison in 1935, for officers likely to receive accelerated promotion, looked hopeful. Six officers attended.[37] But this was not really acceptable to staff either, and the Home Secretary was asked if he knew about discontent among senior officers because of the scheme.[38] The officers were dissatisfied because they have always wanted a 'unified service', that is to say a service where all promotions are selected from the rank next below. Support for this system, where all would begin in the basic grade, is common amongst senior officers for obvious reasons.

Individual officers often express the view that they do not wish the abolition of direct entry. The reasons are complex. A lingering respect for people from upper classes, and resentment at being commanded by an ex-officer are probably uppermost. Du Parcq commented in his Report on the opposition to the Governor of Dartmoor, the first ex-officer to hold the post,[39] and was attacked in the *Prison Officers' Magazine* as a result.[40] But even in the *Magazine* there are occasional letters expressing support for direct entry.[41]

The system of appointing direct to senior grades, then, affected promotion. But the system did something else which in the opinion of the officers was even more disastrous. It gave reformation a priority which, in the opinion of officers, literally wrecked the prison system. The perennial complaints and protests of officers which appeared year after year in the *Magazine* are summed up by Harley Cronin. Cronin writes with authority. He spent thirty-six years in the prison service, mainly as full-time General Secretary of the Prison Officers' Association. His views on prisoners and matters concerned with prison reform have always been supported by prison officers. According to Cronin the influence of direct appointees was widespread, and, as far as he was concerned, disastrous. He wrote in *The Screw Turns*:

The rot—for I think the borstal system is rotten—began, in my view, *when it was decided to introduce people from outside the prison service to act as housemasters*, as they were called. These newcomers vied with each other in advocating relaxation of every reasonable restriction on the boys' behaviour—restrictions that would be enforced in any youth hostel, or even holiday camp—until borstal institutions have become today not unlike public schools, but without public school discipline. (His italics.)

And in a letter to the *Prison Officers' Magazine*, December 1967:

The later blow came when, with the passing of time, some of these 'outsiders' were promoted to the governor grades and transferred into the prisons proper and, in certain cases, conveyed with them their borstal ideas. The process has increased throughout the years with disastrous consequences to normal prison discipline.

Reformation and the officer. II: a lowering of status

The question which is now to be discussed, is whether or not the officer was as little involved in training as is implied by the description of his situation so far. After all, it may be argued, the change of title from warder to officer in 1921, was significant, as was the wearing of civilian clothes in borstal, the discussion of his place in the house team, in *The Principles of the Borstal System*, and his work as a teacher. Furthermore, even in the pages of the *Prison Officers' Magazine* he was once described, in May 1930, as 'a social reformer'. Surely these are indications that he was involved in the new developments?

It must be conceded that some borstal officers were, and still are, involved in training programmes for the inmates to a degree which would surprise colleagues in prison. Such training as they did, however, was in addition to their primarily controlling role. The borstal officer who wants to spend a lot of time on training has either to become a housemaster, or to take up another job. It is important to note too that, although borstal attracted a great deal of attention, the numbers of staff and inmates involved were very small in relation to the total numbers. Most officers then, as now, work in closed prisons.

The officers for their part tried to claim that they were so involved and therefore ought to be paid more, when a committee under Lord Stanhope considered their position in 1923:[42]

It has been impressed on us that a Prison Officer is no longer a mere turnkey and disciplinarian, but is required to take his part in the endeavours which have been increasingly made of recent years to reform the offender and to restore him to sound citizenship.

But the Committee would not accept this. They considered that the new measures had added to the work of superior grades, and had not added 'materially' to the burden of work of individual officers. In a minute to the Home Secretary the PORB vigorously disagreed.[43] In fact Stanhope was right. If the officer's job *was* more onerous under the new regime, it was because he was presented with a more difficult problem of control, and not because he was called upon to use training skills.

The true situation can be adduced from the development of borstal. Here, if anywhere, there was a case for claiming that the officer's job was more complicated because of his involvement in training. But the borstal officer was only marginally concerned with training, and his problems of control were eased by a rewards system of staggering proportion, the peak of which was a movable release date. The borstal principal officer, for example, has had a much easier job since the 1920s. He had been relieved of the responsibility for a wing or house by the housemaster, and was able to contract out of the training system almost completely. The new problems of coping with increasing documentation, and of dealing with aggressive boys, denied promotion or release, has always rested squarely on the housemaster. The paradox was that in a system devoted to training, the officers and more particularly the principal officers, were largely excluded from it. In the prisons, their involvement was negligible. The officer's job was indeed more complicated after 1921, but not through involvement in training.

The Stanhope Committee Report was a depressing document in every way for the officers. It began with the observation that the Committee were 'impressed with the high morale which exists in the service', but its refusal to concede that the officers had a case led to an angry reaction. The *Prison Officers' Magazine* of November 1923 dismissed the Report contemptuously as a 'farce'. The PORB warned the Home Secretary that the Board would lose its credibility if the Report were accepted.[44] The Home Secretary, after discussion with the Board, and no doubt aware of the boost which might be given to the *Prison Officers' Magazine* if the staff got nothing, pointed out to the Treasury that dissatisfaction among officers was strong enough 'to give grounds for some uneasiness'.[45]

The Treasury was very reluctant, and attacked the PORB for bringing pressure when it had no case.[46] The Board met the Home Secretary again and described Stanhope as 'a class report',[47] perhaps because the report was more sympathetic to the position of the governors, who had not had a rise since 1878![48] After great difficulty the Treasury agreed to make small concessions in respect of pay[49] which the officers regarded as quite inadequate. The whole affair badly damaged the image of the PORB as a negotiating body, and provided fuel for Ramsey in his consistent demands for a proper staff association.

The uniformed officer suffered certain other material disadvantages during this period, which naturally affected his attitude to his work. It is reported in the 1925–6 Annual Report that, because of financial stringency twenty-five local prisons were closed between 1914 and 1926. The staff were posted to other prisons. This created a shortage of quarters, and a serious reduction in promotion prospects. Stanhope, pointing this out, reported that, as a result, promotion to principal officer took twenty-four years in local prisons, and twenty-one years in convict prisons. Thus the reduction of promotion prospects to the governor grades because of direct entry, was paralleled by a long delay in promotion to principal and chief officer. To both must be added a third which arose as a result of the steady development of the clerical staff. Although the clerk and schoolmaster/warder had been established in 1895, the civilian clerk was not ousted from the service. In 1921 the Civil Service clerks in the prisons were assimilated to the junior clerical grade of the Civil Service, as were all the clerical staff at Head Office.[50] At the time of the Stanhope Committee, uniformed officers could, after a qualifying examination, be promoted to clerk and schoolmaster or to new-grade clerk or new-grade schoolmaster doing work of a higher standard.[51] In 1931 all these grades were assimilated to the Civil Service. Relationships between these various groups had been very brittle in the 1920s, as the *Prison Officers' Magazine* frequently made clear.

After 1930, clerical staff began to be recruited from the open competition for clerical grades of the Civil Service, or from examinations for members of the minor and manipulative grades. The result was more than just an 'influx of young clerical officers'.[52] Another avenue of promotion had been blocked for uniformed staff.

Prison staff everywhere, faced with change, the introduction of new skills in which they do not share, and a resultant uncertainty of status, tend to take consolation in the belief that their work is dangerous. It is often the last defence against diminishing status. In the United States the cult of the prison official risking his life to quell vicious convicts, has been institutionalised in the cinema. When all is said, the officer is physically vulnerable and must be able to 'handle himself'. Even this consolation was removed, and the belief that progress could only be made because uniformed staff were at the periphery ensuring stability at some personal risk, was denied. In the evidence to the Stanhope Committee the analogy with the police service was claimed yet again. The Committee reported that police work was definitely superior. Policemen had to know law, use more initiative, and were more likely to be injured. The Committee drew up a table to show that the policeman, the railwayman, the miner, and the quarryman, were all much more likely to be injured than the prison officer (see Table 2) and so in every major respect this was an

Table 2   Fatal and serious accidents as a percentage of staffs in a representative year (Stanhope Report, p. 2)

Occupation	Percentage
Railways	2·13
Mines and quarries	7·41
Factories and workshops	1·66
Metropolitan Police	10·87
Prison staff	1·97

The figure for prison staff includes trivial injuries.

unhappy time for the prison officer. In these years of the boldest reforms which the English system had ever seen, the officer was excluded from the socially approved work of rehabilitation. The controlling task, with its coercive overtones, was depressed and the status of its agent, the uniformed officer, was depressed with it.

There was one significant improvement in the officer's position in the period. Following the 1919 strike, the prison staff had been excluded from the Whitley Council negotiating machinery when it was established in that year. In 1939, after twenty years' representation by the PORB—which the Commissioners regarded as satisfactory, and the officers regarded as unsatisfactory—the Commissioners informed the staff that in principle it had been agreed that they could form a staff association. The Prison Officers' Association has since represented the discipline and 'works' staff in the prison service. The first meeting of the new council was in May 1941.[53]

Escapes—measuring task failure

As the years went on, it became increasingly difficult for the uniformed staff to perform their controlling role. Inmates were given more and more freedom, and staff became more and more anxious. It is possible to measure the degree of task failure by an analysis of the figures for escape, and attempted escape, during the period. The figures in Table 3 provide objective evidence that the prison system, as reformative measures were introduced, progressively failed to ensure safe custody.

Table 3   *Escapes and attempts to escape, 1895–1945**

Year	Daily average population (male)		Escapes and attempts (male)	Escapes and attempts per 1,000 of population†
1895	Prison	14,954	9	0·6
1900–1	Prison	14,459	20	1·4
1905–6	Prison	18,398	16	0·9
1910–11	Prison	17,861	5	
	Borstal	462	6	
	Total	18,323	11	0·6
1920–1	Prison	8,667	10	
	Borstal	906	59	
		9,573	69	6·9
1921–2	Prison	9,784	11	
	Borstal	1,007	38	
		10,791	49	4·4
1922–3	Prison	9,536	16	
	Borstal	1,021	45	
		10,557	61	5·5

* Details are in Annual Reports for respective years. The figures for the war years 1914–18 and 1939–45 are omitted since factors such as shortages of staff and bombing can be claimed to artificially distort them.

† Daily average to the nearest thousand.

Year	Daily average population (male)		Escapes and attempts (male)	Escapes and attempts per 1,000 of population
1923–4	Prison	9,180	23	
	Borstal	937	46	
		10,117	69	6·9
1924–5	Prison	8,837	30	
	Borstal	971	37	
		9,808	67	6·7
1925–6	Prison	8,592	23	
	Borstal	1,043	45	
		9,635	68	6·8
1926–7	Prison	8,853	21	
	Borstal	1,119	44	
		9,972	65	6·5
1927	Prison	9,121	32	
	Borstal	1,179	44	
		10,300	76	7·6
1928	Prison	9,102	17	
	Borstal	1,203	56	
		10,305	73	7·3
1929	Prison	8,862	27	
	Borstal	1,232	65	
		10,094	92	9·2
1930	Prison	9,276	24	
	Borstal	1,285	68	
		10,561	92	8·4
1931	Prison	9,396	22	
	Borstal	1,488	66	
		10,884	88	8·0
1932	Prison	10,211	31	
	Borstal	1,781	55	
		11,992	86	7·1
1933	Prison	10,249	34	
	Borstal	1,931	137	
		12,180	171	14·3

Year	Daily average population (male)		Escapes and attempts (male)	Escapes and attempts per 1,000 of population†
1934	Prison	9,606	28	
	Borstal	1,887	102	
		11,493	130	11·9
1935	Prison	8,893	16	
	Borstal	1,694	84	
		10,587	100	9·1
1936	Prison	8,331	15	
	Borstal	1,608	116	
		9,939	131	13·1
1937	Prison	8,162	15	
	Borstal	1,732	135	
		9,894	150	15·0
1938	Prison	8,368	25	
	Borstal	2,020	186	
		10,388	211	21·1

Several points about these figures should be borne in mind. In the Annual Report for 1960 the claim is made that the daily average population is not a fair basis from which to examine escapes. The daily average, it is pointed out, does not represent:[54]

> the total number of individual prisoners who have been in custody during the year, each of whom must be regarded as an escape risk; that total would be more nearly represented by the figure of those in custody at the beginning of the year, together with those received during the year, although some allowance must be made for the fact that some individuals may be received more than once.

Such a total cannot be deduced. For example, there is absolutely no indication of the number of individuals who have been imprisoned more than once. The daily average is the most useful figure, because it conveys some idea of the size of the population through the year. It is the figure incidentally, which is used by the Commissioners themselves when discussing escapes.

Next the meaning of 'escape' must be clarified. The combination of 'escapes' and 'attempts' makes it impossible to discover how many there were in each category. Prison officials everywhere try to keep the figures of escape as low as possible, and avoid reporting attempts unless they are very serious attempts. It is likely therefore that the figures represent more escapes than attempts. Moreover, in 1929 the incidence of incipient, and occasionally actual, escape was further concealed by a subtle reclassification. 'Quitting or attempting to quit, without leave or orders, the appointed place of work, or location, in prison or ranks' was classed as 'insubordination', and appears under that heading.[55] Many occasions will have arisen when a serious escape attempt could be concealed in this way. It follows that the figures quoted in the Reports as escapes or attempts, are likely to be the absolute minimum, especially after 1929.

In spite of this steady increase in escapes there was little articulated complaint from the community. People were apparently assuaged by the Home Secretary's typical assurance in April 1928 that there was 'a careful inquiry' after an escape, or his statement in February 1928, that, in 1927, sixteen prisoners, and forty-two of the forty-four borstal boys who had escaped, had been recaptured. Credit for this, he omitted to add, was due to the police, not to the prison service. In any case people were concerned not that they were escaping justice, but that they committed offences while at large.

The officers did what they could to protest about the increasingly casual attitude to escapes. The first expression of concern was in the *Magazine* for December 1923, when it was claimed that after an escape the 'officer is usually blamed and punished unmercifully'. He was expected to control prisoners as he had in 1895, even though the aids of control had been undermined.

By 1941 the officers' views were being supported in the Commons. In April the Home Secretary was asked to inquire into the increase in assaults and escapes, and whether he would listen to the views of prison officers. He denied an increase in assaults, blamed the blackout and the use of an establishment which was not very secure for increased escapes, and said that the Commissioners were always ready to listen to staff.

This agitation by officers is of the greatest significance. It indicated that, for the first time, the Commissioners and the officers were in open conflict about the task of the prison service. Thus the quality of the differences of opinion between the two had changed dramatically since Victorian times, from arguments about conditions of service to basic disagreement about aims. The 'agitation' also provides the first illustration, that professionals within the prison system were aware that the organisation was not doing its job. This is a characteristic pattern of development in organisations which are moving away from successful task achievement. It is natural that the first people to be aware of an impending crisis should be those most closely concerned.

The Commissioners for their part did not discuss the mounting escape figures. The earliest comment is in the Annual Report for 1945. If the programme of reform was to go ahead, they obviously could not draw too much attention to escapes. The tradition was therefore subtly established that a few escapes are an inevitable, and small price to pay for the benefits of a training regime. Borstal, with its commitment to reform, communicated this attitude to prison. The open institution was a symbol, at one and the same time, of a great advance in penal treatment and a dangerous depression of the custodial priority. The last barrier—the wall—was removed. The Commissioners dealt with this by stating, as a matter of pride, in the Annual Report for 1934 that:

> new institutions are under construction at Lowdham Grange and North Sea Camp in which considerations of security have, as a result of experience, been put aside and buildings have been devised with a view solely to reformative training.

And they were careful to state, in the period after opening, how little trouble there was—a situation which, they neglected to point out, always deteriorated.

Although criticism was muted, it was evident that there was real trouble ahead. After all, events at Dartmoor were without parallel in English experience since the time of the hulks. This behaviour and the protests of officers could not easily be reconciled with the information given by the governors to the Commissioners, and purveyed by them to the public. This described prisoners grateful for the introduction of change, and borstal boys appreciative of the opportunity to indulge in a public school experience. In the Annual Report for 1932, consolation was found in the belief that the service had to deal with a new and more dangerous kind of criminal:

> There has been in recent years a change in the character of the prison population which adds materially to the difficulty of control.

There was discussion in *The Times* about London gangs organising escapes during the mutiny,[56] and in Parliament there was reference to the 'type of dangerous criminals now detained in custody in some of His Majesty's Prisons'.[57] It is possible that the presence of more serious offenders contributed to the unrest. If they were serving long sentences, it would be difficult to maintain the collusion between staff and prisoners which depended for success on the rewards system. However the statement that criminals were more difficult than hitherto, was in direct contradiction to almost every comment in the Reports. The reverse is usually asserted, and, moreover, attention is frequently drawn to the ever improving behaviour of the prisoners, as in the 1923–4 Annual Report (p. 27):

> There is no doubt that there is a different tone in the prison population of today, due partly to the fact that the majority of the persons received are of a less violent type than formerly.

Macartney is correct when he points out that:[58]

> Great play is made with 'gangsters' and 'motor bandits' and 'planned escapes' as the cause of the trouble. There have long been gangsters in prison who have planned escapes, but this did not lead to the burning down of a prison.

In any case, whether or not prisoners were more difficult during this period than previously is not only questionable, but irrelevant. Prison staff suffer from the common tendency to detect 'change and decay' all around. Borstal boys today, for example, are always less promising than they were. The reality was that the inability of the staff to deflect the incipient crises, was revealed. This inability was not the fault of any one member of staff, or of the staff collectively. In the separate system, prisoners, however difficult, could have been contained. Under the new regime they could not. The new regime created an explosive situation where: 'advantage has been taken of improved conditions by ringleaders who have incited others to abuse those improved conditions.'[59] A simple and visible example of this was the reintroduction of shaving in the 1920s. In two incidents leading to the mutiny, razor blades were used to attack staff. One of these was extremely serious and the prisoner was sentenced to twelve years' penal servitude. It also emerged that blades were used for betting.[60]

The effect of the war

The reformative spirit was kept alive right up to 1939. Optimism reached new levels when the Annual Report for 1937 discussed the possible closing of Pentonville, and the replacement of prison for women by some kind of camp. Land for the latter was bought at Stanwell in Middlesex, but the camp was never built. The land is now farmed by Feltham borstal.

The Newson Report, *Half Our Future*, observes how the war swept away the tradition which had been built up in the elementary school. In the same way the effect of the emergency on the prison service was disastrous. The standards which had been built up in the borstal service, and the spirit which was becoming a tradition, were swept away as staff and senior boys joined the forces. Prisons and borstals were reclassified, and had to cope with new problems, notably 'the London recidivist',[61] and the inevitable political prisoners and detainees. There were two main groups of these; aliens, and detainees under Defence Regulation 18B. The aliens were quite co-operative, but the '18Bs' were as difficult as the earlier political groups who have been discussed. Legal action by some detainees against governors failed.[62]

The staff, greatly reduced in numbers, had to cope with these problems in addition to the usual crises of war, such as heavy bombing in some places. In spite of this strain the Commissioners continued to introduce measures which added to it. In 1942 for instance, prisoners at all prisons were allowed to converse at exercise, some privileges were given earlier in the sentence, and Maidstone was converted into a 'training centre'.[63] But the staff situation was becoming really desperate, and the Report for 1945 is notable for the four and a half pages which are devoted to staff matters, the first time for many years that they had been discussed at such length. There was justification for concern, since it seemed as though there might be a 'serious breakdown of the machine'. The autumn of 1945 saw the staffing position reach its nadir. At the end of the war there was a new Chairman, Lionel Fox.[64] And two years later the Paterson era closed. 'A.P.' died in 1947 'in harness, at the age of sixty-three, having worn himself out in the service of his fellow men'.[65]

Notes

1 There is no published biography of Paterson. The sources from
   which this information is taken are: Sir Harold Scott, *Your Obedient*

Servant, ch. 4 and John Watson, *Which is the Justice ?*, ch. 4. The latter in turn is drawn from a 'privately printed biographical essay' by Gordon Hawkins, Watson acknowledgment. There is also some information in the Annual Report for 1947, pp. 5–7. I have also drawn on private material accumulated in conversation with prison staff who worked under him.

2 His collected papers on prison matters were published under the title, *Paterson on Prisons*, edited by S. K. Ruck.

3 Annual Report 1932, p. 30.

4 Annual Report 1947, p. 7.

5 Annual Report 1936, p. 47. Paterson's report on his visit to Devil's Island is reprinted in Ruck, op. cit., ch. 19 and app. 5.

6 Watson, op. cit., p. 63.

7 *Prison Officers' Magazine*, July 1930, p. 204.

8 Scott, op. cit., p. 77.

9 Annual Report 1929, pp. 19–20. For a description of the march, see Llewellin's account, 'Lowdham Grange, a Borstal Experiment', and Scott (who was on the march), op. cit., pp. 69–70.

10 See Rose, *The Struggle for Penal Reform*, pp. 187–8.

11 Scott, op. cit., p. 75.

12 Ibid., p. 72.

13 *Prison Officers' Magazine*, May 1930, p. 136.

14 Macartney, *Walls have Mouths*, p. 237. Macartney, in chapter 11, offers one version and interpretation of events. Macartney was sentenced to ten years' penal servitude for obtaining information calculated to be useful to an enemy. He was not at Dartmoor, but he met some of the mutineers at Parkhurst.

15 *The Times*, 27 January 1932, p. 10.

16 *The Times*, 25 January 1932, p. 13.

17 *The Times*, 8 February 1932, p. 13.

18 *The Times*, 13 December 1932, p. 12 and 28 December 1932, p. 7.

19 *The Times*, 17 November 1932, p. 14; 19 November, p. 10; 21 November, p. 12; 22 November, p. 12; 23 November, p. 12.

20 *The Times*, 5 December 1932, p. 14.

21 *The Times*, 6 December 1932, p. 16.

22 Scott, op. cit., p. 75.

23 Ibid., p. 76.

24 *Prison Officers' Magazine*, August 1945, p. 206.

25 *The Times*, 18 March 1932, p. 4.

26 Paterson, 'The Principles of the Borstal System' (unpublished) is saturated with this spirit, see especially ch. 2.

27 Watson, op. cit., p. 70 (his italics).

28 Italics in original. A charge in that year that the Commissioners did not deal promptly and sympathetically with officers' representations was denied (Hansard, vol. 370, col. 1579).

29 Annual Report 1921–2, p. 29.

30 Annual Report 1922–3, p. 28.

31 Hansard, vol. 274, col. 1030, 15 February 1933.

32 Annual Report 1936, p. 26.
33 *Prison Officers' Magazine*, May 1922, p. 118.
34 Loc. cit.
35 Hansard, vol. 276, col. 2582, 12 April 1933. It was still possible for an outsider to be appointed as a governor directly.
36 Hansard, vol. 274, col. 1030, 15 February 1933. On the other hand, there were 300 outside applicants while only thirteen clerical and subordinate staff applied. Other figures are given at vol. 241, col. 2177, 23 July 1929/30.
37 Annual Report 1933, p. 28; Annual Report 1934, pp. 43–4.
38 Hansard, vol. 296, col. 534, 13 December 1934; vol. 299, col. 540, 14 March 1935; vol. 303, cols. 529–30, 20 June 1935.
39 Du Parcq Report, pp. 9–10.
40 *Prison Officers' Magazine*, March 1932, p. 75.
41 See, for example, the issue of March 1923, pp. 82–3.
42 The Stanhope Committee's Report contains a good deal of information about conditions of service at the time.
43 P.R.O. H.O.45/11966/449102/16, 27 November 1933.
44 P.R.O. H.O.45/11966/449102/16.
45 P.R.O. H.O.45/11966/449102/17, 9 February 1924.
46 P.R.O. H.O.45/11966/449102/21.
47 P.R.O. H.O.45/11966/449102/27.
48 Stanhope Report, p. 15.
49 P.R.O. H.O.45/11966/449102/27.
50 Annual Report 1921–2, p. 28.
51 Stanhope Report, p. 7.
52 Annual Report 1939–41, p. 18.
53 Annual Report 1939–41, p. 16. See also the triumphant editorials in the *Prison Officers' Magazine*, November and December 1938.
54 Annual Report 1960, p. 116.
55 Annual Report 1932, p. 64.
56 For example, 27 January 1932, p. 12.
57 Hansard, vol. 261, col. 1166, 12 February 1931/2.
58 Macartney, op. cit., p. 241.
59 *The Times*, 26 January 1932, p. 12.
60 *The Times*, 4 March 1932, p. 16; 12 March, p. 7; 14 May, p. 7; 28 April, p. 9.
61 Annual Report 1939–41, p. 7.
62 For an account, see Annual Report 1939–41, pp. 9–11.
63 Annual Report, 1942–4, pp. 33–4.
64 Fox was a career civil servant. Born in 1895, he had been Secretary of the Commission in 1925, Assistant Commissioner and Inspector in 1930, and had later gone to Scotland Yard. He became Chairman in 1942 and died in 1962 shortly after retirement.
65 Scott, op. cit., pp. 78–9.

1945–68: the crisis erupts

Further reforms

The prison service had coped well with the enormous problems created by the war. During the 1914–18 war there had been a decrease in the prison population, which had alleviated the difficulties caused by the call up of staff. In the second world war on the other hand, the daily average population did not fall and in some years increased due largely to longer sentences being awarded.[1] Numbers increased after 1945, into the 1950s and 1960s. In 1945 there was a daily average population of 12,910. By 1950 this had risen to 20,474 and 1951 saw the highest number of prisoners since just after 1877. From a total of 27,099 in 1960, the numbers soared to 29,580 in 1965.

The Commissioners were naturally desperate for accommodation and they applied two main remedies. The first was the building of open and medium-security prisons and borstals, by now approved as a reformative measure. This began with Leyhill in Gloucestershire in 1946. Between 1945 and 1952, seventeen of these were opened. But this expedient could not solve the problem, and a new device was introduced into English prison administration—'threeing up'. The political decision to allow this led to considerable controversy, and a great deal of misery to many prisoners, to say nothing of the under-mining of control. By 1948 an average of 2,000 men were sleeping three to a cell, with a claim by the Commissioners in their 1948 Report, that prisoners 'find that the advantages of company outweigh the drawbacks'. By 1958 the number of prisoners enjoying these 'advantages' had risen to 6,000, all of them in local prisons.

The most important piece of legislation in the decade, the Criminal Justice Act of 1948 increased these burdens. Under the Act two new kinds of institutions were to be administered by the Commissioners, remand centres and detention centres, and the restrictions on the imprisonment of people under twenty-one was to contribute to an increase in borstal committals. An especially strenuous job was to follow from the innovation of a new sentence for younger recidivists, the ill-fated corrective training.[2] There were also changes in the form of preventive detention which resulted in an increase in numbers.[3]

The history of this period must be viewed against this background of overcrowding. For a great deal of the time, as in the early years of the century, this must have appeared to the Commissioners as the first and last problem, day after day. The complexity of institutions resulted too in the changing of institutions from prison to borstal or vice versa, and the changing of borstals to detention centres. The status of borstal received a serious setback when North Sea Camp became a detention centre in 1963. It appeared, in spite of the Commissioners' description of this as 'an interesting experiment',[4] as though the deliberate punishment, which was the policy of the centres, was winning its war against the allegedly unequivocal 'training' of borstal. The latter received another blow in the 1961 Criminal Justice Act, when the training period was reduced from three years to two years ostensibly so that training could be brisker, but in fact because the borstals were filled to overflowing.

Especially in the post war period, as the prison population increased, the staff situation deteriorated.[5] Even if the regime had remained as it had been in 1895, the situation would have been difficult. With the opening of new institutions, and the introduction of reformative measures, it was impossible for the staff to maintain effective control. It will be seen that control over intra-personal behaviour amongst prisoners was almost non-existent, and that escapes could only be prevented by luck, and the fact that most prisoners did not wish to escape. The routine tasks such as feeding and locking-up were carried out, but it is to the credit of the prison service that complete breakdown was avoided, a possibility which seemed more than likely to those aware of the gravity of the situation.

In spite of this central difficulty of overcrowding and shortage of staff, the Commissioners persisted in the effort to maintain the impetus of the Paterson era. Those interested in prison reform could not fail to be impressed by some developments in training and treatment. Some of the more remarkable of these were the increase in open institutions already mentioned, the 'Norwich system', the hostel scheme, home leave for prisoners, the proliferation of specialists, the extension of staff training, and the introduction of research work into the prison system.

The Norwich system was started at Norwich prison. It is described in the Annual Report for 1956. It had three main features: dining in association for all convicted prisoners; an increase in the hours of labour from twenty-six to thirty-five a week without increasing staff; and an attempt to improve officer/inmate relationships by the allocation of groups of prisoners to specific officers. The scheme soon spread through the prison system, establishing the important tradition that association was usual, and advantageous. The hostel scheme, which was begun at Bristol in 1953, allowed selected prisoners to work away from the prison in normal civilian employment. They had to return to the prison to sleep, and their pay was used for their upkeep, and for that of their families. It was soon introduced to other prisons, and survived some almost disastrous publicity, notably in 1963 when a hostel resident murdered in the course of a robbery, and allegations of political influence and favouritism, shown towards a notorious criminal who was put on the scheme.[6] On security grounds Mountbatten was critical of them, since the majority were within the walls. As a result some were closed.[7] The privilege of five days' parole—'home leave'—which had been granted to borstal inmates for some time, was introduced into prison in 1951.

The growth of specialist departments in the prison service, is one of the signal characteristics of the period. Because it had important effects on the uniformed staff, it will be appropriate to deal with it later. Staff training, upon which the Gladstone Committee had laid such stress, reached its peak in this period. Although the period of initial training had to be reduced after the war because of staff short-age, by the early 1960s considerable attention had been paid to training needs, and the training organisation at Wakefield was expanded and developed to cater for a wide range of courses. In addition, from 1956 the developing skills of groupwork and casework were introduced into the service, albeit at a limited level, through the secondment of members of the governor grades to university and other professional courses. Research by Home Office and University staff became a feature of policy during the period, and from 1952 the Annual Reports carry an account of research work being carried out. Finally, although this account is not concerned with women's establishments, no account of the development of training and treatment would be complete without reference to the remarkable progress of the female service which can be traced in all the Annual Reports.

These reforms were all the more impressive since the social context within which they took place was very different from that before the war. The change may be illustrated by reference to the Criminal Justice Act of 1948. This had been presented as a Bill in 1938, but the outbreak of war prevented its enactment. When it was introduced

ten years later: 'the experience of the war and post-war years sharp-
ened the feeling that punitive measures were needed.'[8] Perhaps the
most important formative experience which society underwent at
that time was a rapid rise in the crime rate. And the most evident
example of the movement away from 'liberalism' was the institution
of the detention centre, an organisation unlike any other in the penal
system since it was starkly punitive and committed to the idea of
deterrence.

A mounting crisis

The confusion about the task of the prison service reached its zenith
in 1949. The Prison Rules of that year set out the task as follows:[9]
'The purposes of training and treatment of convicted prisoners shall
be to establish in them the will to lead a good and useful life on discharge, and to fit them to do so.' This *manifest* task was frequently
restated by policy makers and senior officials.[10] 'A prison today
serves three purposes, which may be described as custodial, coercive,
and correctional . . . the last of these . . . now takes the primary place.'

But the law courts continued to issue warrants, the legal authority
for imprisonment, which in various ways instructed the staff to secure
the prisoners, making no reference to reform. This put the prison
service in the position of having two manifest tasks, one of which had
political and official weight, and one of which had the necessary legal
authority to cause imprisonment in the first place. The success of the
system would be judged by the achievement of the latter, but the
regime necessary to effect it was undermined by the official emphasis
given to the former. It was a progression which had its origins in the
Gladstone Report and had been gaining momentum with the ever
increasing amounts of freedom being given to prisoners, as an
inevitable concomitant of the reforms which were introduced. This
progression, together with the overcrowding situation, meant that
effective achievement of the controlling task was impossible. It is
true that there had been escapes, assaults, and indeed a riot before
the war, and these were evidence of task failure. But although these
were on a scale which would have been regarded as quite intolerable
fifty years before, they were tolerated because they were isolated,
sporadic, and because their proportions were accepted as a reasonable risk by the community, which was led in its opinion by groups

who were interested in, and sympathetic to what the prison service was trying to do. After the war the mood of the community was rather different, and the worst fears of the public about penal institutions were continually being confirmed by a new powerful organ, the Prison Officers' Association. The role of the Association will be discussed later; at this point it is necessary to note its contribution to every increase in public concern, through its constant allegations of defects at Annual Conferences, in its magazine and elsewhere.

Escapes

During the period the rate of escapes from all kinds of penal institutions soared. The figures are given in Table 4.[11]

Table 4   Escapes and attempts to escape (male), 1946–66

Year	Daily average population		Escapes and attempts	Per 1,000*
1946	Prison	12,328	322	
	Borstal	2,228	542	
	Total	14,556	864	57·6
1947	Prison	13,360	224	
	Borstal	2,626	1,070	
		15,986	1,294	80·8
1948	Prison	15,736	262	
	Borstal	2,885	1,192	
		18,621	1,454	76·5
1949	Prison	15,785	197	
	Borstal	2,998	1,127	
		18,783	1,324	69·5
1950	Prison	16,490	134	
	Borstal	2,877	1,209	
		19,367	1,343	70·5
1951	Prison	17,741	127	
	Borstal	2,946	1,203	
		20,687	1,330	63·3

* Daily average to the nearest thousand.

Year	Daily average population		Escapes and attempts	Per 1,000
1952	Prison	19,346	111	
	Borstal	3,212	1,131	54·1
	Detention centre	10	3	
		22,568	1,245	
1953*	Prison	19,237	172	
	Borstal	3,193	1,028	56
	Detention centre	43	12	
		22,473	1,212	
1954†	Prison	18,288	132	
	Borstal	2,941	902	50
	Detention centre	108	18	
		21,337	1,052	
1955	Prison	17,427	148	
	Borstal	2,605	555	35·8
	Detention centre	124	13	
		20,156	716	
1956	Prison	17,203	171	
	Borstal	2,573	747	46·6
	Detention centre	165	14	
		19,941	932	
1957	Prison	18,457	241	
	Borstal	3,051	890	51·8
	Detention centre	234	9	
		21,742	1,140	
1958	Prison	20,474	356	
	Borstal	3,714	913	53·7
	Detention centre	271	21	
		24,459	1,290	
1959	Prison	21,419	542	
	Borstal	4,034	914	56·6
	Detention centre	274	26	
		25,727	1,482	
1960	Prison	21,808	485	
	Borstal	4,115	975	56·8
	Detention centre	275	17	
		26,198	1,477	

* From this year the term 'abscond' was used in respect of borstal and detention centre escapes.

† From this year the prison escape figures include breaches of parole.

Year	Daily average population		Escapes and attempts	Per 1,000
1961	Prison	23,188	700	
	Borstal	4,444	899	58·7
	Detention centre	462	46	
		28,094	1,645	
1962	Prison	24,612	536	
	Borstal	4,701	897	49·1
	Detention centre	753	41	
		30,066	1,474	
1963	Prison	24,156	618	
	Borstal	4,755	974	54·6
	Detention centre	1,014	47	
		29,925	1,639	
1964	Prison	22,990	791	
	Borstal	4,456	1,173	72·0
	Detention centre	1,272	126	
		28,718	2,090	

Year				Escapes	Attempts	Escapes while at other establishments
1965*	Prison		23,427	412	168	103
	Borstal		4,652	693	270	146
	Detention centre		1,501	59	46	1
			29,580	1,164	484	250

Total escapes = 1,414 (47·1 per thousand)
Total escapes and attempts = 1,898 (63.2 per thousand)

Year				Escapes	Attempts	Escapes while at other establishments
1966	Prison		25,461	325	163	104
	Borstal		5,063	571	239	369
	Detention centre		1,603	44	48	8
			32,127	940	450	481

Total escapes = 1,421 (44·4 per thousand)
Total escapes and attempts = 1,871 (58·4 per thousand)

* From this year the figures are divided into three categories: escapes, attempts, and escapes while at other establishments.

The attitude of the Commissioners to this deteriorating situation was based on a realistic assessment of what *was* possible, bearing in mind the ever present pressure for reform with which, it appeared, they had a great deal of sympathy. But they were conscious that the situation was actually highly unsatisfactory. They expressed concern in the Annual Reports, initiated investigations into causes, disciplined staff where appropriate[12] and, in the 1952 Report, tried to introduce a distinction between escaping and absconding. They defended themselves by pointing out that 98 per cent of borstal escapers were caught almost immediately[13] and that only escapes from secure conditions ought to be considered since escapes from outside parties or open prisons 'are an inevitable risk which must be accepted.[14] This was a view consistently supported by the Howard League.[15] With regard to causes of the increase in escapes, the Commissioners were as certain that 'changes in the methods of treatment' were not a cause,[16] as the Prison Officers' Association was certain of the opposite.[17] This basic divergence of view, the culmination of an historical process, is the keynote of relationships between the two during the period.

The prison service was not helped by the escapes of dangerous patients from Broadmoor. This is a special hospital for which the Ministry of Health is responsible and is not under the control of the Prison Commissioners. Nevertheless, the extremely serious offences committed by some escaping patients, notably John Thomas Straffen and Frank Mitchell, were further evidence of a generally unsatisfactory state of security. Organisational distinctions between Ministries did not communicate themselves to a community aware only that people who should have been locked up were, in fact, at large.

All the efforts of the Commissioners, and all their investigations, which were never described because of their confidential nature, had very little effect, unless it was to make the situation worse. Nor is their failure to make any inroad on the problem in any way remarkable. Whether or not society ought to have accepted the risks, the reality was that it had to. These were now firmly built into the fabric of the system. To have made any major inroad into the escape rate would have involved the closing of open institutions, a custodial priority being introduced into borstal which had never been there, and the cessation of marginal security flaws such as home leave and the hostel scheme. To have contained the really dangerous offender, it would have been necessary to re-establish the civil guard. All of these solutions at that time were not only ideologically unthinkable, but were economically impossible. And so the system lurched on. It was becoming apparent however that this degree of task failure was intolerable, and it was already evident that a crisis had to come.

'*Discipline*'

There was not only concern about increasing loss of control, demonstrated by the escape rate. It was becoming clear that the staff were losing the power to direct the behaviour of inmates, both towards staff, and towards each other. The staff were somewhat concerned about how inmates behaved towards each other; but they were very concerned indeed about the behaviour of inmates to staff. During these years complaints about 'discipline' dominated discussions by officers and became increasingly prominent in the Annual Reports and the extracts from governors' reports which appeared in them. What does the term 'discipline' mean to the prison officer?

There will be in any group of inmates of a penal institution a number of people whose behaviour, for whatever reason, is likely to be violent. This violence is unlikely to be consistent, and can be expressed at almost any time, frequently or hardly ever, for reasons which are obscure, debatable, and, in the everyday situation of the prison officer, irrelevant. There is uncertainty about all human response, but in penal institutions this uncertainty is heightened by the personal characteristics, the social commitment, and perennial refusal to concede the legitimacy of the rule of law, which characterises the prisoner community. It is dealing with this uncertainty which makes penal work difficult. And the greater the degree of uncertainty, the greater is likely to be the degree of anxiety on the part of the officer. 'Discipline' to the officer means the reduction (elimination is impossible) of this uncertainty. This reduction can be achieved by greater control over the movement of inmates, through closer supervision, and by ensuring that respect is given to staff instructions—a respect which may be either commanded or demanded. This can be achieved, the officer believes, through swift and certain punishment if there is misbehaviour.

It can be seen, therefore, that the historical process of reformation, which has been described so far, has, in the officer's view, brought only erosion of what officers call 'discipline'. Reform did not only mean to the officer the 'pampering' of prisoners, of which he, like others in society, may have disapproved. It meant the usurpation of his control. Not only was this a blow to the dignity which follows from approval because of successful job performance. It created anxiety about the possibility of being physically assaulted, which it would appear was more likely than at any time since 1877 and certainly was more likely than it was at the time of the Stanhope Committee.

Assaults on staff were constantly being discussed. The Prison Officers' Association continually raised the matter, frequently urging the Commissioners to do something about increasing violence against staff.[18] Generally the Commissioners conceded that there had been an increase in assaults, but in the earlier years were not prepared to agree that there was any real cause for alarm.[19] By 1960, however, it was stated that 'the persistence of assaults upon the staff continues to cause the Commissioners grave concern' and it was announced in the Annual Report that the worst offenders would be segregated in a special wing. But 1961, a year which was full of crises, saw a rise in assaults on officers to 228, for which ten prisoners were sentenced to corporal punishment (seven of these sentences were carried out).[20]

Throughout the period there were acts of insubordination, sometimes concerted, which caused concern. There was, for instance, serious trouble at Portland in 1950, which led Portland UDC to appeal to the Home Secretary for a public inquiry into the management of the borstal.[21] Cardiff and Birmingham had sit-down strikes in 1959[22] and the preventive detainees were always turbulent over the operation of the Advisory Board, which decided whether a prisoner would gain one-third, or one-fifth, remission of his sentence.[23]

If the staff found that it was becoming extremely difficult to regulate the behaviour of inmates towards them, it is clear that it was impossible to control the behaviour of inmates to each other. It will be remembered that the justification for maximising contact in association was that it was normal, likely to be beneficial, and preferred by the inmates themselves. The 'contamination' problem, which had so worried the Victorians and which had been avoided in the inter-war period, continued to be ignored. When the subject was raised, which was only rarely, classification was regarded as the solution.[24]

In the conditions of freedom now prevailing in closed prisons and the almost total absence of constraint in the open prisons, it was inevitable that, while some inmates might benefit from contact with their fellows, others would suffer, since in training prisons 'prisoners move freely about the place without the direct supervision of officers.'[25] The more malign result was the growth of an elaborate inmate sub-culture, actively anti-therapeutic, and socially damaging, especially to the weaker or less sophisticated. This was the period when the 'baron' reached the height of his power, when violence between prisoners became usual, when the strong terrorised the weak, and homosexual practices were made easy. At Parkhurst, where between 400–500 men were in association outside the cell block:[26]

> it must be admitted . . . that this compound association time is used by prisoners for the passing of contraband goods, the indulgence of gambling, and for the various activities of the barons.

In borstal, where the twin problems of bullying and homosexual practices were never really faced, the staff were advised to watch for bullying and indecency.[27] A *cause célèbre* occurred in 1954 when eleven boys were sent to prison and two to further borstal training for indecent offences committed at Usk.[28]

The POA Conference in 1959, discussed the rise in the incidence of homosexuality in prisons, and one delegate asked:[29]

> How can we as prison officers do anything about it when there is not sufficient staff even to keep security, let alone supervision over the moral conduct of these men?

These expressions of concern from the officers about their inability to control inmates' behaviour, highlight an important strain in institutional work which needs emphasising. The demands for more freedom for inmates, do not take account of the fact that, in the institutional situation, there is a limited amount of freedom. An important part of the role of institutional staff, and a most difficult one, is the adjudication on rival claims for the limited amount of freedom which is available. The staff member often has to restrain one prisoner, so that another can be left in peace. It is often assumed that the only ceiling to freedom of action for prisoners is a desire on the part of staff to suppress it. In reality, it frequently happens that a staff member who is restricting the freedom of an inmate is doing so to preserve the freedom of another inmate. If this adjudicatory function is lost sight of, a situation arises which is described in the Mountbatten Report. The price that was paid for allowing Mitchell freedom, was that large numbers of prisoners went in terror.

Another contribution to this loosening of control over the intra-group behaviour of the inmates, which led to a weakening of 'discipline', was the reappearance of the inmate who was given authority over others. In his study of the defects of total power in New Jersey prison, Sykes describes how the power of staff is eroded by collusion of various kinds with prisoners. A feature of this erosion is the performance by inmates of tasks which properly belong to the staff.[30] In the English system, the repression of the inmate/officer could not be sustained when massive association created the need for a multitude of simple tasks to be performed by selected inmates. This was a significant contribution to the erosion of the officer's capability to control.

Du Cane had reduced this to a minimum and by 1900 there remained only the 'red collar' man whose activities were carefully circumscribed and who had no authority whatever. First appearing at Dartmoor in 1852, he was the nucleus of a movement which was to make a significant contribution to the usurpation of the officer's authority. The transition which followed, from the minimal super-vision of the 'red collar' to no supervision at all, was drastic, but the enormity of the difference was clouded because of the rehabilitive overtones which gave approval to such a development:[31]

> The main purpose of this was not to save staff, or to facilitate administration of the Prison but to introduce a reforming agency in convict prisons.

The 'red collar' may have appeared in locals as early as 1902,[32] but it was not until 1910 that the system, but called 'red bands', was formally extended to locals which might 'in many cases lead to economy in staff, and reduce the need of temporary officers'.[33] After an inquiry in 1921 about the high cost of staff at Camp Hill, the 'honour party', a variant of the red band system, was set up.[34] This consisted of a group of prisoners working without supervision inside the walls. In 1922, after a governors' conference, the honour party was extended to locals.[35]

With the Paterson era, the next stage was inevitable. This was to set a prisoner in authority over others, continuing to argue from reforma-tive principles, and always making the dangers clear. 1933 brought a threat to this development, as to others. After the escape of a prisoner from Norwich it seemed as though the process might be reversed. But like everything else in the reformative movement, it survived.[36] A kind of super red band, wearing a blue band and called a 'stroke', appeared in Wakefield Prison heading a 'crew' of prisoners, who wore blazers with crossed oars.[37] Although the crew system of workers has finished, the 'stroke' remains.

Borstal too developed a 'leader' system, without which many borstals could never have been administered. The leader organised the work of the house, supported the staff and, in theory, set an example. This sometimes happened, but the usual experience of the leader system was that it gave the official imprimatur to violence which was quickly administered by leaders who had no experience of exercising authority and who saw violence as a ready solution to problems posed by their groups. All of these undermined the control which officers exercised and increasingly the latter became unaware of what inmates were doing and thinking. Here and there, appeared echoes of the prisoner participation which had been fostered in American prisons by Thomas Mott Osborne in the 1920s. One governor at least of a local prison reported, in 1950, that he held meetings between leaders, red bands, and representative staff. Because the 'leaders' did so much work, the officers were prepared to approve of them. Harley Cronin, in an account which is almost unrelieved in its disapproval of the prison system, states that 'the trust reposed in leaders and red bands was very rarely abused.'[38]

The context of the officer's role

The abolition of the Prison Commission

The point has been stressed that the uniformed staff were becoming emotionally and politically alienated from the organisation. It is necessary now to examine in more detail the main factors which contributed to this alienation. The first of these was the abolition of the Prison Commission.

At the time when the Commission was set up there was increasing involvement of the central government in what had been local affairs. Thus the Commission was one of several 'Boards' established during that period. In the same way its abolition was paralleled by the abolition of other quasi-autonomous Boards, which were brought under direct ministerial control, such as the Board of Control, abolished by the Mental Health Act, 1959. But the Prison Commission was unique in the degree of centralised power which it wielded. Inefficiency or remoteness in the Head Office had devastating effects, as we have seen. Its abolition was rather more traumatic, therefore, than the abolition of similar bodies.

As early as 1895, in evidence to the Gladstone Committee, it was stated that the Commissioners were being excluded by administrators from crucial information about events and decisions. At the same time it emerged that relationships between Head Office and the institutions were defective. Perhaps because of the work of Ruggles-Brise and certainly because of the work of Paterson, relationships improved and seem indeed, at times, to have been reasonably good. Paterson was not interested in administration but, because of his power, he retained a grip on administrative affairs. His contact with the institutions was deep rooted and it was reinforced by the fact that he personally selected every member of staff who joined.[39] The several factors contributing to at least a modicum of sense of unity were helped by the relatively small size of the service.

In the 1946 Report, a radical change in the structure of the Commission was announced. Administrative class civil servants were introduced at a very senior level, and at that time the three Commissioners were all members of that class. The 'professionals' such as the Director of Prison Administration and the Director of Borstal Administration were to carry out 'the day-to-day control and inspection of the establishments'. They were also to advise on general questions of policy and administration. This development was accompanied by bureaucratisation of the administration of the prison service in the field, which was most visible in the evolution of the various clerical and executive hierarchies. The executive and clerical departments of the institutions soon came to regard Head Office, not the governor, as their superior authority. Early in the 1960s the steward, the senior clerk in the prison, changed his title to 'the administration officer'. This together with a newly awarded authority which allowed him to send and receive letters from Head Office, without consulting the governor, further damaged the governor's relationship with the Commissioners. The increasing dominance of the adminstrative and executive civil servants is one of the most significant features of the period and it had important administrative, as well as psychological, effects.

The first hint of an attempt to abolish the Commission altogether appeared in the Criminal Justice Bill of 1938. The Bill was not enacted, but was resurrected in 1948. The clause proposing abolition was rejected, but the instigators were not so easily dissuaded. In the

Criminal Justice Act of 1961, it was enacted that, by Order in Council, the functions of the Prison Commission could be transferred to the Secretary of State. And in 1963 the one reason which was ever given for the transfer was outlined in Parliament. It was, it appeared, rational to deal with crime in one organisation since 'the handling of offenders does not begin and end in prison'.[40]

The opposition to the proposal was considerable. During the debate it was pointed out that the merger was opposed by the *Lancet*, the *Observer*, *The Times*, the *Guardian*, *The Economist* and the *Sunday Telegraph*. It was pointed out further that in 1961 everyone who spoke in the debate was opposed to it, except for the government front bench.[41] Opposition expressed in two leaders in *The Times*[42] was supported by letters from Harold Scott, Llewellin and other ex-governors.[43] Only one correspondent supported the proposal.[44] In spite of these pressures, enough MPs seemed to have been reassured about the proposed change. On 1 April 1963 the Commission was dissolved.[45] The former Chairman became Assistant Under Secretary of State in charge, and the Commissioners became Directors.

The uniformed staff did not officially express strong views about abolition, probably because they felt that any change was bound to lead to an improvement, since the rift between them and the Head Office was already wide. The position was, of course, complicated by the fact that the service was growing all the time and there were problems of the relationship between the size of the organisation and morale which were never properly examined. The total situation after 1963 was calculated to produce a lowering of the indefinable entity known as morale. As early as April 1961 an article in the *Prison Officers' Magazine* had claimed that morale had never been 'at such a low ebb'. It will be seen that nothing happened to improve this situation, so that Mountbatten observed that: 'I do not believe the morale of the prison service is as high as it should be.'[46] The Chairman of the Prisons Board later said that talk of a 'bad period of morale' was exaggerated.[47]

But the effect of the abolition on the officers was indirect and had as its source the direct effect on the governors. The latter had, of course, not commented publicly at the time of abolition. Had they done so, they might have given weight and depth to the opposition. It had been impossible for opponents to quantify their objections in any arithmetical form. They were based on experience, on intuition and on a consciousness that an indefinable sense of cohesion, of belonging, would be lost. None of these were very impressive or rational arguments. Fortunately, the governor grades did have the opportunity later to discuss the change. The Prison Governors' Branch of the Society of Civil Servants submitted a memorandum to an Estimates Committee in 1967, and followed this up with oral evidence.[48] This short memorandum is an astute summary of the defects in the relationship between Head Office and the institutions which had been deteriorating and which abolition made worse. One of the results was an increase in distance between Directors and Assistant Directors on the one hand, and governors on the other. Since the former had been governors themselves, this relationship had been crucial. It became ineffective because the Directors too were confused, and increasingly being pushed out by the civil servants. The governors summed up their position as 'the Directors [who] do not direct in any real sense'.[49]

The administrative and psychological effects of these changes were disastrous. Increasingly the Head Office began to appear to governors and officers as remote,[50] 'grossly over-centralised and consequently inefficient'[51] and as a place where 'matters of mainly human interest' were dealt with by 'people who are predominantly concerned with administrative matters'.[52] The staff, during the latter part of the period, found themselves dealing with a central organisation which was rapidly becoming incomprehensible. It was no longer possible to identify the decision makers in major or minor matters. Staff could not get to the centre of the decision-making apparatus, because there was no centre; they could not go to the top, because there was no top. The memorandum of the Howard League sets out very clearly the results of a situation where the nominal head of the Prison Department, unlike the Chairman of the Commissioners, had 'other duties' besides the prisons. This official, a Deputy Under Secretary of State, and the Assistant Secretary in charge were both senior to the 'Chief Director'. The latter, like other Directors, presumably directed nothing.[53] A confused, angry, and demoralised staff looked for sensitive, intelligent direction from the central authority. They did not get it. The centre and the institutions continued to draw apart, and the inevitable result was that described by Mountbatten, with an over-zealous sense of fair play:[54]

> The Head Officer has clearly to some extent lost touch with the establishments under its control.

The specialist era

The other important contextual factor which influenced the development of the role of the officer, was the proliferation of specialists, which had begun in the 1930s. These were allegedly introduced to increase the pace and depth of training and treatment of inmates. But the process was also a microcosm of what Marsh called the 'never ending birth of professions which is a characteristic of occupational trends in this century'.[55]

At first sight there seems little in this development which bears on the role of the officer. The specialist is the 'authority on', has no place in the traditional hierarchical pyramid and is restricted to serving it. The classical theoretical assessment of the specialist is that his kind of authority should not be confused with the authority of the traditional structure. The terms 'line' and 'staff' are generally utilised to distinguish them.

This description is over simple. The specialist is not content merely to serve. He has views about administration, the nature of his professional contribution and his place in the organisation. This debate is sometimes regarded as a somewhat tiresome discussion about 'status', but it is more basic than that. It is a debate about organisational goals and how decisions about implementing these should be made. In the industrial organisation where success or failure is visible, the contribution of the professional can be controlled and evaluated. The engine that is a tribute to the ingenuity of the engineer is of little value to the firm if nobody will buy it.

In organisations with no means of measuring success or failure, there are infinite possibilities for specialist groups to set up sub-organisations with their own definitions of what the organisation is supposed to be doing. In organisations where there is no commonly accepted task, a substantial part of the activity of the specialist is devoted to battles with other specialist groups and with administrators.

The growth of specialist departments in the prison service meant more than increased facilities for the training and treatment of inmates. It was to introduce complications in management which were to contribute, in no small measure, to the increasingly confused situation with which officers had to cope. They were not alone in this: nurses, for example, have witnessed the introduction of occupational therapists, physiotherapists and others, with a consequent depressing of the status of the 'generalist'. As new techniques for training and rehabilitation were introduced, it became clear to the officers that they were not going to be involved in them. Clearly they were not qualified for some of the work of the 'full fledged' professions[56] but they felt strongly that they could undertake the work of some of the others with great success. Their exclusion from teaching and clerical work was gradual, and had a mixed reception. In the 1946 Report, after a pioneer scheme in co-operation with the Durham LEA it was announced that further education for prisoners was an appropriate function for an education authority. By 1954 the instructors, and the vocational trade trainers, were civilians and, while an officer could still become a physical education instructor, physical education experts were being brought in from outside. Clerical work was no longer part of the officer's duty. He was left with two other specialist posts: as a cook and baker, or hospital officer. There were two growth semi-professions for which the uniformed staff believed themselves to be singularly well suited: assistant governor and welfare officer.

The normal point of entry to the governor grade was, by now, assistant governor.[57] The uniformed staff during this period, through the POA, continued to express the view, as they had since 1915, that there were enough officers of suitable calibre to be promoted to this grade. The Commissioners disagreed, as did successive Home Secretaries, and the Wynn Parry Committee,[58] which reviewed the situation very carefully. As the number of assistant governors was increased, the officers became increasingly vociferous about direct entry.

The first social worker was appointed in 1946.[59] But in 1953 social work took a leap forward when the Maxwell Committee reported, recommending the appointment of prison welfare officers. It was considered desirable for them not to be members of the prison staff and that they should be trained social workers. The first was appointed in 1955.[60] They were employed by the National Association of Discharged Prisoners' Aid Societies.

In 1963 the Advisory Council on the Treatment of Offenders published its report called *The Organisation of After-Care*. It recommended an expansion of the welfare services, even, it was hinted, to borstal.[61] Further, the appointment in the detention centres, of a social worker, was welcomed. A specific recommendation that the welfare officers should not be members of the probation service was obviously the subject of an interdepartmental struggle in the Home

Office and it was announced, with no public or professional discussion, that they were to be probation officers.[62]

The prison officer saw the post of welfare officer as one for which he was admirably suited. This presented an opportunity for him to achieve status by working in an expanding area of rehabilitation. The POA was certain that welfare officers:[63]

should, in future, come from the ranks of Prison Officers. [They have] obvious, almost overwhelming advantages . . . to offer.

Naturally individual officers did become welfare officers, but then they were no longer prison officers. The officers considered that welfare work had no acknowledged professional skills, other than the magical 'experience'. Both Maxwell and ACTO, however, envisaged a 'qualified', 'professional' social worker for prison welfare work. The role envisaged for a prison social worker by the Howard League was also incompatible with the uniformed officers' perception of it. The secretary of the Howard League considered that a welfare officer might even act as a prisoner's 'friend' in disciplinary proceedings in prison.[64]

The officers' attempt to become involved in reform will be discussed more fully later. It is important to note at this stage that the introduction of specialists had two effects on the prison service. The first was to narrow the role of the officer, to heighten its coercive overtones and to contribute to its definition as starkly custodial. The second was to add to the overall deterioration in the administration of the service. The needs of the officers for support and understanding in coping with the problems thrown up by the changes which have been described had never been greater. But the Head Office's ability to meet these needs had never been so slight. The central organisation was absorbed in its own internal problems which were, in many ways, a replica of what was going on in the prisons. As each specialist group was established, the situation grew worse. The organisational chaos which resulted was summed up by the Prison Governors' Branch of the Society of Civil Servants:[65]

each of these additions, usually concerned with specialist needs and techniques, is equipped with its own hierarchy, channels of departmental communication, and Head Office pressure group. In the absence of agreement on basic aims, which would facilitate integration and the establishment of priorities, the department can be reasonably described as an aggregation of secondary interests more or less continually in conflict with each other.

'The pampered scum'[66]

The uniformed staff had other problems besides trying to cope with a remote Head Office and an ever growing galaxy of specialists. The developments in the reformative programme which have been outlined continued to foster the belief, by now firmly held by the officers, that more was being done for prisoners than for staff, and that in the conflict between the two groups the best that could be said about the attitude of the community was that it was ambivalent. The worst that could be said in the officers' view was that it was 'pro-prisoner'. And, significantly, a number of influential people seemed to be contributing to the process of lionising prisoners and consequently attacking the staff.

In material terms, the Wynn Parry Report states categorically the discrepancy in the allocation of resources to the two groups:

> we saw living and working conditions which can only be described as Dickensian. Substantial improvements have been made for the prison population with the emphasis now on training and rehabilitation, but in our view parallel improvements have not been made for the staff.

Within the institutions, the feeling had been growing for many years that governors were likely to take the part of prisoners if there was a difference between them and staff:[67]

> 'Don't upset the men,' was the governor's watchword. The men ran the place. Their superior rating over the staff was so accepted . . . he suggested that the officers who had joined from the Scrubs could be accommodated in some empty cells in the prison! After all, they were good enough for the men!'

The community and Parliament, in the view of officers, went much further. They exposed the staff to serious risk of injury or death by the abolition of corporal and capital punishment. The *de facto* abolition of the former may be seen in Table 5.[68]

Table 5 *Corporal punishment in prisons*

Year	Number sentenced	Number confirmed by Secretary of State
1961	10	7
1962	4	3*
1963	2	Nil
1964	1	Nil
1965	1†	Nil
1966	1	Nil

* *Not* 4 as recorded in all Annual Reports since.
† The only one in these years sentenced to the 'cat'.

On 1 October 1967, Section 65 of the Criminal Justice Act 1967, abolishing corporal punishment in prison, came into force.[69] Murder of a prison officer fell into the category of 'capital' offences in the 1957 Homicide Act, but in 1965 when the decision was made to suspend capital punishment, the murder of a prison officer became a non-capital offence.

Officers interpreted this as a kind of betrayal, and a removal of such protection as they had from extreme forms of violence:[70]

> . . . these measures have increased the risks to which prison
> officers are liable and have removed what were, to some
> prisoners at any rate, deterrents against acts of violence perpet-
> rated on the prison staff.

Officers were angry too at what they believed to be an undue readiness to set up investigations into misconduct by the staff. There were two noteworthy investigations. One at Durham, and a much more controversial one at Liverpool. Although both inquiries largely vindicated the staff, feeling amongst the officers ran high, partly because, in the case of Liverpool, the operation of the inquiry was biased in favour of the prisoners, but mainly because their very existence, and concomitant debate, inevitably cast doubt on the conduct of the staff. The expressions of pro-prisoner sympathy by politicians were continued when members of the several nuclear disarmament groups emerged from prison, and wrote of their experiences.[71] Even in the early days of the events leading to the 1966 crisis, when the first mail train robber escaped, it was clear that the anger of the community at prison service failure was tempered by admiration for the apparent ingenuity of the escapers.[72]

The attitude of some sections of the public and Parliament to the prisons, increased the officer's sense of uncertainty and confusion about his role and his value as a member of the organisation. From the Victorian situation where, within clearly defined limits, he was able to control prisoners with public approval, he had moved to a situation where remoteness at the head, ineffective rule within many institutions and a keenly felt sense of condemnation from the community, gave him a strong feeling of isolation. All around was hostility and he had the strenuous task of trying to cope with it. The situation was especially complicated by the realisation that public support of the criminal was in fact very fragile and did not extend to toleration of the escape of violent offenders. He began deeply to resent being put in a position by the community, and by his own superiors, where he could be held up to ridicule and turned into a classic scapegoat. This experience was not confined to the prison officer. Since 1945 it has been shared by others in positions of authority—schoolmasters, police officers and social welfare workers, to name but three.

'The modern prison officer'

Put at its mildest then, this was a difficult time for prison staff. They had to cope with conflicting priorities and variations in instructions as to how those priorities had to be carried out, which seemed to them to be capricious. The solution which was adopted at an extant level was to reject both priorities, in the way that people living in a situation of 'culture conflict'[73] will reject all the rival cultures and will be propelled into a state of anomie. The strain created by the concerted confusion associated with this task conflict was too great to be carried indefinitely. The only way in which the staff could survive was to contract out, to refuse to collude in the concealment of the chaotic situation in the service. In their daily work they operated pragmatically. As an article in *The Times* on 8 May 1950 said, in dealing with prisoners being strict gave way to being clever.

At a national level the situation was extremely serious. The disagreement between the uniformed officers and the Commissioners was so basic, so apparently irreparable, that the only satisfactory way in which the situation can be described is to say that the officers set up in opposition to the reformative pressures which were, it seemed to them, being subscribed to by the Commissioners. The POA went unchallenged by its membership as it argued with the Commissioners, denied the latter's assurances that all would be all right and resisted almost every innovation which brought new stresses. It was only very rarely in the years 1945–65, that the Commissioners' account, and the POA account, of what was happening in prison, bore any relation to each other.

This can be seen through an examination of the accounts given by the two camps of the reasons for the progressive collapse of control which has been described. The explanation given by the officers was that the root of the problem was the increase in 'liberalism'. The agents of this liberalism were many. The kinds of staff (almost all members of the governor grades) who subscribed to it were caustically referred to as 'Paterson's Light Horse'.[74] 'The psychiatrists' were another visible target for blame, since they 'do not help in maintaining discipline'.[75] The effects of this liberalism were felt everywhere. The officers claimed that 'the relaxation of discipline was a cause of the big increase in the prison population',[76] that there was mob rule in prisons[77] and that liberalism had caused the increase in escapes.[78] Above all, it led to attacks on staff which were not punished severely enough. A delegate to the POA Conference in 1958 stated that 'in some cases they get awards tantamount to being deprived of their boot-laces for a fortnight.[79] As has been shown, during this period corporal punishment in prison became less frequent and eventually ceased altogether.

The anger of the officers can be gauged from the evidence which they presented to a Select Committee on Estimates,[80] and to the Franklin Committee. This Committee's Report, published in 1951, is odd in one interesting respect. Unlike all of the official inquiries and reports discussed so far, as Rose points out, its origins and sources are obscure. It is very likely that the relentless criticism by the officers on the system contributed to the demand for the Inquiry. Indeed, there is no evidence of any other pressure.

Statements of the staff to both Committees, especially about borstal, reflect the gulf which was developing between them and the Commissioners. These statements could only have come from people who were alienated from the organisation, and were designed to arrest developments with which they had no sympathy. The officers put forward the assertion that discipline had deteriorated since the war, that bad behaviour was more common and often went unreported, that subordinate officers were discouraged from reporting misconduct, and that reports were suppressed. These were amongst the most serious allegations ever made against the administration of the prison service by anyone, including ex-prisoners. The open conflict was summed up by the Committee as a:

> wide difference of opinion between the governing and subordinate grades of the Borstal Service on the kind of discipline necessary.

The Commissioners disagreed.[81] And when the POA was invited to supply concrete instances, the Committee reported that their response was 'less fruitful' than had been expected in view of the 'emphatic language' which had been used. Nevertheless the Committee accepted that there had been suppression of reports in the past. And they were not overimpressed with what they saw in borstals:

> We saw lads with long matted hair, unkempt in their clothing, slovenly and untidy, slouching without any form of respect past the officers of whatever rank whom they met or passed.

The officers had made quite an impact. It was as though officers were writing when, in an attack on the assistant governors, the Committee commented that 'too much leniency' was being interpreted as 'sloppy sentimentality'. 'Discipline,' they concluded, 'in general requires tightening.' It was. The 1952 Annual Report announced new Prison and Borstal Rules which set out to do this, and a borstal institution was set aside for troublemakers.

The officers' views were rammed home again in their evidence in the *Seventh Report from the Select Committee on Estimates*. The claim about the suppression of reports was repeated. At Portland it was alleged the boys were in charge and housemasters were apparently 'sensible' if they 'never interfere with the staff in any way whatsoever'. From about 1938 there had developed, it was claimed, an 'appeasement policy'.[82] This fundamental division grew worse. In 1962 *The Times* reported a 'gap between enlightened policies and the outlook of the ordinary prison officers'.[83]

The Commissioners' explanation of the increase in escapes and violence was more tempered. They were only rarely critical of officers. In 1952 they reported that 'the reports of Governors on their junior staff are more encouraging than those of a few years ago', which meant presumably that they had been dissatisfied earlier. The Governor of Parkhurst stated that the standard of officers had deteriorated since the war.[84] The temptation to accuse the uniformed staff of disloyalty at best, or prosecute for offences under the Official Secrets Act at worst, must have been very strong. It was, however, resisted.

Instead the Commissioners attributed the trouble to overcrowding, shortage of staff, to violence in society and, inevitably, to a decline in the standard of prisoner being received. Especially in respect of the corrective trainee and the borstal boy, each year brought reports of further deterioration. It is impossible to be sure whether this explanation was any more valid than it had been in 1933. Corrective trainees were after all recidivists, and a realistic expectation might well have been that they would be indifferent training material. With regard to borstal, it is likely that the extension, and increased use of, detention centres affected the quality of boy sent to borstal. But this was not until the early 1960s, and the official observations about deterioration went back for many years before that.

One factor which may have affected the attitude of these groups, as indeed of all prisoners, to their environment and their 'training' was the subtle shift in the operation of the system of privileges. This may be seen as early as 1937. In June of that year the Home Secretary announced that it was better to give an inmate privileges at once, with the threat of losing them, rather than to offer 'the rather indefinite hope of getting something better later on if he behaves well'. Remission is an example. Originally a prisoner had to earn it; now it is automatic and he can lose it for misbehaviour. In fact it is much more difficult to remove a privilege once given, than to award it as a culmination of good behaviour. Privileges which are given almost at once, cease to be privileges. They become accepted as rights, and their value as stimuli to good behaviour and hard work is lost. The 'deterioration' which is commented upon may be a consequence of this shift.

How then could the officers deal with this situation? The familiar clichés about how crucial their part was in the new reformative measures were sustained.[85] And of course this was true in a negative sense. The extensive contact which the officers had with inmates could well inhibit, diminish, or even wreck, any attempts at reformation which might have been made. Indeed, unconvinced of the feasibility, and perhaps the desirability, of reform, relationships between staff and inmates may well have *deteriorated*, since each new reform laid new stress on the officer;[86] but it was the underlying concern for the prisoner which made him very angry. It led, as I have described, to a demand for more 'discipline', which increased the worsening hostility between the two groups:[87]

> By now I was seething with rage, not so much at the behaviour of the mutineers but at the system which I knew had encouraged them. I suggested that some of us, with the Camp Hill crowd, should belt into the rabble with riot sticks, round them up and teach them that they were in prison. The governor looked shocked as if I'd made an indecent proposal.

It was in the person and role of the officer that the confusion of tasks reached its most visible, as well as its most disastrous, expression. For at the same time as they were protesting about the ill-effects of reformation, they were demanding that they be involved in it. In 1957 it was reported that the officers wished to become involved in group psychotherapy. The practice of allocating groups of prisoners to officers, which was one of the features of the Norwich system, was extended to several institutions at different times. Where there was a hostel, it was usually a principal officer who was in charge of it. He was often responsible for liaison with employers in the district, and performed an almost exclusively training role. At one borstal the most promising re-examination of the borstal system of the decade involved officers, for the first time in borstal, closely in the training of boys.[88] The adoption of group-counselling techniques also provided an opportunity for uniformed staff to become associated with reform. Although the extent and quality of this association varied from the extensive to the merely nominal, involvement in counselling was the closest that the officer was ever to come to a rehabilitative role.[89] When discussing this involvement in any of these aspects of reform, it is always essential to bear in mind three points. First, that the number of institutions which made any pretence at wishing to develop the officer's role in this way, was very small. Second, that there was by no means universal involvement of all the staff in these few institutions; and third, that the quality of the reformative work carried out, with the possible exception of that by hostel wardens, was not high.

Because of the ever increasing eminence of the reformative aim, and the consequent depression of the controlling task, the prison officer began to express some distaste for his work. In 1963 the POA published a three-page document, 'The Role of the Modern Prison Officer' (referred to here as the 'POA Memorandum'), which is unique since it set out an account of the officer's position as he saw it. It begins with a precise and accurate description of the bulk of the work performed by the majority of the officers:

a day's duty for an officer usually comprises nothing more or less than unlocking the men and locking them up again; escorting them to exercise, to the workshops and back again inside the prison; feeding them and, at the end of the day, finally locking them up and checking them in for the night.

This document was unanimously adopted at the POA Annual Conference in 1963. In essence, it proposes that there should be five aspects of the role of the officer, which would mean five grades of officer. First, there would be 'group work' officers who had 'passed through the group work training part of the programme' for which 'no great academic learning is necessary'. Next come the 'rehabilitation officers', another group role whose difference from the previous grade is not clear, except that their training would be 'to a higher standard'. The fourth grade would be welfare officers, who would do what welfare officers do at the moment, and finally there would be a grade which would work in liaison with the after-care associates. The document concludes with the hope that the proposals will eradicate 'a common attitude amongst prison officers which reflects a bitter hopelessness'.

Apart from the major disadvantages of an entirely wrong structure, the proposals were not realistic because of staff attitudes to, and expectations of, the role of the officer. Governors for their part were sometimes willing to initiate a group-counselling programme, but only rarely were they involved in it themselves, and equally rarely did they understand the implications of such a programme. Often there was a need to rearrange work schedules, to pay overtime and so forth, which was opposed by the senior uniformed staff, who were usually highly suspicious of these new activities by junior staff, and made their disapproval clear to them.[90] There is very little evidence, even in the *Prison Officers' Magazine*, other than the 'unanimous vote', that many officers either properly understood the proposals, or agreed with them. The POA like other trade unions, has to make suggestions and take up positions with which the membership does not really agree. The most easily demonstrable of these is on overtime. As the POA has admitted, if their demand that this be cut down or eliminated were met, there would be an angry reaction from the officers.[91]

Why then was the memorandum drawn up, if it had so little real chance of success? It was, above all, a kind of wild blow at the forces whose encroachment was lowering the status of the officer. The memorandum was not so much motivated by a wish to be involved in reformation, as from a desire to arrest the process of status erosion which the officer, correctly, felt was the most significant development in his situation. Thus for instance, it was not long before the POA, commenting on the introduction of courses for staff which followed the memorandum, was expressing the hope that, with the introduction of these courses, direct entry might soon be ended.

The problem for the Prison Department was how to deal with these demands of the officer for a reformative role, which culminated in the 1963 Memorandum. This was the year of *The Organisation of After-Care*, which had recommended an extended welfare service. Nothing could stop this and the most that the official side would concede was that it did 'not rule out the possibility of Prison Officers, if suitably qualified, becoming welfare officers'.[92] The reform groups themselves, as well as 'progressive' governors, were also anxious to see the uniformed staff in a kind of reformative role, although there was, inevitably, a great deal of vagueness about exactly how this was to be achieved.

In the early years of the period the reduction of formality between staff and inmates associated with the Norwich system and similar schemes represented a great change, and could be acclaimed as contributing to the general reformative endeavour. The consultative committee, which was a kind of staff meeting, at first was acclaimed, because of the novelty of any 'upward' communication at all. Consultative committees were introduced in 1955 and were reported as being successful for some years. Because they were mere appendages to the system, their uselessness soon became apparent, and they petered out. They have not been mentioned since the Annual Report for 1962. But these, after all, were modest innovations. Group counselling, and the Huntercombe system, could be contained, without interfering too much with the traditional framework of institutional life. Both however began to press against the framework and needed a serious commitment by governors to sustain the crises which such novelty brought. The POA Memorandum was entirely different. This involved more than 'much hard work', it meant revolution. Yet it could not be rejected, and so it was received 'sympathetically'.[93]

The Home Secretary, on 5 March 1964, in answer to a question about involving prison officers in rehabilitation and the steps he was taking to enable them 'to qualify as social workers in prison', expressed pleasure at the desire of officers to be involved. A Joint Working Party was set up and made its first report in June 1964.[94] The second interim report indicated clearly what the response of the Department was going to be. It was first to emphasise the insuperable difficulties of implementing staff proposals. For example, the staff thought little could be done with a pilot scheme at Pentonville, until the population had been reduced to 850. The official reply was that this was impossible. The second was to emphasise the value of training. Extra-mural training was to be encouraged, and officer training at Wakefield was 'redesigned to bring it more into line with the modern role of the prison officer'.[95]

Organisations often look to training as a means of coping with difficulties, not because it will solve them, but because training has overtones of professionalism and intellectual attainment, which can keep demands for radical change at bay. This was the role of training in this scheme of things. Officers were encouraged to go to courses of all kinds,[96] no doubt with the expectation on their part that they would become in some vague kind of way trained in social work. They certainly hoped that their training would be put to some novel use. Once again, the implications of this situation had barely been considered. No doubt many, if not all, of the courses were good and worthwhile. No doubt many officers enjoyed them and gained a great deal from them. But they did not produce qualified social workers, nor was the situation in the institution influenced by this training. The role remained that of the controller. It may be that an officer, after a course, knew more about criminality, perhaps his approach to the prisoner was more informal, but this is not social work. And he was still occupied in traditional tasks. In a later discussion the staff side expressed concern that 'the most effective use should be made of officers who had undertaken special training'.[97] But in fact, as often happens, training was encapsulated and regarded as something which happens elsewhere.

The officers soon began to protest at the lack of activity in implementing their proposals.[98] But they never could be implemented. The extent of a uniformed officer's involvement in reform is that he should be sensitive to the complicated fabric of the prisoner's situation: conscious of the complexity of a background which propelled him into crime, aware of the effects of the experience of imprisonment during and after sentence, and knowledgeable about such organisational resources as can be called upon to aid the process of reformation. Such an aim may appear modest. But it is usually absent, and its encouragement is the most significant, as well as the greatest, contribution that a uniformed officer can make to a regime which seeks to introduce reformative measures. Occasionally he may become involved in techniques such as group counselling. But the numbers of officers, and indeed of inmates, so involved will be small, and the amount of time spent on such activities will be slight. Even in borstal, where the officer has always been regarded as part of 'the treatment team', as recently as the 1964 Annual Report it was stated that: 'the staff have traditionally spent very little time discussing the lads' offences with them.' When all the proposals, assertions about development, and accounts of 'change' are scrutinised, it emerges that all prison officers, for nearly all the time, are engaged in work which is, in all important essentials, the same as it was in 1877; which is precisely what the POA had said in the Memorandum.

Events leading to the Mountbatten Report

The 1950s, and early 1960s, saw the prison service trying to cope with a situation of appalling confusion. There were now two contradictory manifest tasks—Rule 6, which ordained reformation, and the warrant, which ordained custody. Within the service, the assumed task varied from grade to grade and often from person to person within the grade. Commissioners were committed to Rule 6, governors were probably divided and officers probably rejected reformation in favour of custody and deterrence. The specialist groups were oriented to reformation, but differed about the best means of setting about it. The prisoners themselves saw the task as primarily deterrent. The extant task was custody. To members of the service who saw little discrepancy between the manifest, assumed and extant tasks, the requisite task did not arise. Those, on the other hand, including most officers, who saw that the equilibrium was seriously disturbed, defined the requisite task as the restoration of a controlling task.

These conflicts had led to increases in escapes, loss of control of inmate affairs, an unwieldy central administration complicated by the growth of specialists and a loss of personal contact as a consequence of the abolition of the Commission. Morale was low amongst officers because of the depressed status of control (which was their work), the overwhelming concern for inmates, and the lack of guidance, direction and support from the Head Office. The paramilitary structure which was originally associated with supervision *and* support, now only manifested its coercive overtones. Guidance was rare, but reprimand, in the event of unsatisfactory behaviour, was certain. And so the officers coped by 'opting out'.

Many of the governor grades were unhappy, for most of the same reasons. Although a formal description of the role of the governor would have been identical with that of the governor of 1877, there were cardinal differences. The governor in later years did not have anything like the authority of his predecessor. The growth of specialists, and the transfer of power to the Head Office, had made important inroads on his authority. This process was not easily seen, and the governor was still regarded as one of the last of the autocrats wielding a power which could be used to implement reform. But as the governors themselves said:[99]

> The preservation of a certain hierarchy does not entail the preservation of particular roles.

The people who work in the middle and lower strata of an organisation are usually the first to be aware that there is something wrong. In the evolution of a crisis they may be aware of this for some considerable time, but in the absence of effective communication with the administrative heads and policy makers, they may not be able to demonstrate that they know. The POA, as we have seen, attacked the system and drew attention to its defects for many years. And both the officers and the governors stated in evidence to the 1967 Estimates Committee that they had been aware that the situation of conflict could not go on indefinitely:

> Our evidence to the Mountbatten inquiry indicated our lack of surprise at the extent to which the present prison crisis has developed. Most of us have worked in an atmosphere of

incipient crisis for many years. (The governors.[100])

—there have been times when the prison service was near to a far more serious situation than that of a number of individual escapes; there have been occasions on which there could have been mass indiscipline and collective breaking out on a serious scale. (The officers.[101])

It was apparent then, that all the ingredients were present for a major crisis in the organisation. What was needed was a catalyst to bring the crisis to a head. Two developments contributed to this catalyst: the reduction and ultimate abolition of capital punishment, and the appearance in England of a novel kind of professional criminal.

The change in the law relating to capital punishment resulted in the award of life sentences to murderers who were unlikely to be released for a very long time, if at all. Previously, life-sentence prisoners expected to be considered for release after a long period of imprisonment. As Sir Harold Scott said in evidence to the Royal Commission on Capital Punishment, 1953, this 'prospect of release . . . was an important factor in the maintenance of discipline in prison.' They, like all other prisoners, were induced to collaborate with the system through techniques which were compounded of bluff and privilege. The problem of the prisoner who had little or no hope, was obviously going to be a worsening one. This development has been a *reinforcing* influence in the process of re-establishing control rather than a causative one, although the presence of this group was certainly an important factor. In the years from 1966 to 1969 it became even worse as murderers, convicted of offences which appalled the public, were added to the numbers serving life imprisonment.

The second and more central development was the appearance, for the first time, of two new kinds of offender: the spy, whose offences receive very long sentences,[102] and the professional criminal whose offences make world headlines. Increasingly skilful police work had resulted in the prosecution and conviction of growing numbers of these professional criminals[103] and lesser known but equally serious offenders who have been given long sentences.[104] The most important group from the point of view of this analysis, were the mail train robbers. When their appeals were dismissed, the chance of holding them in prisons which had not been secure in any real sense for forty years, was very slight. This was primarily a task for the traditional prison, with its emphasis on effective containment. But by this time there were none able to contain a prisoner with any real certainty of success. The latest institution, the new psychiatric prison at Grendon Underwood was of no help with its three tasks, none of which was security, and whose aim, above all, was to 'establish a successful therapeutic community'.[105]

One of the many problems of this period was the reappearance of a phenomenon which had not been experienced since medieval times.[106] This was breaking into prisons to aid escape, or to 'plant' aids to facilitate it. As early as 1956 revolvers and keys had been passed into Dartmoor[107] and in 1959 outsiders tried to help prisoners escape from Camp Hill, Wandsworth and Dartmoor.[108] A direct contribution of this practice to the final critical situation occurred in August 1964, when a group of men broke into Birmingham prison and 'released' Charles Wilson, a mail train robber serving thirty years.

This novel, dramatic and highly damaging event attracted only brief mention in the 1964 Annual Report, although new security measures were announced, including a notice that Assistant Directors would concentrate on security in their visits, the setting up of a working party, and the intention to establish special security wings. There was a political storm and criticism from the press. *The Times* in a leading article described the episode as 'a monumental scandal' and said that it made 'the prison service a laughing stock among the criminal classes'.[109]

Worse was to come. In July 1965, a gang of men with the aid of a furniture van and a shotgun, removed Ronald Biggs, another mail train robber, from Wandsworth. This escape led to more demands for improvement in security and the appointment of a security adviser.[110] This appointment was one of a number of indignities to which prison staff had to submit. The person appointed was a police officer. The inability of prison officers to perform their basic job was emphasised in 1965 and early 1966 by the employment of soldiers to patrol Durham and the use of armed police to guard Leicester. It was as though the prison system was changing from open conditions to security for the first time. In all these moves little account could have been taken of the repository of experience which already existed in the prison service.

During 1966 'a number of measures designed to improve security' were instituted or extended.[111] These were expedited by the escape of five prisoners from Wormwood Scrubs in June 1966. But before these measures could be properly introduced, George Blake escaped from Wormwood Scrubs in October 1966. In political terms this was the most important escape and was the reason for the appointment of the Mountbatten Inquiry. There was little comment in the press or in Parliament about the choice of Lord Mountbatten or his assessors. The reaction was one of approval that at last a rigorous inquiry had been put in hand. As if to give the demand a boost, Frank Mitchell, serving life imprisonment for robbery with violence, absconded from an outside working party at Dartmoor.

One of the interesting questions which arises was the political response to the expressions of dissatisfaction which accompanied these events. The parallels with the 1932–3 crisis are striking, but the response of the respective Home Secretaries is quite different. Gilmour in 1933 refused to yield to pressures which advocated a 'tightening up', Jenkins in 1966 did yield to these. It is impossible, without a great deal of information which is not yet available, to develop the comparison of responses which were political, decisions which were based in varying degree on political expedience and outcomes which were to be so crucial to the administration of the English prison system.

The Mountbatten Report and recommendations

The Report dealt with the escapes, which, beginning with Wilson, had caused alarm. These were the escapes of Wilson, Biggs, six prisoners from Wormwood Scrubs, a group from a coach between Winchester and Parkhurst, Mitchell and Blake. For the most part the investigation examined how each escape took place in some detail and from the results drew up a number of recommendations. The Report drew attention to obvious defects in security, such as the presence of hostels inside the prison walls, the 'rudimentary' communications at Dartmoor and so on. The overall view of the system expressed in the Report was summarised in paragraph 204 as follows:

> . . . taking account of the difficulties, the daring and resource of determined escapers has not been matched by a superior imagination, alertness and vigour.

More important than the detailed evidence which the Report furnishes, are the recommendations which Mountbatten made. Not surprisingly, these are dominated by considerations of security. For the purpose of this analysis the recommendations in respect of staff are more relevant than the recommendations about prisoners, although they naturally overlap at times. The principal recommendations about prisoners were that a new maximum security prison should be built, and that prisoners should be classified and allocated according to their security risk. All kinds of resources were seen as contributing to this end, even the recommended increase in welfare facilities.

The recommendations affecting the staff structure were major. One of their more remarkable features was that, unlike the usual proposals for organisational change, they began at the top. Of Head Office, Mountbatten stated that he was 'convinced that matters cannot be left as they stand.' He recommended the establishment of a new post called 'Inspector-General'. This 'high-level and vital post' needed unusual ability, 'and the first may have to come from outside the prison service'. Existing expertise was passed over (the Chief Director's was an office job) and with no examination of what was meant by the term 'professional', the accolade 'professional head of the service' was bestowed on the proposed Inspector-General.

Another important recommendation was that a new grade of senior officer should be established. He would rank between the officer and the principal officer. This change formalised an existing informal extant situation. The term senior officer had been used, unofficially, for many years. Mountbatten envisaged a greater degree of supervision as a result of its establishment. He recommended that the proportion of time given to instruction in security should be increased. The operation of closed circuit television systems, and later the use of dogs, deployed staff on duties exclusively concerned with security. The Report recommended the appointment of a 'security officer' who would be in charge of security matters and who would be a specialist. Finally, it was suggested that officers should gradually take over the work of night patrols. Other changes were recommended, such as that Assistant Directors should have staff officers, but these were mainly designed to increase efficiency in existing parts of the organisation.

It is remarkable, even uncanny, that such recommendations should have been made, for they re-established the staff structure of the pre-Gladstone prison service. All of the changes which had been made in the structure of the uniformed staff since 1877 were reversed and, although the designations of grade are different and functions vary slightly, the staff structure is the same as that which Du Cane established, following Jebb.

The title 'Inspector-General' itself is one which Du Cane held, though in respect of military prisons. The 'introduction' of the 'senior officer' means that there are now three ranks below the chief officer: principal officer, senior officer and officer. Thus the situation is restored to the original gradation: principal warder, warder and assistant warder.[112] The security staff which Mountbatten recommended, was also not new. The significance of this development is that for the first time since the abolition of the civil guard in 1919, there are prison officers who do not have face-to-face dealings with prisoners. After the abolition of the guard, who only stood at a distance, every officer had some contact however slight, however peripheral, with prisoners. The new security staff, watching their banks of television screens, or patrolling with dogs, do not have this contact. It is true that Mountbatten believed it would be a 'mistake to create two classes of prison officer', but, if security is given a high priority, it is inevitable. Security staff will develop new skills and expertise which it would be economically unwise to waste by transfer to other duties. Current advertisements announce another complication which is symptomatic—that security staff will receive extra allowances.

Not only is the security staff structure a resurrection of the old civil guard, but the 'security officer' is a resurrection of the old superintendent. An awareness of the history of prisons would have warned of a basic organisational flaw. There is a built-in clash with the chief officer who has always been regarded as in some way 'responsible' for security, although it is only rarely that he is held to account for it. Security is now an activity which accrues status, evidenced by extra pay. The inevitable, increasing independence of the security staff, with the chief officer's control of them diminishing, will lead to conflict; a conflict which may incidentally lead to a defect in security. This is why the superintendent's post was abolished by Du Cane, and the guard was put under the chief officer.

Mountbatten considered the question of firearms for certain officers, but recommended against it. The old civil guard was armed, and so inexorable seems this reversion to the old structures, that even this feature of security has now been recommended.[113] Lastly the introduction of night duty for officers was, in fact, also a reintroduction. It was usual until 1912. The only real novelty in the post-Mountbatten situation was the use of dogs in the centralised system, although they had been used in Gloucester Prison in 1820.

Conclusion

This analysis of the role of the English prison officer has been structured round the historical evolution of the prison system. Empirical evidence has been drawn from that evolution to account for the development of his role within the framework of the overall primary task of the system, which is control.

It has been shown that any prison system must be examined within the context of a dynamic relationship with the community. The latter expresses its disapproval of the system if evidence appears that control is not being exerted. This evidence takes the form of riot, or an intolerable level of escaping, or very rarely cruel treatment of inmates. Very rarely, partly because having little sympathy with the prisoner the community does not become so agitated at revelations of ill-treatment, partly because such ill-treatment is difficult to prove, but mainly because modern prison systems usually ensure that supervision is effective in preventing it happening.

Whether it is rioting or escaping which becomes the manifest disaster, depends on the particular prison system. If there is perimeter security there will be riots, if there is not, escapes will soar. Both problems can be removed if prisoners are not allowed to associate or communicate freely. Contact between prisoners is an essential preliminary to either. If such association is allowed, crises will arise, and the community must tolerate them, or remove their means—communication.

It is, of course, possible to speculate endlessly about how the attention of the community is drawn to the evidence of task failure. The press may be blamed and accused of creating a panic. The role of the mass media may be examined, perhaps deplored. The attitude of the community may be deprecated. The very use of the term community may be challenged. Those are interesting questions. But the fact is that, for whatever reason, and by whatever means, the community from time to time expresses displeasure at the workings of its prison system, and correctives are applied to reassert the controlling priority.

I have shown that in the English system until recently, the central debate was not about this primary task of control, but was about the secondary task, a discussion which hinged on the classic debate about reformation and deterrence. Until 1895 the secondary task was deterrence. There was no conflict in the system, because the regimes necessary to achieve deterrence and control are compatible. When reformation was defined as a task, then a conflict between it and control was inevitable.

The English prison service from 1877 to 1895, in which most of the features of the English officers' role were established, had a clear task. It was a small service, tightly knit and organised in a para-military structure. Since there was clarity of task there was clarity of role. As a result the Commissioners knew what kind of officers they were looking for. This is not to say that the Victorian service had no problems. I have discussed two inquiries into staff grievances. It is important to note, however, that these grievances were almost entirely about material matters and were dealt with in this way mainly because there was no machinery for consultation. It is hardly necessary to add that the prison service was by no means unique in this respect in Victorian England. However one very ominous defect in the organisation had already begun to make itself felt towards the end of Du Cane's regime. This was the gradual breakdown in communication between Head Office and the prisons, which was to contribute in no small measure to the crises of the 1960s.

The Gladstone Committee began that process of organisational confusion which, even at a distance of seventy years, culminated in the Mountbatten Report. These years saw the increasing alienation of the prison officer from the aims of the organisation, aims which he found confusing, and in some cases, repugnant. A very important factor in this alienation was the drawing together of the Commissioners and governor grades, and the prisoners. In the Victorian service, officers and governors were able to identify with each other in pursuit of a common task. The variation of the governor's role to that of a reformer, led the officers to believe that they were now second in importance to the prisoners. Commissioners' and governors' concern for prisoners was repeated in the work of the reform organisations, from whom the officers finally broke in the 1920s. Later, the officers detected hostility from other groups in society, a hostility which was a feature of social attitudes in the 1950s and 1960s. I have shown that as the service became more complex, the attempts to involve the officer in specialist work and his attempts to become involved in it, failed. As time went on, he was progressively excluded from nearly every role which was not custodial. The struggle, which came to a head in the 1950s and 1960s, and which he lost, was over a welfare role. The extended social work provision in prisons was to be carried out by professional social workers.

But at the centre of this process of alienation was the deteriorating relationship between the Commissioners and the prisons. As early as 1895, there was evidence that civil servants were taking over the decision-making machinery in the Home Office. This consolidation of the civil servants' power in London had its parallels in the prisons where increasingly the clerks were establishing an identity of their own. They eventually established links with other civil servants in Head Office, which led to a communication system which bypassed governors and Commissioners, and created a separate power structure which deserves prolonged examination. The result of this increasing remoteness of the Head Office was a feeling of hopelessness on the part of officers, and a conviction that 'the people in London' did not know anything about prisons. Those who did, Inspectors and Commissioners, were powerless. Head Office came to be regarded as a place from whence correction, but not approval, was certain to come.

Prison officers were not the only people to face these problems. The influx of specialists, who collectively reduced the status of the generalists, occurred in the hospital service. The head of the organisation who bypasses the entire staff to deal with inmates personally, is a commonplace in the psychiatric hospital. The officers' struggle to form a staff association is paralleled in the experience of other workers. Responsibility for social and welfare services other than prisons lay in a Ministry in London. But the prison officer's experience of all these developments was more intense than most. The skills of some of the specialists who went into the prison service were not readily acknowledged by the officers as skills worthy of the name. The Physician Superintendent who practises his skills on a patient is more readily conceded as having a treatment role by nurses, than is the governor by his officers. The struggle for recognition for a staff association was longer and, in its way, more damaging than that of many other workers. Finally the prison system is more centralised than any other service. There is no parallel with the local education authority, or the hospital management committee, which act as buffers. Ineffective communication with the centre of the prison service leaves prison staff completely isolated.

As the years went on the English prison officer coped by dissociating himself from the way in which prisons were run. The *Prison Officers' Magazine* and later the Prison Officers' Association, expressed the contempt of the body of staff for the confusion in which the service lay. Officers carried out their routine tasks, and tried to draw attention to the defects in the system. They occasionally, for example, drew attention to the worst dangers in association. When no notice was taken they could only survey the growth of an inmate sub-culture over which they could have no control.

And so the prison service moved inevitably towards crisis, which took the form of escapes which the community was not prepared to tolerate. Changes in policy before and after the Mountbatten Report applied correctives which have reasserted the custodial priority, and reaffirmed the controlling role of the prison officer. His role has not been drastically altered as a result of the Mountbatten Report. The most significant change is that his work is now regarded as necessary and it is the work which his predecessors were carrying out in 1877.

What conclusions can be drawn from this analysis? The most important is that whatever manifest tasks may be declared, the community perceives the prison primarily as a coercive organisation and measures its competence as such. In the real world of prisons, the burden of carrying out this task rests on the basic-grade uniformed officer. This is his role, and it cannot be combined with a reformative role. The perennial reality is that the officer has to spend most, if not all, of his time in custodial tasks—checking bars, counting knives, locking, unlocking and supervising prisoners. Although this is a repressive role it need not be performed in a cruel or vicious way. Officers who are aware of the complexities of criminal behaviour and conscious of the effects of institutionalisation, can treat prisoners with courtesy and kindness without custody being undermined. But this does not mean that he has a reformative role in any real sense.

This has been a study of alienation. How has this process taken place, and how can it be avoided? Clearly the development of a reformative regime has been the principal cause. The resistance of officers to reformative measures has traditionally been reduced to pseudo-psychological discussion about 'punitive personalities' and so on. While there may be aberrant people in the prison service as there are in other occupations, I have tried to show that this is not an adequate reason. The introduction of reformative measures created colossal, *real* problems for the prison officer, which were never faced.

As the years went on it would have been remarkable if he had not become increasingly anxious. Nor was he very distorted in his perception of the situation as one where scarce organisational resources were being deployed to improve the inmates' situation, while his own very real material needs were being ignored.

Must the conclusion be then that no reformative skills can be introduced because the officers may be upset. Of course not. But before they can be introduced two facts must be faced. The first is simply that the possibilities of training and treatment in a prison system are few and limited because of the very nature of imprisonment. Once in the prison system, the reformative agent is regarded by the prisoners as part of the coercive structure ensuring their confinement. The second is that the uniformed staff must be accepted as a constraint upon what is possible. They will resist change, which is only to say that they will behave as other men do in other organisations. How can their understandable resistance to change be minimised, and perhaps eliminated ? These are questions which must be faced by the developing, expanded, social welfare departments in prison. These departments, in time, should be able to make a valuable contribution to the knowledge about prisons.

A situation must be created in which the officers must feel reasonably contented, secure and able to identify with the organisation. The role of the Head Office is absolutely crucial to this end. The officers must feel that the heads of the service accept that the whole organisation is responsible for ensuring effective control of the prison population, not that this rather distasteful task is carried out by unpleasant, reactionary people who in some way are different from other people in the service. It must be clear to the officers that the heads are sympathetic to their problems and that vigilance over staff includes the positive element of support in difficult situations. Above all, officers, and indeed all staff in the field, must have access to the men who make decisions affecting them. The peripatetic powerless delegate from the centre who has haunted the service must disappear.

If this relationship between centre and field can be re-established, with a consequent rise in morale, then the introduction of reformative measures will have some chance of success. If the uniformed staff feel secure, then they will not immediately feel threatened or aggrieved if resources are deployed to develop inmate training or treatment.

The chances of success will be further increased if it is appreciated that the introduction of reformative measures will affect the officers probably more than it will affect any other group, including the prisoners. The effect of change on the officers' work must therefore be fully explored *with them*. The question may well arise whether, if all these preliminaries have to be completed, any reformative measures would ever be introduced. The answer must be that any attempt to do so without the support, in the most general terms, of the officers, is doomed to certain failure. For one thing above all has emerged from this analysis: that the uniformed officer *is* the English prison service.

Notes

1 For an outline of the trends, see Annual Report 1939–41, pp. 7–11; Annual Report 1942–4, pp. 6–8.
2 For an account of 'C.T.', see Fox, *The English Prison and Borstal Systems*, p. 307 et seq. An account of prisoners undergoing the sentence by a prison psychologist is in the Annual Report for 1951, p. 90. Norman, *Bang to Rights*, gives one prisoner's view. Annual Reports examine the failure, actual and incipient, of corrective training. The intention to abolish it, announced in *The Adult Offender*, 1966, was carried out in the Criminal Justice Act 1967.
3 Rose, *The Struggle for Penal Reform*, p. 237.
4 Annual Report 1963, p. 25.
5 For details, see Annual Reports: 1945, pp. 7–8; 1947, pp. 7–9; 1948, pp. 7–8.
6 These allegations excited attention in Parliament. See Hansard, vol. 709, cols. 1355–64.
7 Mountbatten Report, paras 304–6; Annual Report 1967, p. 26.
8 Rose, op. cit., p. 232. Rose discusses both Bills and Act in ch. 16.
9 Prison Rules 1949, rule 6. This was slightly altered and elevated to become rule 1 in the 1964 Prison Rules. Rule 2 in 1964 advised that: 'Order and discipline shall be maintained with firmness, but with no more restriction than is required for safe custody and well-ordered community life.'
10 Newsam, *The Home Office*, p. 144 (Sir Frank Newsam was Permanent Under Secretary at the Home Office). See also *Penal Practice in a Changing Society*, 1959.
11 The remarks made about the figures in Table 3 (see pp. 174–5) are still applicable. A distinction between escapes from 'secure' conditions and others, is made by Mountbatten on page 55 of his

Report. He sets out the number of escapes from secure conditions as follows:

1955	*1960*	*1962*	*1963*	*1964*	*1965*	*1966*
29	76	56	71	93	79	72

The figure for 1966 is for 1 January to 1 December and was later increased to 79 in the Annual Report for 1966, p. 1.

12 See, for example, *The Times*, 18 February 1952, p. 2 and Annual Report 1954, p. 2.
13 Annual Report 1945, p. 47.
14 Annual Report 1947, p. 35.
15 See, for example, *The Times*, 28 June 1951, p. 7 and 8 June 1966, p. 13. The League protested at 'an exaggerated emphasis on security' in a letter to the Home Secretary in 1970 (the *Observer*, 18 February 1970).
16 Annual Report 1958, p. 27.
17 *The Times*, 10 June 1966, p. 13.
18 See, for example, the report of the POA Conference in *The Times*, 28 May 1954, p. 3.
19 See, for example, Annual Report 1952, p. 45.
20 Annual Report 1961, p. 13. In 1960 there were 197 assaults and 213 in 1959.
21 *The Times*, 6 January 1951, p. 4.
22 Annual Report 1959, p. 24.
23 Annual Report 1951, p. 30. See also *Seventh Report from the Select Committee on Estimates, Session 1951–2*, pp. XV–VI and 148.
24 Annual Report 1955, p. 15.
25 Fox, op. cit., pp. 151–2.
26 Annual Report 1952, p. 124. For an account of how association gave free rein to a vicious rule by 'barons' see Cronin, *The Screw Turns*, p. 143.
27 Annual Report 1956, p. 92.
28 Annual Report 1954, p. 71.
29 *The Times*, 22 May 1959, p. 7.
30 Sykes, *The Society of Captives*, p. 57.
31 P.R.O. H.O.45/15189/570791/1984. See also Annual Reports: 1910–11, pp. 23–4; 1911–12, pp. 10–11.
32 P.R.O. H.O.45/15189/570791/1984.
33 Circular 19/1910, P.R.O. H.O.45/15189/570791/1984.
34 P.R.O. H.O.45/15189/570791/1984. As well as the advantages of allowing freedom, 'substantial economies' were noted (Annual Report 1921–2, p. 12 and p. 49).
35 P.R.O. H.O.45/15189/570791/1984. 'Most local prisons have at least one' (Annual Report 1922–3, p. 24).
36 P.R.O. H.O.45/15189/570791/1984.
37 Fox, op. cit., p. 152. Hansard, vol. 324, col. 1348, 4 June 1937. At Maidstone they were called 'leaders' (Fox, op. cit., p. 152).
38 Cronin, op. cit., pp. 51–2.
39 Seventh Estimates Committee Report, p. 178.

40 Hansard, vol. 673, col. 1243, 12 March 1963.

41 Hansard, vol. 673, cols 1256–8, 1241–4, 1251–1314, 12 March 1963.

42 *The Times*, 11 April 1961, p. 11, col. B; 6 February 1963, p. 11, col. C.

43 *The Times*, 8 February 1961, p. 13; 10 February, p. 13; 13 February, p. 11; 14 February, p. 13; 17 February, p. 15; 21 February, p. 11; 23 February, p. 13.

44 *The Times*, 18 February 1961, p. 9.

45 Prison Commissioners Dissolution Order, 1963 (S.I.1963, No. 597).

46 Mountbatten Report, p. 4. But at p. 60 he reports 'morale appeared to me to be surprisingly high in the prisons I visited.' From his general description, however, the first quotation is a more adequate summary of his views.

47 *Eleventh Report from the Estimates Committee, Session 1966–7, Prisons, Borstals and Detention Centres*, p. 58. This report gives a much fuller account of the prison service than does the Mountbatten Report.

48 Ibid., pp. 64–9, 69–80.

49 Ibid., p. 66.

50 Mountbatten Report, para. 224.

51 Eleventh Estimates Committee Report, p. 65.

52 Prison Officers' Association, 'The Role of the Modern Prison Officer', p. 3.

53 'Memorandum submitted by the Howard League for Penal Reform' in the Eleventh Estimates Committee Report, pp. 277–8.

54 Mountbatten Report, para. 224. Mountbatten, in one of several confused statements, goes on to express the view that the abolition of the Commission was necessary in itself (para. 245).

55 Marsh, *The Changing Social Structure of England and Wales 1871–1961*, p. 141.

56 The term is Etzioni's. The first psychologist, for example, was appointed in 1946 (Annual Report 1963, p. 9).

57 'Housemaster' was no longer an official rank after 1947. From that year they became governors, class V (Annual Report 1947, p. 9). In 1949, their title was changed again—to assistant governor class II (Annual Report 1949, p. 9).

58 Wynn Parry Report, 1958, pp. 6–8.

59 Annual Report 1946, p. 11.

60 Annual Report 1955, p. 85.

61 ACTO, *The Organisation of After-Care*, ch. 4. The report revealed how little was known about the borstal housemaster or his training.

62 The decision was announced, 'after consultation', in Parliament (Hansard, vol. 716, cols 83–4, 14 July 1965). The recommendation is made on p. 23 of *The Organisation of After-Care*.

63 *Prison Officers' Magazine*, November 1963, p. 329. The *Magazine* also claimed a 'changeover from turnkey to social worker' (October 1963, p. 297).

64 *The Times*, 29 June 1951, p. 5.

65 Eleventh Estimates Committee Report, p. 65.
66 This term was used to describe prisoners at an Annual POA Conference (*The Times*, 20 May 1966, p. 14).
67 Cronin, op. cit., p. 135.
68 Annual Reports: 1961, pp. 133–4; 1962, p. 123; 1963, p. 91; 1964, p. 87; 1965, p. 77; 1966, p. 69.
69 Annual Report 1967, p. 67.
70 POA Memorandum in the Eleventh Estimates Committee Report, p. 82.
71 In 1963, for example, allegations by the 'Prison Reform Council' were supported by Lord Stonham (*The Times*, 13 February 1963, p. 56).
72 Mountbatten Report, para. 221.
73 The term is Thorsten Sellin's. See 'The Conflict of Conduct Norms', in *The Sociology of Crime and Delinquency*, ed. Wolfgang *et al.*, Wiley, 1962.
74 See Cronin, op. cit., p. 24 and elsewhere.
75 *The Times*, 30 May 1952, p. 3.
76 *The Times*, 29 May 1958, p. 7.
77 *Prison Officers' Magazine*, April 1961, p. 86.
78 *The Times*, 13 June 1966, p. 13.
79 *The Times*, 30 May 1958, p. 8.
80 Seventh Estimates Committee Report.
81 Franklin Report, 1951, p. 89. See also Annual Report 1951, p. 67.
82 Seventh Estimates Committee Report, pp. 151–2.
83 *The Times*, 15 January 1962, p. 11.
84 Seventh Estimates Committee Report, p. 142.
85 See, for example, Franklin Report, p. 12; ACTO, *The Organisation of After-Care*, p. 25; Annual Report 1955, p. 20; Wynn Parry Report, p. 5.
86 At the POA Conference 1952, reference was made to the 'appalling strain mentally and physically to which we are being exposed' (*The Times*, 30 May 1952, p. 3).
87 Cronin, op. cit., p. 139.
88 For accounts by the Governor of Huntercombe and an officer, see *Prison Officers' Magazine*, May 1965, p. 120 and December 1966, p. 319.
89 See Prison Department, *Group Work in Prisons and Borstals*.
90 This very common experience is mentioned in a letter to the *Prison Officers' Magazine* (June 1965, p. 170) where the writer complains that after training they are 'told to forget what we have been taught.' The Chairman of the POA deplored the teaching of 'sociology and goodness knows what' instead of the basic job—'to learn the security' (Eleventh Estimates Committee Report, p. 91).
91 Seventh Estimates Committee Report, p. 30 and p. 52.
92 Joint Working Party on the Role of the Prison Officer, Interim Report, *Prison Officers' Magazine*, June 1964, p. 165.
93 Ibid., p. 164.

94 Ibid.
95 *Prison Officers' Magazine*, July 1965, p. 168.
96 Lists of extra-mural courses appeared in the Annual Reports for two years—1964, p. 8 and 1965, p. 9. They disappeared as the crisis built up.
97 *Prison Officers' Magazine*, July 1966, p. 172.
98 See, for example, 57th meeting of the Prison Department Whitley Council, 12 May 1966, reported in *Prison Officers' Magazine*, July 1966, p. 172.
99 Eleventh Estimates Committee Report, p. 65.
100 Ibid., p. 64.
101 Ibid., p. 81.
102 George Blake was given the longest fixed sentence ever awarded—forty-two years. An account of some others appears in an article in *The Times*, 5 November 1969, p. 8.
103 Latterly the 'Richardson Gang' and the 'Kray Gang'. See Lucas, *Britain's Gangland*.
104 The length of sentences is discussed in the Radzinowicz Report, 1968.
105 Annual Reports: 1962, p. 60; 1963, p. 58.
106 See Pugh, *Imprisonment in Medieval England*, pp. 222–4.
107 Annual Report 1956, p. 35.
108 Annual Report 1959, p. 25. See also Annual Report 1958, p. 27.
109 *The Times*, 13 August 1964, p. 11.
110 *The Times*, 10 July 1965, p. 9.
111 Annual Report 1966, p. 8. By now all the 'advantages' of sharing cells had gone: now this was a 'threat to security' (ibid., p. 10).
112 This was varied to principal warder and warder classes I and II in 1909 (Annual Report 1909–10, p. 25). The two classes of warder were amalgamated in 1920 (*Prison Officers' Magazine*, September 1920, p. 9).
113 Radzinowicz Report, pp. 23–4.

10   Postscript

Some results of the implementation of the Mountbatten recommendations

There was an immediate effort to tighten up security after the Report. The measures which were taken must have cost a great deal of money, but the amount is not distinguishable from other expenditure in the Annual Reports. Some idea of the capital outlay can be gauged from the statement that in one small prison, Hull, the 'conversion' cost one million pounds.[1] At Wakefield the figure quoted was £180,000–£200,000.[2] The effect on staff was no less drastic:[3]

> Staff who had long been encouraged to develop treatment relationships towards prisoners had little time for this important work after discharging tasks arising from the need to concentrate on security. There was some curtailment of prisoners' activities, a reduction in the number of outside working parties and of educational classes. Hostels at Cardiff, Chelmsford and Wandsworth were closed.

The officers made no complaint. They felt that they would now get the guidance and support they had wanted. The appointment of an ex-regular soldier[4] to be Inspector-General[5] was of the greatest significance and is yet another example of the process of restoration which was at work. Reformative pretensions in respect of the officer's role had not diminished the proportions of ex-regular servicemen who were attracted to prison work, and the complaints about these proportions were sustained. With a restored primary task, and the overtones of militarism once again respectable, it might appear that there were few real problems to resolve. In fact, despite the expense and the 'change', which seemed radical, there was not as much impact in respect of really fundamental matters, as might appear.

There have already been several interesting developments. The first is that although the intention was that the Inspector-General should be the 'professional head', well known, close to the Home Secretary and so on, the prison service was very much more complicated than it was when Du Cane was appointed. The flaw in Mountbatten's expectation was that he took no account of the place of the senior civil servants in the revised service. In 1969 a 'management review team' investigation resulted in a reconstituted Prisons Board. How far this review arose from Mountbatten is not clear. The Chairman was to be an administrative class civil servant, and the Inspector-General was to be one of five members of the Board. The danger here is evident from the historical analysis. It is that the Inspector-General's role will become like that of the Inspectors and Commissioners of earlier years, consisting essentially of a round of visits made ineffective through lack of executive authority.

This departmental reconstruction has led to more involvement of field prison staff in the central administration. Two of the five members nominated had been prison governors and, since 1968, there appears to have been a studied attempt to bring staff, including senior uniformed staff, into Head Office. The most optimistic view of this development is that it may draw Head Office and the field together, since staff in the prisons may be able to identify the decision makers at the centre. The prison staff moved to Head Office, for their part, may be very much more conscious of despair felt by people in the field, and may try to bridge the gap. This is the best that can happen. The worst that can happen is that the administrative and executive classes will contain the people with field experience and ensure that they are neutralised. The sum total of the historical evidence is that precisely this will happen. This remains to be seen.

But the Mountbatten crisis was about security. While gestures could be made in the shape of changes in staff structures, and a great deal of money could be spent on security devices, the really basic problem could not be tackled. The prison system was so committed to minimum security that the process which had been going on could not be reversed for political, and even more to the point, for economic reasons. After all, the crisis leading to Mountbatten was over escapes, the Report was about escapes and the recommendations were intended to reduce escapes. The success of the new security policy must therefore be judged on *its effectiveness in the prevention of escapes*. The figures of escapes for 1967 and 1968 are given in Table 6.

The Prison Department persists in its claim that only escapes from closed prisons should count as escapes. In the 1968 Annual Report, it is stated that strengthened physical security has produced encouraging results and attention is drawn to the reduction of escapes from closed prisons and remand centres:

1965	1966	1967	1968
77	79	23	21

Table 6   Escapes and attemps to escape, 1967–8

Daily average population	Escapes*	Attempts	Escaping offences punished which were committed at another establishment
1967			
Prison and remand centre 26,909	178	108	136
Borstal 5,562	599	155	388
Detention centre 1,585	49	31	2
34,056	826	294	526

Total escapes 1,352 = 39·7 per thousand
Total escapes and attempts 1,646 = 48·4 per thousand.

1968			
Prison and remand centre 24,712	165	95	125
Borstal 5,389	786	200	434
Detention centre 1,555	54	40	2
31,656	1,005	335	561

Total escapes 1,566 = 48·7 per thousand.
Total escapes and attempts 1,901 = 59·4 per thousand.

* Borstal and detention centre 'absconds' are now classed as escapes in the Annual Report.

It can be seen therefore that the various elements in the new security apparatus have reduced 'maximum security' escapes by 56 since 1965. Or, to put the best construction on these figures, escapes of this kind have been cut by approximately two-thirds. A consideration of the total escape pattern, however, demonstrates that the numbers of people who escaped from all kinds of prison establishments increased.

It has been shown, both from theoretical propositions and from practical experience, notably at Dartmoor in 1932, that the refusal to condone escape as a release from institutional pressure must result in internal disturbances. This will happen in the English system as security is increasingly strengthened. Indeed there have already been serious disturbances at Durham and Parkhurst, which led to the prosecution of prisoners for very serious offences and to a demand from officers for effective riot equipment.

The number of potential trouble spots has been increased by the policy of 'dispersal' of the most dangerous prisoners, consequent upon the Radzinowicz Report. Mountbatten had recommended the establishment of a new super-security prison. But, it was decided, for a number of reasons, that these prisoners should be dispersed throughout several prisons. It is only fair to say that the Advisory Council on the Penal System recognised that the choice between concentration and dispersal is difficult.

Given the restored emphasis on security, it is natural that governors and staff of prisons to which dangerous prisoners are sent, will make security the first and last consideration, to be absolutely certain that they will not escape. It follows that unnecessary restrictions will be placed on large numbers of prisoners in those prisons, a possibility which was recognised by the Radzinowicz Committee. Also, the prospect of recreating the Dartmoor situation, where a whole prisoner community has to suffer from the depredations of a violent, powerful man, or group of men, is very gloomy indeed.

Society should not be surprised when, over the next few years, serious disturbances increase in prisons. This will not be due, necessarily, to harsh treatment by staff, but it is almost certain to be a consequence of the increase in security which followed the Mountbatten Inquiry. Such disturbances are inevitable in top-security prisons. If dangerous prisoners were confined to one prison, then in other prisons, the stress, and the danger of disturbance would be reduced.

The alternative to such disturbance is to condone a certain amount of escaping, which would appear to be inevitable in a prison system which has reformative pretensions. This is an issue for society to discuss and decide upon.

Notes

1 Hull *Daily Mail*, 6 February 1970, p. 1.
2 Eleventh Estimates Committee Report, p. XVIII; further information about costs is given on p. XIX.
3 Annual Report 1967, p. 5.
4 Dr N. A. Jepson, in an unpublished survey, found that 34 per cent of officers attending two-year and five-year courses at Wakefield from 1964 to 1966 had completed *regular* engagements. This figure excluded national service and wartime experience.
5 Prison officers approved of the establishment of the post, and of the reappointment of Brigadier M. S. K. Maunsell to fill it (*Guardian*, 12 February 1969, p. 4).

Appendix

The closing of prisons in 1878

The Prisons Act came into force on 1 April 1878. There is an extra-ordinary amount of confusion in reports, newspapers and books about the precise number of local prisons which were taken over, and the number and names of subsequent closures. Since the opportunity has presented itself, I should like to clear this up. The First Local Report stated that the actual number taken over was 113. But the first official list, in this First Report of the Prison Commissioners, which 'shows the prisons which came into our possession on the 1st April' consists of 112 prisons. This discrepancy seems to have arisen because the Appendix, while intended to be a list of prisons, is headed:

> Return showing the number of *prisoners* in every prison in England and Wales on the 29th September 1876 and the 25th September 1877. (My italics.)

The prison missing from the list is Buckingham, since Buckingham did not have any prisoners on 1 April. If Buckingham is added to the first official list then the total becomes 113.

There is further confusion about closures. On p. 6 of the First Report, the Commissioners state: 'we were able to show to your satisfaction that 37 might be dispensed with in May', and Appendix 7 to the First Report shows 'The population of each prison on 2nd April and 2nd July 1878, showing the redistribution after 37 gaols had been closed.' But Du Cane wrote later that: 'On that day, after due preparation, an order was issued by which 38 prisons of the 113 were closed in the month of May.'[1] *The Times* reported that the order 'made on the 1st April' ordered no less than 38 prisons to be dis-continued in the month of May,[2] but in fact lists 37. The elusive Buckingham had still not been included in the official lists, once again because these lists were primarily concerned with prisoner population. If Buckingham is added the number is 38.

The Times's list included Buckingham, which was singled out for special mention. 'In this list will be found several which have been a frequent mark for the shafts of penal reformers—Buckingham

Borough which managed to secure the services of a governor, matron, chaplain, and surgeon, not to mention other minor officials, all for the sum of £12 10s. 0d. per annum.' However, the list omitted Ipswich Borough, probably because the 'Borough' was merged with the 'County'.

In fact the number of May closures *was* 38, as can be deduced from subsequent lists in Annual Reports. The prisons which were closed were:

Cambridge	Sandwich	Peterborough Liberty
Isle of Ely	Lincoln County	Berwick on Tweed
Wisbech	Falkingham	Borough
Barnstaple Borough	Lincoln City	Nottingham County
Tiverton	Grantham	Oxford City
Devonport	Stamford Borough	Portsmouth Borough
Poole	Beaumaris County	Bury St Edmunds
Ilford	Cardigan County	Appleby
Bristol City Bridewell	Mold County	Beverley County
Ipswich Borough	Dolgelley County	Scarborough County
Buckingham	Montgomery County	Ripon Liberty
Hereford City	Wymondham County	Presteign County
Hertford	(for women)	
Dover	Norwich City	

Total 38

These closures left 75 local prisons. The situation was promptly confused by the opening of 'new' Portsmouth on 22 August 1878[3] bringing the total up to 76. By 31 August, Petworth, Bath, Brecon, Haverfordwest, Oakham and Southampton had been closed.[4] Newington was closed by the end of September. This left 69, but the position with regard to Leicester's two prisons is confused. In a rather unclear footnote on p. 6 of the First Report, it is stated that 'the Leicester County and Borough prisons are also to be worked administratively as one.' On p. 7 of the Second Report it is stated that 'the old borough prison at Leicester has been closed since our last report.' These two prisons are distinguished in some reports (for example in appendix 5 to the Second Report), but apparently reckoned as one in others (as in appendix 2 to the same report). To arrive at the total of 68 prisons claimed by the Commissioners,[5] Leicester must be reckoned as one.

From the Third Report (1879–80) it can be seen that Northampton (Lower) and Southall were closed by February 1880. This ought to have left 66 prisons, but in fact the total was 67 on 31 March 1880.[6] This discrepancy is accounted for by the reopening of Brecon on 21 February 1880.[7] There was no change in the Fourth Report, 1880–1. On 1 November 1881, Morpeth was closed[8] and Newgate, one of the most famous prisons of all time, was closed on 7 February 1882. The closing of Newgate was a relatively complicated matter, necessitating an Act of Parliament. Newgate continued to function as a lock-up during sittings of the Central Criminal Court, but its local prison function was taken over by Clerkenwell.

At the end of the reporting period 1881–2 there were 65 local prisons. During the period of the Sixth Report 1882–3, there were no closures, but in 1883–4 the closures began again. Spalding had closed by March 1884.[9] In October 1883 Westminster (Tothills) was closed, and Westminster (Millbank) was substituted for it. The total was then 64. The Eighth Report 1884–5 reports that in the period, Chester, Taunton and Huntingdon were closed. The first two in fact closed on 1 October 1884, but Huntingdon still had 19 prisoners on 3 March 1885.[10] This reduced the number to 61. The next prisons to be closed were Coldbath Fields Prison and Clerkenwell House of Detention, in March and June 1886 respectively. The prisons at Holloway and Pentonville were improved and adapted to cater for the extra numbers.[11] Pentonville thereby changed its status from convict to local prison. In March 1887, therefore, there were 60 locals.

Notes

1 Du Cane, *The Punishment and Prevention of Crime*, p. 74.
2 *The Times*, 12 June 1878, p. 4.
3 Second Local Report, p. 50, app. 13.
4 Ibid., app. 5.
5 'The number of prisons in use has been reduced from 113 to 68 or nearly by one half' (Second Local Report, p. 1).
6 Third Local Report, p. 7, para. 21.
7 Ibid., app. 12, p. 35, footnote.
8 Fifth Local Report, p. 3.
9 Precise dates can be seen from the return of monthly prisoner population figures, appendix 3 in each Report.
10 Eighth Local Report, app. 3.
11 Tenth Local Report, p. 5, para. 22.

Bibliography

Statutes

16 Geo. III c. 43	'Hard Labour' or 'Hulks Act' 1776, *cont.* by 18 Geo. III c. 62 1778 and 19 Geo. III c. 54 1779
19 Geo. III c. 74	Penitentiary Act 1779
24 Geo. III c. 12	Transportation Act 1784
24 Geo. III c. 54	Gaol Building Act 1784
24 Geo. III c. 56	Transportation Act 1784
31 Geo. III c. 46	Gaol Act 1791
55 Geo. III c. 50	Gaol Fees Abolition Act 1815
56 Geo. III c. 116	Act to Amend and Explain Gaol Fees Abolition Act 1816
4 Geo. IV c. 64	Gaol Act 1823
5 Geo. IV c. 85	Gaol Act 1824
5 and 6 Will. IV c. 38	Prisons Act 1835
2 and 3 Vic. c. 56	Prison Act 1839
5 and 6 Vic. c. 98	Prisons Act 1842
5 and 6 Vic. c. 53	Act for encouraging the establishment of District Courts and Prisons 1842
7 and 8 Vic. c. 50	Act to extend powers in above Act 1844
8 and 9 Vic. c. 114	Gaol Fees Abolition Act 1845
13 and 14 Vic. c. 39	Convict Prisons Act 1850
16 and 17 Vic. c. 99	Penal Servitude Act 1852
20 and 21 Vic. c. 3	Penal Servitude Act 1857
28 and 29 Vic. c. 126	Prisons Act 1865
40 and 41 Vic. c. 21	Prisons Act 1877
44 and 45 Vic. c. 64	Central Criminal Court (Prison) Act 1881
54 and 55 Vic. c. 69	Penal Servitude Act 1891
61 and 62 Vic. c. 41	Prison Act 1898
7 Edw. VII c. 17	Probation of Offenders Act 1907
8 Edw. VII c. 67	Children Act 1908
8 Edw. VII c. 59	Prevention of Crime Act 1908
3 and 4 Geo. V c. 38	Mental Deficiency and Lunacy Act 1913
4 and 5 Geo. V c. 58	Criminal Justice Act 1914
11 and 12 Geo. VI c. 58	Criminal Justice Act 1948
15 and 16 Geo. VI and 1 Eliz. II c. 52	Prison Act 1952
7 and 8 Eliz. II c. 72	Mental Health Act 1959
9 and 10 Eliz. II c. 39	Criminal Justice Act 1961
10 and 11 Eliz. II c. 15	Criminal Justice Administration Act 1962
10 and 11 Eliz. II c. 80	Criminal Justice Act 1967

Official papers and reports

Hansard's Parliamentary Debates.
Annual Reports of the Directors of Convict Prisons, Commissioners of
  Prisons, and the Prison Department, 1851–1968.
The Public Records: H.O. 180 and H.O. 45.
Prison Rules, Borstal Rules, Detention Centre Rules.
Report of the House of Commons Committee on the State of the Gaols,
  1820.
Parliamentary Select Committee on Secondary Punishments, 1833.
House of Lords Committee on the State of the Gaols and Houses of
  Correction, 1835.
Report of the House of Commons Committee on Transportation, 1838.
Parliamentary Select Committee on Prison Discipline, 1850.
Report on the Discipline and Management of the Convict Prisons, by
  Lieutenant-Colonel Jebb, 1851.
Report from the Select Committee of the House of Lords on the Present
  State of Discipline in Gaols and Houses of Correction, 1863 (Carnarvon
  Committee).
Officers' Fees, Salaries, Emoluments. House of Correction, Coldbath
  Fields, 1872.
Departmental Committee on Treatment of Treason Felony Convicts in
  English Convict Prisons, 1867.
Report of the Commissioners Appointed to Inquire into the Treatment of
  Treason Felony Convicts in English Prisons, 1871.
Inquiry as to the Alleged Ill-treatment of the Convict Charles M'Carthy
  in Chatham Convict Prison, 1878, C. 1978.
Report of the Committee of Inquiry on the Wearing of Prison Dress, 1889.
Report of the Visitors of HM Convict Prison at Chatham as to the
  Treatment of Certain Prisoners Convicted of Treason Felony, 1890,
  C. 6016.
Minutes of Evidence taken by the Departmental Committee on Prisons
  with Appendices and Index, 1895, C. 7702–1.
Report from the Departmental Committee on Prisons, 1895 (Gladstone
  Committee), C. 7702.
Observations of Prison Commissioners on Recommendations of Depart-
  mental Committee, 1895.
Departmental Committee on Education and Moral Instruction of Prisoners
  in Local and Convict Prisons, 1896.
Report of the Departmental Committee Appointed by the Secretary of
  State for the Home Department to Inquire into the Representations
  made by the Clerical Staff of HM Prisons, 1903.
Report of Allegations against the Acting Governor of Wandsworth Prison,
  1918, Cmd. 131.
Report of the Departmental Committee Appointed to Inquire into the Pay
  and Conditions of Service at the Prisons and Borstal Institutions in
  England and Scotland and at Broadmoor Criminal Lunatic Asylum,
  1923 (Stanhope Committee), Cmd. 1959.

Report of the Committee Appointed to Inquire into claims of the Men Dismissed from the Police and Prison Services on account of the Strike of 1919, 1925, Cmd. 2297.

Report on the Circumstances Connected with the Recent Disorder at Dartmoor Convict Prison, 1932 (Du Parcq Report), Cmd. 4010.

Report of a Committee to Review Punishments in Prison, Borstal Institutions, Approved Schools and Remand Homes, Parts I and II, 1951 (Franklin Report), Cmd. 8256.

Seventh Report from the Select Committee on Estimates, Session 1951–52.

Report of the Committee on Discharged Prisoners' Aid Societies, 1953 (Maxwell Report), Cmd. 8879.

Allegations of Ill-treatments of Prisoners in HM Prison Liverpool. Report of Inquiry by Sir Godfrey Russell Vick QC, 1958.

Report of the Committee on Remunerations and Conditions of Service of Certain Grades in the Prison Services, 1958 (Wynn Parry Report), Cmd. 544.

Penal Practice in a Changing Society, 1959, Cmnd. 645.

Prisons and Borstals, 1960.

The War against Crime in England and Wales 1959–1964, 1964.

Report of an Inquiry Held by the Visiting Committee into Allegations of Ill-treatment of Prisoners in HM Prison, Durham, 1962 Cmd. 2068.

The Adult Offender, 1966.

Report of the Inquiry Into Prison Escapes and Security, 1966 (Mountbatten Report).

Eleventh Report from the Estimates Committee, 1966–67.

The Regime for Long-term Prisoners in Conditions of Maximum Security, 1968 (Radzinowicz Report).

Reports on crises in institutions other than prisons

Findings and Recommendations following enquiries into allegations concerning the care of elderly patients in certain hospitals, N.H.S., 1968.

Report of the Committee of Inquiry into Allegations of Ill-treatment of Patients and other Irregularities at the Ely Hospital, Cardiff, N.H.S., 1969.

Disturbances at the Carlton Approved School on 29 and 30 August 1959, Home Office, 1959.

Administration of Punishment at Court Lees Approved School, Report of Inquiry by Mr E. B. Gibbens QC, Home Office, 1967.

Report of the Committee of Inquiry Appointed by the Leeds Regional Hospital Board to Inquire into Allegations Concerning the Care and Treatment of Children at the Hornsea Children's Convalescent Hospital, 1970.

Royal Commissions

Royal Commission on the Penal Servitude Acts, 1863.
Royal Commission on Courts Martial and Military Punishments, 1868.
Royal Commission on the Penal Servitude Acts, 1879.
Royal Commission on Capital Punishment, 1953.

Books, pamphlets and articles

'A Prison Matron', *Memoirs of Jane Cameron, Female Convict*, Hurst & Blackett, 1864.
Association of Social Workers, *New Thinking about Administration*, 1966.
Association of Social Workers, *New Thinking about Institutional Care*, 1968.
Banton, M., *Roles*, Tavistock, 1965.
Barton, R., *Institutional Neurosis*, Wright, 1959.
Behan, B., *Borstal Boy*, Hutchinson, 1958.
Blake, W., *Quod*, Hodder & Stoughton, 1927.
Blizard, Sir William, *Desultory Reflections on Police, with an essay on the Means of Preventing Crime and Amending Criminals*, 1785.
Brown, J. A. C., *Social Psychology of Industry*, Pelican, 1964.
Brown, W., *Exploration in Management*, Heinemann, 1960.
Burns, T., and Stalker, G., *Management of Innovation*, Tavistock, 1961.
Burt, The Revd J. T., *Results of the System of Separate Confinement as Administered at the Pentonville Prison*, Longman, Brown, Green and Longmans, 1852.
Buxton, Thomas Fowell, *An Inquiry whether Crime and Misery are Produced or Prevented by our Present System of Prison Discipline*, 1818.
Chamberlain, R. W., *There is no Truce*, Routledge, 1936.
Chesterton, G. L., *Revelations of Prison Life*, 1856.
Clapham, J. H., *An Economic History of Modern Britain*, Cambridge University Press, 1932.
Clark, D. H., *Administrative Therapy*, Tavistock, 1964.
Clay, The Revd W. L., *The Prison Chaplain*, Macmillan, 1861.
Clemmer, D., *The Prison Community*, Holt, Rinehart and Winston, 1940.
Cloward *et al.*, *Theoretical Studies in Social Organisation of the Prison*, SSRC 1960.
Conrad, J. P., *Crime and its Correction*, Tavistock, 1965.
Council of Europe, *The Status, Selection and Training of Prison Staff*, Strasbourg, 1963.
Council of Europe, *Third European Conference of Directors of Criminological Research Institutes*, Strasbourg, 1966.
Cressey, D. R. (ed.), *The Prison: Studies in Institutional Organisation and Change*, Holt, Rinehart and Winston, 1961.
Cronin, H., *The Screw Turns*, John Long, 1967.
D'Harcourt, P., *The Real Enemy*, Longmans, 1967.
Dixon, W. Hepworth, *London Prisons*, 1850.

Donnison, D., and Chapman, V., *Social Policy and Administration*, Allen & Unwin, 1965.

Du Cane, Sir Edmund, *An Account of Penal Servitude in England*, London, 1882. (Almost all of this account is reprinted in his second book.)

Du Cane, Sir Edmund, *The Punishment and Prevention of Crime*, Macmillan, 1885.

Duffy, C., *San Quentin*, Four Square Books, 1958.

Elkin, W. A., *The English Penal System*, Penguin, 1957.

Etzioni, A., *Modern Organizations*, Prentice-Hall, 1964.

Fox, Sir Lionel, *The Modern English Prison*, Routledge, 1934.

Fox, Sir Lionel, *The English Prison and Borstal Systems*, Routledge and Kegan Paul, 1952.

Goffman, E., *Asylums*, Anchor, 1961.

Gordon, J. W., *Borstalians*, Hopkinson, 1932.

Grew, B. D., *Prison Governor*, Herbert Jenkins, 1958.

Grygier, T., Jones, H., and Spencer, J. C., *Criminology in Transition*, Tavistock, 1965.

Hamblin Smith, M., *Prisons*, The Bodley Head, 1934.

Hobhouse, S., and Brockway, Fenner, *English Prisons Today*, Longmans, 1922.

Holland, Vyvyan, *Son of Oscar Wilde*, Penguin, 1957.

Hood, R., *Borstal Reassessed*, Heinemann, 1965.

Howard, D. L., *The English Prison*, Methuen, 1960.

Howard, D. L., *John Howard—Penal Reformer*, Christopher Johnston, 1958.

Howard, John, *The State of the Prisons in England and Wales, with Preliminary Observations and an Account of some Foreign Prisons*, Warrington, 1778.

Jackson, W. A., *The Irish in Britain*, Routledge & Kegan Paul, 1963.

Jacques, E., *The Changing Culture of a Factory*, Routh, 1951.

'J. H.', *Observations, Moral and Political, particularly respecting the Necessity of Good Order and Religious Economy in our Prisons*, 1784.

Johnston, N., Savitz, L., and Wolfgang, M. E., *The Sociology of Punishment and Correction*, Wiley, 1962.

Jones, K., *Lunacy, Law and Conscience 1744–1845: The Social History of the Care of the Insane*, Routledge and Kegan Paul, 1955.

Jones, K., *Mental Health and Social Policy 1845–1959*, Routledge & Kegan Paul, 1960.

Jones, K., and Sidebotham, R., *Mental Hospitals at Work*, Routledge & Kegan Paul, 1962.

Labor Information M.S.A. Mission to the United Kingdom, *Economic Development in the United Kingdom 1850–1900*, n.d.

Leopold, N. F., *Life + 99 years*, Gollancz, 1958.

Leslie, S., *Sir Evelyn Ruggles-Brise*, Murray, 1938.

Llewellin, W. W., 'Lowdham Grange, A Borstal Experiment', *Howard Journal*, vol. 3, no. 4, 1933.

Lucas, N., *Britain's Gangland*, Pan Books, 1969.

Macartney, W. F. R., *Walls have Mouths*, Gollancz, 1936.

Marsh, D. C., *The Changing Social Structure of England and Wales 1871–1961*, Routledge & Kegan Paul, 1958.

Martin, J. B., *Break Down the Walls*, Gollancz, 1955.

Mathiesen, T., *The Defences of the Weak*, Tavistock, 1965.

McCabe, S., and Dunlop, A., *Young Men in Detention Centres*, Routledge & Kegan Paul, 1965.

Merrow-Smith, L. W., *Prison Screw*, Herbert Jenkins, 1962.

Merton, R., *Social Theory and Social Structure*, Free Press of Glencoe, 1946.

Mikes, G., *The Prison*, Routledge and Kegan Paul, 1963.

Mooney, J. D. and Reiley, A. C., *Onward Industry!*, Harper, 1931.

Morris, T. and P., *Pentonville*, Routledge & Kegan Paul, 1963.

Morrison, The Revd W. D., 'Are our Prisons a Failure?', *Fortnightly Review*, April 1894.

Morrison, The Revd W. D., 'The Increase of Crime', *Nineteenth Century*, June 1892.

Moseley, S. A., *The Convict of Today*, Palmer, 1927.

Mosca, G., *The Ruling Class* (ed. Livingston), McGraw-Hill, 1939.

Mulholland, B., *Almost a Holiday*, Macmillan, 1966.

Neild, James, *State of the Prisons in England, Scotland and Wales etc.*, 1812.

Newsam, Sir Frank, *The Home Office*, Allen and Unwin, 1954.

'No. 7' [Anon.], *Twenty-five Years in Seventeen Prisons*, Robinson, 1904.

Nokes, P. L., *The Professional Task in Welfare Practice*, Routledge & Kegan Paul, 1967

Norman, E. R., *Anticatholicism in Victorian England*, Allen and Unwin, 1968.

Norman, F., *Bang to Rights*, Secker and Warburg, 1958.

'One who has tried them' [Anon.], *Her Majesty's Prisons: Their Effects and Defects*, London, 1881.

Parker, C. S. (ed.), *Sir Robert Peel*, Murray, 1891.

Paterson, Sir Alexander, *Across the Bridges*, Edward Arnold, 1911.

Paterson, Sir Alexander, *Our Prisons*, Hugh Rees, 1911.

Pears, E. (ed.), *Prisons and Reformatories at Home and Abroad*, Maidstone Prison, 1912.

Porter, W., *History of the Corps of Royal Engineers* (London, 1889).

Prison Department, *Group Work in Prisons and Borstals*, HMSO, 1966.

Prison Officers' Association, 'The Role of the Modern Prison Officer', *Prison Officers' Magazine*, November 1963, pp. 1–3.

Pugh, R. B., *Imprisonment in Medieval England*, Cambridge University Press, 1968.

Read, C., *It is Never too Late to Mend*, Nisbet, n.d.

Reynolds, G. W., and Judge, A., *The Night the Police went on Strike*, Weidenfeld and Nicolson, 1968.

Rice, A. K., *Productivity and Social Organization*, Tavistock, 1958.

Rice, A. K., *The Enterprise and its Environment*, Tavistock 1963.

Robb, B., *Sans Everything*, Nelson, 1967.

Roberts, D., *Victorian Origins of the Welfare State*, Yale University Press, 1960.

Roethisberger, F. J., and Dickson, W. J., *Management and the Worker*, Cambridge University Press, 1939.

Rose, G., *The Struggle for Penal Reform*, Stevens, 1961.

Ruck, S. K. (ed.), *Paterson on Prisons*, Muller, 1951.

Ruggles-Brise, Sir Evelyn, *The English Prison System*, Macmillan, 1921.

Ruggles-Brise, Sir Evelyn, *Prison Reform at Home and Abroad*, Macmillan, 1925.

Rutledge, Dom Denys, *The Complete Monk*, Routledge & Kegan Paul, 1966.

Scott, Sir Harold, *Your Obedient Servant*, Deutsch, 1959.

Shaw, A. G. L., *Convicts and the Colonies*, Faber & Faber, 1966.

Simon, H. A., *Administrative Behaviour*, Free Press, 1945.

Simon, Smithburg, and Thompson, *Public Administration*, Knopf, 1958.

Slater, G., *The Growth of Modern England*, Constable & Co., 1932.

Society for the Improvement of Prison Discipline and for the Reformation of Juvenile Offenders, *Rules Proposed for the Government of Gaols, Houses of Correction and Penitentiaries* (printed T. Bensley, London), 1820.

Stanton, A. H., and Schwarz, M. S., *The Mental Hospital*, Basic Books, 1954.

Sykes, G., *The Society of Captives*, Princeton, 1958.

Tallack, W., *Defects in the Criminal Administration and Penal Legislation of Great Britain and Ireland with Remedial Suggestions*, 1872.

Tobias, J. J., *Crime and Industrial Society in the 19th Century*, Batsford, 1967.

Turner, M., *A Pretty Sort of Prison*, Pall Mall Press, 1964.

Tyndall, N. J., *Prison People*, Educational Explorers, 1967.

Vaizey, J., *Scenes from Institutional Life*, Faber & Faber, 1959.

Vidler, J., *If Freedom Fail*, Macmillan, 1964.

Watson, J., *Which is the Justice?*, Allen Unwin, 1969.

'W.B.N.' *Penal Servitude*, Heinemann, 1903.

Webb, S. and B., *English Prisons under Local Government*, Longmans, 1922.

Wedderburn, A., *Observations on the State of the English Prisons etc.*, 1793.

Wildeblood, P., *Against the Law*, Weidenfeld & Nicolson, 1956.

Williams, T. G., *The Main Currents of Social and Industrial Change 1870–1924*, Pitman, 1925.

Wolfgang, M. E., *et al.*, *The Sociology of Crime and Delinquency*, Wiley, 1962.

Remarks by the County Chairman upon the Tables published by David Ricardo Esq. February 1850 in his pamphlet upon the appointment of a Government Auditor, Gloucester, 1850.

Reports from the Advisory Council on the Treatment of Offenders

Alternatives to Short Terms of Imprisonment, 1957.
Corporal Punishment, 1960.
The Organisation of After-Care, 1963.
Preventive Detention, 1963.

Unpublished material

'Report of the Committee Appointed to Inquire into the Position and
   Prospectus of Convict Wardens and Broadmoor Asylum Attendants.'
   Marked 'Confidential', 1883 (Rosebery Committee).
'Report of the Committee Appointed to Inquire into the Hours of Duty,
   Leave, Pay and Allowances, and Terms of Retirement of the
   Subordinate Officers in the Convict and Local Prisons and of the
   Officials of the Broadmoor Criminal Lunatic Asylum,' 1891 (De
   Ramsey Committee).
Paterson, Sir Alexander, 'The Principles of the Borstal System', circa
   1932.
Leng, Anne (University of Hull), 'The Positive Uses of Care', Lecture
   delivered at Hull, March 1968.
Jepson, N. A. (University of Leeds), Survey on the Prison Officer (still
   proceeding).

Journals, periodicals and newspapers

British Journal of Criminology.
British Journal of Sociology.
Civil Service Gazette.
Contemporary Review.
Daily Chronicle.
Fortnightly Review.
Globe.
Journal of Management Studies.
Nineteenth Century.
Prison Officers' Magazine.
Prison Service Journal.
The Times.

Index

International Library of
Sociology

Edited by
John Rex
University of Warwick

Founded by
Karl Mannheim

as The International Library of Sociology
and Social Reconstruction

*This Catalogue also contains other Social Science
series published by Routledge*

Routledge & Kegan Paul   London and Boston

68-74 Carter Lane   London EC4V 5EL
9 Park Street   Boston   Mass 02108

Contents

● *Books so marked are available in paperback*
All books are in Metric Demy 8vo format (216 × 138mm approx.)

GENERAL SOCIOLOGY

Belshaw, Cyril. The Conditions of Social Performance. *An Exploratory Theory. 144 pp.*

Brown, Robert. Explanation in Social Science. *208 pp.*

Cain, Maureen E. Society and the Policeman's Role. *About 300 pp.*

Gibson, Quentin. The Logic of Social Enquiry. *240 pp.*

Homans, George C. Sentiments and Activities: *Essays in Social Science. 336 pp.*

Isajiw, Wsevold W. Causation and Functionalism in Sociology. *165 pp.*

Johnson, Harry M. Sociology: *a Systematic Introduction. Foreword by Robert K. Merton. 710 pp.*

Mannheim, Karl. Essays on Sociology and Social Psychology. *Edited by Paul Keckskemeti. With Editorial Note by Adolph Lowe. 344 pp.*
   Systematic Sociology: *An Introduction to the Study of Society. Edited by J. S. Erös and Professor W. A. C. Stewart. 220 pp.*

Martindale, Don. The Nature and Types of Sociological Theory. *292 pp.*

● **Maus, Heinz.** A Short History of Sociology. *234 pp.*

Mey, Harald. Field-Theory. *A Study of its Application in the Social Sciences. 352 pp.*

Myrdal, Gunnar. Value in Social Theory: *A Collection of Essays on Methodology. Edited by Paul Streeten. 332 pp.*

Ogburn, William F., and **Nimkoff, Meyer F.** A Handbook of Sociology. *Preface by Karl Mannheim. 656 pp. 46 figures. 35 tables.*

Parsons, Talcott, and **Smelser, Neil J.** Economy and Society: *A Study in the Integration of Economic and Social Theory. 362 pp.*

● **Rex, John.** Key Problems of Sociological Theory. *220 pp.*

Stark, Werner. The Fundamental Forms of Social Thought. *280 pp.*

FOREIGN CLASSICS OF SOCIOLOGY

● **Durkheim, Emile.** Suicide. *A Study in Sociology. Edited and with an Introduction by George Simpson. 404 pp.*
   Professional Ethics and Civic Morals. *Translated by Cornelia Brookfield. 288 pp.*

● **Gerth, H. H.,** and **Mills, C. Wright.** From Max Weber: *Essays in Sociology. 502 pp.*

Tönnies, Ferdinand. Community and Association. *(Gemeinschaft und Gesellschaft.) Translated and Supplemented by Charles P. Loomis. Foreword by Pitirim A. Sorokin. 334 pp.*

SOCIAL STRUCTURE

Andreski, Stanislav. Military Organization and Society. *Foreword by Professor A. R. Radcliffe-Brown. 226 pp. 1 folder.*

● **Cole, G. D. H.** Studies in Class Structure. *220 p.*

Coontz, Sydney H. Population Theories and the Economic Interpretation. *202 pp.*

Coser, Lewis. The Functions of Social Conflict. *204 pp.*

Dickie-Clark, H. F. Marginal Situation: *A Sociological Study of a Coloured Group. 240 pp. 11 tables.*

Glass, D. V. (Ed.). Social Mobility in Britain. *Contributions by J. Berent, T. Bottomore, R. C. Chambers, J. Floud, D. V. Glass, J. R. Hall, H. T. Himmelweit, R. K. Kelsall, F. M. Martin, C. A. Moser, R. Mukherjee, and W. Ziegel. 420 pp.*

Glaser, Barney, and **Strauss, Anselm L.** Status Passage. *A Formal Theory. 208 pp.*

Jones, Garth N. Planned Organizational Change: *An Exploratory Study Using an Empirical Approach. 268 pp.*

Kelsall, R. K. Higher Civil Servants in Britain: *From 1870 to the Present Day. 268 pp. 31 tables.*

König, René. The Community. *232 pp. Illustrated.*

● **Lawton, Denis.** Social Class, Language and Education. *192 pp.*

McLeish, John. The Theory of Social Change: *Four Views Considered. 128 pp.*

Marsh, David C. The Changing Social Structure in England and Wales, 1871-1961. *272 pp.*

Mouzelis, Nicos. Organization and Bureaucracy. *An Analysis of Modern Theories. 240 pp.*

Mulkay, M. J. Functionalism, Exchange and Theoretical Strategy. *272 pp.*

Ossowski, Stanislaw. Class Structure in the Social Consciousness. *210 pp.*

SOCIOLOGY AND POLITICS

Crick, Bernard. The American Science of Politics: *Its Origins and Conditions. 284 pp.*

Hertz, Frederick. Nationality in History and Politics: *A Psychology and Sociology of National Sentiment and Nationalism. 432 pp.*

Kornhauser, William. The Politics of Mass Society. *272 pp. 20 tables.*

Laidler, Harry W. History of Socialism. *Social-Economic Movements: An Historical and Comparative Survey of Socialism, Communism, Co-operation, Utopianism; and other Systems of Reform and Reconstruction. 992 pp.*

Mannheim, Karl. Freedom, Power and Democratic Planning. *Edited by Hans Gerth and Ernest K. Bramstedt. 424 pp.*

Mansur, Fatma. Process of Independence. *Foreword by A. H. Hanson. 208 pp.*

Martin, David A. Pacificism: *an Historical and Sociological Study. 262 pp.*

Myrdal, Gunnar. The Political Element in the Development of Economic Theory. *Translated from the German by Paul Streeten. 282 pp.*

Verney, Douglas V. The Analysis of Political Systems. *264 pp.*

Wootton, Graham. Workers, Unions and the State. *188 pp.*

FOREIGN AFFAIRS: THEIR SOCIAL, POLITICAL AND ECONOMIC FOUNDATIONS

Bonné, Alfred. State and Economics in the Middle East: *A Society in Transition. 482 pp.*
Studies in Economic Development: *with special reference to Conditions in the Under-developed Areas of Western Asia and India. 322 pp. 84 tables.*
Mayer, J. P. Political Thought in France from the Revolution to the Fifth Republic. *164 pp.*

CRIMINOLOGY

Ancel, Marc. Social Defence: *A Modern Approach to Criminal Problems. Foreword by Leon Radzinowicz. 240 pp.*
Cloward, Richard A., and **Ohlin, Lloyd E.** Delinquency and Opportunity: *A Theory of Delinquent Gangs. 248 pp.*
Downes, David M. The Delinquent Solution. *A Study in Subcultural Theory. 296 pp.*
Dunlop, A. B., and **McCabe, S.** Young Men in Detention Centres. *192 pp.*
Friedlander, Kate. The Psycho-Analytical Approach to Juvenile Delinquency: *Theory, Case Studies, Treatment. 320 pp.*
Glueck, Sheldon, and **Eleanor.** Family Environment and Delinquency. *With the statistical assistance of Rose W. Kneznek. 340 pp.*
Lopez-Rey, Manuel. Crime. *An Analytical Appraisal. 288 pp.*
Mannheim, Hermann. Comparative Criminology: *a Text Book. Two volumes. 442 pp. and 380 pp.*
Morris, Terence. The Criminal Area: *A Study in Social Ecology. Foreword by Hermann Mannheim. 232 pp. 25 tables. 4 maps.*
Trasler, Gordon. The Explanation of Criminality. *144 pp.*

SOCIAL PSYCHOLOGY

Bagley, Christopher. The Social Psychology of the Child with Epilepsy. *320 pp.*
Barbu, Zevedei. Problems of Historical Psychology. *248 pp.*
Blackburn, Julian. Psychology and the Social Pattern. *184 pp.*
● **Fleming, C. M.** Adolescence: *Its Social Psychology: With an Introduction to recent findings from the fields of Anthropology, Physiology, Medicine, Psychometrics and Sociometry. 288 pp.*
● The Social Psychology of Education: *An Introduction and Guide to Its Study. 136 pp.*
Homans, George C. The Human Group. *Foreword by Bernard DeVoto. Introduction by Robert K. Merton. 526 pp.*
Social Behaviour: *its Elementary Forms. 416 pp.*

Klein, Josephine. The Study of Groups. *226 pp. 31 figures. 5 tables.*

Linton, Ralph. The Cultural Background of Personality. *132 pp.*

Mayo, Elton. The Social Problems of an Industrial Civilization. *With an appendix on the Political Problem. 180 pp.*

Ottaway, A. K. C. Learning Through Group Experience. *176 pp.*

Ridder, J. C. de. The Personality of the Urban African in South Africa. *A Thematic Apperception Test Study. 196 pp. 12 plates.*

● **Rose, Arnold M.** (Ed.). Human Behaviour and Social Processes: *an Interactionist Approach. Contributions by Arnold M. Rose, Ralph H. Turner, Anselm Strauss, Everett C. Hughes, E. Franklin Frazier, Howard S. Becker, et al. 696 pp.*

Smelser, Neil J. Theory of Collective Behaviour. *448 pp.*

Stephenson, Geoffrey M. The Development of Conscience. *128 pp.*

Young, Kimball. Handbook of Social Psychology. *658 pp. 16 figures. 10 tables.*

SOCIOLOGY OF THE FAMILY

Banks, J. A. Prosperity and Parenthood: *A Study of Family Planning among The Victorian Middle Classes. 262 pp.*

Bell, Colin R. Middle Class Families: *Social and Geographical Mobility. 224 pp.*

Burton, Lindy. Vulnerable Children. *272 pp.*

Gavron, Hannah. The Captive Wife: *Conflicts of Household Mothers. 190 pp.*

George, Victor, and **Wilding, Paul.** Motherless Families. *220 pp.*

Klein, Josephine. Samples from English Cultures.
  1. Three Preliminary Studies and Aspects of Adult Life in England. *447 pp.*
  2. Child-Rearing Practices and Index. *247 pp.*

Klein, Viola. Britain's Married Women Workers. *180 pp.*
  The Feminine Character. *History of an Ideology. 244 pp.*

McWhinnie, Alexina M. Adopted Children. *How They Grow Up. 304 pp.*

Myrdal, Alva, and **Klein, Viola.** Women's Two Roles: *Home and Work. 238 pp. 27 tables.*

Parsons, Talcott, and **Bales, Robert F.** Family: *Socialization and Interaction Process. In collaboration with James Olds, Morris Zelditch and Philip E. Slater. 456 pp. 50 figures and tables.*

SOCIAL SERVICES

Bastide, Roger. The Sociology of Mental Disorder. *Translated from the French by Jean McNeil. 264 pp.*

Carlebach, Julius. Caring For Children in Trouble. *266 pp.*

Forder, R. A. (Ed.). Penelope Hall's Social Services of Modern England. *352 pp.*

George, Victor. Foster Care. *Theory and Practice. 234 pp.*
  Social Security: *Beveridge and After. 258 pp.*

● **Goetschius, George W.** Working with Community Groups. *256 pp.*

Goetschius, George W., and **Tash, Joan.** Working with Unattached Youth. *416 pp.*

Hall, M. P., and **Howes, I. V.** The Church in Social Work. *A Study of Moral Welfare Work undertaken by the Church of England. 320 pp.*

Heywood, Jean S. Children in Care: *the Development of the Service for the Deprived Child. 264 pp.*

Hoenig, J., and **Hamilton, Marian W.** The De-Segration of the Mentally Ill. *284 pp.*

Jones, Kathleen. Lunacy, Law and Conscience, *1744-1845: the Social History of the Care of the Insane. 268 pp.*

Mental Health and Social Policy, 1845-1959. *264 pp.*

King, Roy D., Raynes, Norma V., and **Tizard, Jack.** Patterns of Residential Care. *356 pp.*

Leigh, John. Young People and Leisure. *256 pp.*

Morris, Pauline. Put Away: *A Sociological Study of Institutions for the Mentally Retarded. 364 pp.*

Nokes, P. L. The Professional Task in Welfare Practice. *152 pp.*

Timms, Noel. Psychiatric Social Work in Great Britain (1939-1962). *280 pp.*

● Social Casework: *Principles and Practice. 256 pp.*

Trasler, Gordon. In Place of Parents: *A Study in Foster Care. 272 pp.*

Young, A. F., and **Ashton, E. T.** British Social Work in the Nineteenth Century. *288 pp.*

Young, A. F. Social Services in British Industry. *272 pp.*

SOCIOLOGY OF EDUCATION

Banks, Olive. Parity and Prestige in English Secondary Education: a Study in Educational Sociology. *272 pp.*

Bentwich, Joseph. Education in Israel. *224 pp. 8 pp. plates.*

● **Blyth, W. A. L.** English Primary Education. *A Sociological Description.*

1. Schools. *232 pp.*

2. Background. *168 pp.*

Collier, K. G. The Social Purposes of Education: *Personal and Social Values in Education. 268 pp.*

Dale, R. R., and **Griffith, S.** Down Stream: *Failure in the Grammar School. 108 pp.*

Dore, R. P. Education in Tokugawa Japan. *356 pp. 9 pp. plates*

Evans, K. M. Sociometry and Education. *158 pp.*

Foster, P. J. Education and Social Change in Ghana. *336 pp. 3 maps.*

Fraser, W. R. Education and Society in Modern France. *150 pp.*

Grace, Gerald R. Role Conflict and the Teacher. *About 200 pp.*

Hans, Nicholas. New Trends in Education in the Eighteenth Century. *278 pp. 19 tables.*

● Comparative Education: *A Study of Educational Factors and Traditions. 360 pp.*

Hargreaves, David. Interpersonal Relations and Education. *432 pp.*
● Social Relations in a Secondary School. *240 pp.*
Holmes, Brian. Problems in Education. *A Comparative Approach. 336 pp.*
King, Ronald. Values and Involvement in a Grammar School. *164 pp.*
● **Mannheim, Karl,** and **Stewart, W. A. C.** An Introduction to the Sociology of Education. *206 pp.*
Morris, Raymond N. The Sixth Form and College Entrance. *231 pp.*
● **Musgrove, F.** Youth and the Social Order. *176 pp.*
● **Ottaway, A. K. C.** Education and Society: *An Introduction to the Sociology of Education. With an Introduction by W. O. Lester Smith. 212 pp.*
Peers, Robert. Adult Education: *A Comparative Study. 398 pp.*
Pritchard, D. G. Education and the Handicapped: *1760 to 1960. 258 pp.*
Richardson, Helen. Adolescent Girls in Approved Schools. *308 pp.*
Simon, Brian, and **Joan** (Eds.). Educational Psychology in the U.S.S.R. *Introduction by Brian and Joan Simon. Translation by Joan Simon. Papers by D. N. Bogoiavlenski and N. A. Menchinskaia, D. B. Elkonin, E. A. Fleshner, Z. I. Kalmykova, G. S. Kostiuk, V. A. Krutetski, A. N. Leontiev, A. R. Luria, E. A. Milerian, R. G. Natadze, B. M. Teplov, L. S. Vygotski, L. V. Zankov. 296 pp.*
Stratta, Erica. The Education of Borstal Boys. *A Study of their Educational Experiences prior to, and during Borstal Training. 256 pp.*

SOCIOLOGY OF CULTURE

Eppel, E. M., and **M.** Adolescents and Morality: *A Study of some Moral Values and Dilemmas of Working Adolescents in the Context of a changing Climate of Opinion. Foreword by W. J. H. Sprott. 268 pp. 39 tables.*
● **Fromm, Erich.** The Fear of Freedom. *286 pp.*
The Sane Society. *400 pp.*
● **Mannheim, Karl.** Diagnosis of Our Time: *Wartime Essays of a Sociologist. 208 pp.*
Essays on the Sociology of Culture. *Edited by Ernst Mannheim in co-operation with Paul Kecskemeti. Editorial Note by Adolph Lowe. 280 pp.*
Weber, Alfred. Farewell to European History: *or The Conquest of Nihilism. Translated from the German by R. F. C. Hull. 224 pp.*

SOCIOLOGY OF RELIGION

Argyle, Michael. Religious Behaviour. *224 pp. 8 figures. 41 tables.*
Nelson, G. K. Spiritualism and Society. *313 pp.*

Stark, Werner. The Sociology of Religion. *A Study of Christendom.*
  Volume I. *Established Religion. 248 pp.*
  Volume II. *Sectarian Religion. 368 pp.*
  Volume III. *The Universal Church. 464 pp.*
  Volume IV. *Types of Religious Man. 352 pp.*
  Volume V. *Types of Religious Culture. 464 pp.*
Watt, W. Montgomery. Islam and the Integration of Society. *320 pp.*

SOCIOLOGY OF ART AND LITERATURE

Beljame, Alexandre. Men of Letters and the English Public in the Eighteenth
  Century: *1660-1744, Dryden, Addison, Pope. Edited with an Introduction
  and Notes by Bonamy Dobrée. Translated by E. O. Lorimer. 532 pp.*
Jarvie, Ian C. Towards a Sociology of the Cinema. *A Comparative Essay
  on the Structure and Functioning of a Major Entertainment Industry.
  405 pp.*
Rust, Frances S. Dance in Society. *An Analysis of the Relationships between
  the Social Dance and Society in England from the Middle Ages to the
  Present Day. 256 pp. 8 pp. of plates.*
Schücking, L. L. The Sociology of Literary Taste. *112 pp.*
Silbermann, Alphons. The Sociology of Music. *Translated from the German
  by Corbet Stewart. 222 pp.*

SOCIOLOGY OF KNOWLEDGE

Mannheim, Karl. Essays on the Sociology of Knowledge. *Edited by Paul
  Kecskemeti. Editorial note by Adolph Lowe. 353 pp.*
Stark, Werner. The Sociology of Knowledge: *An Essay in Aid of a Deeper
  Understanding of the History of Ideas. 384 pp.*

URBAN SOCIOLOGY

Ashworth, William. The Genesis of Modern British Town Planning: *A Study
  in Economic and Social History of the Nineteenth and Twentieth Centuries.
  288 pp.*
Cullingworth, J. B. Housing Needs and Planning Policy: *A Restatement of
  the Problems of Housing Need and 'Overspill' in England and Wales.
  232 pp. 44 tables. 8 maps.*
Dickinson, Robert E. City and Region: *A Geographical Interpretation.
  608 pp. 125 figures.*
  The West European City: *A Geographical Interpretation. 600 pp. 129 maps.
  29 plates.*
● The City Region in Western Europe. *320 pp. Maps.*

Humphreys, Alexander J. New Dubliners: *Urbanization and the Irish Family. Foreword by George C. Homans. 304 pp.*

Jackson, Brian. Working Class Community: *Some General Notions raised by a Series of Studies in Northern England. 192 pp.*

Jennings, Hilda. Societies in the Making: *a Study of Development and Re-development within a County Borough. Foreword by D. A. Clark. 286 pp.*

Kerr, Madeline. The People of Ship Street. *240 pp.*

● **Mann, P. H.** An Approach to Urban Sociology. *240 pp.*

Morris, R. N., and **Mogey, J.** The Sociology of Housing. *Studies at Berinsfield. 232 pp. 4 pp. plates.*

Rosser, C., and **Harris, C.** The Family and Social Change. *A Study of Family and Kinship in a South Wales Town. 352 pp. 8 maps.*

RURAL SOCIOLOGY

Chambers, R. J. H. Settlement Schemes in Africa: *A Selective Study. 268 pp.*

Haswell, M. R. The Economics of Development in Village India. *120 pp.*

Littlejohn, James. Westrigg: *the Sociology of a Cheviot Parish. 172 pp. 5 figures.*

Williams, W. M. The Country Craftsman: *A Study of Some Rural Crafts and the Rural Industries Organization in England. 248 pp. 9 figures. (Dartington Hall Studies in Rural Sociology.)*

The Sociology of an English Village: *Gosforth. 272 pp. 12 figures. 13 tables.*

SOCIOLOGY OF INDUSTRY AND DISTRIBUTION

Anderson, Nels. Work and Leisure. *280 pp.*

● **Blau, Peter M.,** and **Scott, W. Richard.** Formal Organizations: *a Comparative approach. Introduction and Additional Bibliography by J. H. Smith. 326 pp.*

Eldridge, J. E. T. Industrial Disputes. *Essays in the Sociology of Industrial Relations. 288 pp.*

Hetzler, Stanley. Technological Growth and Social Change. *Achieving Modernization. 269 pp.*

Hollowell, Peter G. The Lorry Driver. *272 pp.*

Jefferys, Margot, *with the assistance of Winifred Moss.* Mobility in the Labour Market: *Employment Changes in Battersea and Dagenham. Preface by Barbara Wootton. 186 pp. 51 tables.*

Millerson, Geoffrey. The Qualifying Associations: *a Study in Professionalization. 320 pp.*

Smelser, Neil J. Social Change in the Industrial Revolution: *An Application of Theory to the Lancashire Cotton Industry, 1770-1840. 468 pp. 12 figures. 14 tables.*

Williams, Gertrude. Recruitment to Skilled Trades. *240 pp.*

Young, A. F. Industrial Injuries Insurance: *an Examination of British Policy.* *192 pp.*

ANTHROPOLOGY

Ammar, Hamed. Growing up in an Egyptian Village: *Silwa, Province of Aswan. 336 pp.*

Brandel-Syrier, Mia. Reeftown Elite. *A Study of Social Mobility in a Modern African Community on the Reef. 376 pp.*

Crook, David, and **Isabel.** Revolution in a Chinese Village: *Ten Mile Inn.* *230 pp. 8 plates. 1 map.*

The First Years of Yangyi Commune. *302 pp. 12 plates.*

Dickie-Clark, H. F. The Marginal Situation. *A Sociological Study of a Coloured Group. 236 pp.*

Dube, S. C. Indian Village. *Foreword by Morris Edward Opler. 276 pp. 4 plates.*

India's Changing Villages: *Human Factors in Community Development.* *260 pp. 8 plates. 1 map.*

Firth, Raymond. Malay Fishermen. *Their Peasant Economy. 420 pp. 17 pp. plates.*

Gulliver, P. H. Social Control in an African Society: a Study of the Arusha, Agricultural Masai of Northern Tanganyika. *320 pp. 8 plates. 10 figures.*

Ishwaran, K. Shivapur. *A South Indian Village. 216 pp.*

Tradition and Economy in Village India: *An Interactionist Approach. Foreword by Conrad Arensburg. 176 pp.*

Jarvie, Ian C. The Revolution in Anthropology. *268 pp.*

Jarvie, Ian C., and **Agassi, Joseph.** Hong Kong. *A Society in Transition. 396 pp. Illustrated with plates and maps.*

Little, Kenneth L. Mende of Sierra Leone. *308 pp. and folder.*

Negroes in Britain. *With a New Introduction and Contemporary Study by Leonard Bloom. 320 pp.*

Lowie, Robert H. Social Organization. *494 pp.*

Mayer, Adrian C. Caste and Kinship in Central India: *A Village and its Region. 328 pp. 16 plates. 15 figures. 16 tables.*

Smith, Raymond T. The Negro Family in British Guiana: *Family Structure and Social Status in the Villages. With a Foreword by Meyer Fortes. 314 pp. 8 plates. 1 figure. 4 maps.*

DOCUMENTARY

Meek, Dorothea L. (Ed.). Soviet Youth: *Some Achievements and Problems. Excerpts from the Soviet Press, translated by the editor. 280 pp.*

Schlesinger, Rudolf (Ed.). Changing Attitudes in Soviet Russia.

2. *The Nationalities Problem and Soviet Administration. Selected Readings on the Development of Soviet Nationalities Policies. Introduced by the editor. Translated by W. W. Gottlieb. 324 pp.*

SOCIOLOGY AND PHILOSOPHY

Barnsley, John H. The Social Reality of Ethics. *A Comparative Analysis of Moral Codes. 448 pp.*

Douglas, Jack D. (Ed.). Understanding Everyday Life. *Toward the Reconstruction of Sociological Knowledge. Contributions by Alan F. Blum. Aaron W. Cicourel, Norman K. Denzin, Jack D. Douglas, John Heeren, Peter McHugh, Peter K. Manning, Melvin Power, Matthew Speier, Roy Turner, D. Lawrence Wieder, Thomas P. Wilson and Don H. Zimmerman. 358 pp.*

Jarvie, Ian C. Concepts and Society. *216 pp.*

Roche, Maurice. Phenomenology, Language and the Social Sciences. *About 400 pp.*

Sklair, Leslie. The Sociology of Progress. *320 pp.*

International Library of Social Policy

General Editor   Kathleen Janes

Jones, Kathleen. Mental Health Services. *A history, 1744-1971. About 500 pp.*

Thomas, J. E. The English Prison Officer since 1850: *A Study in Conflict. 258 pp.*

Primary Socialization, Language and Education

General Editor   Basil Bernstein

Bernstein, Basil. Class, Codes and Control. *2 volumes.*
  1. *Theoretical Studies Towards a Sociology of Language. 254 pp.*
  2. *Applied Studies Towards a Sociology of Language. About 400 pp.*

Brandis, Walter, and **Henderson, Dorothy.** Social Class, Language and Communication. *288 pp.*

Cook, Jenny. Socialization and Social Control. *About 300 pp.*

Gahagan, D. M., and **G. A.** Talk Reform. *Exploration in Language for Infant School Children. 160 pp.*

Robinson, W. P., and **Rackstraw, Susan, D. A.** A Question of Answers. *2 volumes. 192 pp. and 180 pp.*

Turner, Geoffrey, J., and **Mohan, Bernard, A.** A Linguistic Description and Computer Programme for Children's Speech. *208 pp.*

Reports of the Institute of Community Studies and the Institute of Social Studies in Medical Care

Cartwright, Ann. Human Relations and Hospital Care. *272 pp.*
  Parents and Family Planning Services. *306 pp.*
  Patients and their Doctors. *A Study of General Practice. 304 pp.*
Dunnell, Karen, and **Cartwright, Ann.** Medicine Takers, Prescribers and Hoarders. *About 140 pp.*
● **Jackson, Brian.** Streaming: *an Education System in Miniature. 168 pp.*
Jackson, Brian, and **Marsden, Dennis.** Education and the Working Class: *Some General Themes raised by a Study of 88 Working-class Children in a Northern Industrial City. 268 pp. 2 folders.*
Marris, Peter. Widows and their Families. *Foreword by Dr. John Bowlby. 184 pp. 18 tables. Statistical Summary.*
  Family and Social Change in an African City. *A Study of Rehousing in Lagos. 196 pp. 1 map. 4 plates. 53 tables.*
  The Experience of Higher Education. *232 pp. 27 tables.*
Marris, Peter, and **Rein, Martin.** Dilemmas of Social Reform. *Poverty and Community Action in the United States. 256 pp.*
Marris, Peter, and **Somerset, Anthony.** African Businessmen. *A Study of Entrepreneurship and Development in Kenya. 256 pp.*
Runciman, W. G. Relative Deprivation and Social Justice. *A Study of Attitudes to Social Inequality in Twentieth Century England. 352 pp.*
Townsend, Peter. The Family Life of Old People: *An Inquiry in East London. Foreword by J. H. Sheldon. 300 pp. 3 figures. 63 tables.*
Willmott, Peter. Adolescent Boys in East London. *230 pp.*
  The Evolution of a Community: *a study of Dagenham after forty years. 168 pp. 2 maps.*
Willmott, Peter, and **Young, Michael.** Family and Class in a London Suburb. *202 pp. 47 tables.*
Young, Michael. Innovation and Research in Education. *192 pp.*
● **Young, Michael,** and **McGeeney, Patrick.** Learning Begins at Home. *A Study of a Junior School and its Parents. 128 pp.*
Young, Michael, and **Willmott, Peter.** Family and Kinship in East London. *Foreword by Richard M. Titmuss. 252 pp. 39 tables.*

Medicine, Illness and Society
General Editor W. M. Williams

Robinson, David. The Process of Becoming Ill.
Stacey, Margaret. *et al.* Hospitals, Children and Their Families. *The Report of a Pilot Study. 202 pp.*

Routledge Social Science Journals

The British Journal of Sociology. *Edited by Terence P. Morris. Vol. 1, No. 1, March 1950 and Quarterly. Roy. 8vo. Back numbers available. An international journal with articles on all aspects of sociology.*

Economy and Society. *Vol. 1, No. 1. February 1972 and Quarterly. Metric Roy. 8vo. A journal for all social scientists covering sociology, philosophy, anthropology, economics and history.*

Printed in Great Britain by Lewis Reprints Limited
Brown Knight & Truscott Group, London and Tonbridge   21972